# Private Institutions and Global Governance

# Private Institutions and Global Governance

The New Politics of Environmental Sustainability

Philipp H. Pattberg

*Vrije Universiteit Amsterdam, The Netherlands*

**Edward Elgar**

Cheltenham, UK • Northampton, MA, USA

Published by
Edward Elgar Publishing Limited
Glensanda House
Montpellier Parade
Cheltenham
Glos GL50 1UA
UK

Edward Elgar Publishing, Inc.
William Pratt House
9 Dewey Court
Northampton
Massachusetts 01060
USA

A catalogue record for this book
is available from the British Library

**Library of Congress Cataloguing in Publication Data**

Pattberg, Philipp H., 1975-
  Private institutions and global governance : the new politics of environmental sustainability / Philipp H. Pattberg.
      p. cm.
  Includes bibliographical references and index.
  1. Environmental policy–International cooperation. 2. Environmental management–International cooperation. 3. Industrial management–Environmental aspects. 4. Corporations–Environmental aspects. 5. International economic relations. I. Title.
  GE170.P746 2007
  333.72–dc22

                           2006037183

Freie Universität Berlin, D188

ISBN 978 1 84720 231 4

Printed and bound in Great Britain by MPG Books Ltd, Bodmin, Cornwall

# Contents

# List of Figures

# List of Tables

# List of Acronyms and Abbreviations

| | |
|---|---|
| ACCA | Association of Chartered Certified Accountants |
| AFL-CIO | The American Federation of Labor and Congress of Industrial Organizations |
| AIP | Apparel Industry Partnership |
| BHB | Verband der Baumärkte Deutschland |
| BSR | Business for Social Responsibility |
| CAR | Corrective action request |
| CB | Certification body |
| CBD | Convention on Biological Diversity |
| CEO | Chief Executive Officer |
| CEPI | Confederation of European Paper Industries |
| CERES | Coalition for Environmentally Responsible Economies |
| CFP | Certified forest products |
| CITES | Washington Convention on International Trade in Endangered Species of Wild Flora and Fauna |
| CMT | Change management team |
| CoC | Chain of custody |
| CSA | Corporate social accountability |
| CSR | Corporate social responsibility |
| DIY | Do-it-yourself |
| ED | Executive Director |
| ECOSOC | United Nations Economic and Social Council |
| EMAS | European Eco-management and Audit Scheme |
| EMS | Environmental management system |
| EPA | US Environmental Protection Agency |
| ETI | Ethical Trading Initiative |
| FAO | United Nations Food and Agriculture Organisation |
| FASB | Financial Accounting Standards Board |
| FDI | Foreign Direct Investment |
| FFSC | Finnish Forest Certification Scheme |
| FLA | Fair Labor Association |
| FoE | Friends of the Earth |
| FSC | Forest Stewardship Council |
| GA | General Assembly |

| GATT | General Agreement on Tariffs and Trade |
|------|----------------------------------------|
| GDP | Gross domestic product |
| GEMI | Global Environmental Management Initiative |
| GM | General Motors |
| GNI | Gross national income |
| GRI | Global Reporting Initiative |
| Ha | Hectares |
| HCVF | High conservation value forest |
| HES | Health, safety and environmental performance |
| IAD | Institutional Analysis and Development Approach |
| ICC | International Chamber of Commerce |
| ICCA | International Council of Chemical Associations |
| IFF | International Forum on Forests |
| IFOAM | International Federation of Organic Agriculture Movements |
| IIED | International Institute for Environment and Development |
| ILO | International Labour Organisation |
| INCR | Investor Network on Climate Change |
| IPE | International Political Economy |
| IPF | International Panel on Forests |
| IR | International Relations |
| ISO | International Organization for Standardization |
| ITO | International Trade Organisation |
| ITTA | International Timber Trade Agreement |
| ITTC | International Timber Trade Council |
| ITTO | International Timber Trade Organisation |
| IUCN | World Conservation Union |
| MAC | Marine Aquarium Council |
| MSC | Marine Stewardship Council |
| MTCC | Malaysian Timber Certification Council |
| NGO | Non-governmental organisation |
| NIEO | New International Economic Order |
| NSMD | Non-state market-driven governance |
| OECD | Organisation for Economic Cooperation and Development |
| P&C | Principles and Criteria |
| PEFC | Pan-European Forest Certification Council |
| PERI | Public Environmental Reporting Initiative |
| PwC | PricewaterhouseCoopers |
| RA | Rainforest Alliance |
| RC | Responsible Care |
| SFI | Sustainable Forestry Initiative |
| SFM | Sustainable forest management |
| SIF | Social Investment Forum |

| SRI | Socially responsible investing |
| STCS | Sustainable Tourism Certification Scheme |
| TFAP | Tropical Forestry Action Plan |
| TNC | Transnational Corporation |
| TRI | Toxic Release Inventory |
| UN | United Nations |
| UNCED | United Nations Conference on Environment and Development |
| UNCTAD | United Nations Conference on Trade and Development |
| UNCTC | United Nations Centre on Transnational Corporations |
| UNECE | United Nations Economic Commission for Europe |
| UNEP | United Nations Environment Programme |
| UNEP DTIE | United Nations Environment Programme, Division of Technology, Industry and Economics |
| UNGASS | United Nations Assembly Special Session |
| WBCSD | World Business Council on Sustainable Development |
| WCED | World Commission on Environment and Development |
| WCS | World Conservation Strategy |
| WRAP | Worldwide Responsible Apparel Production |
| WRI | World Resources Institute |
| WSSD | World Summit on Sustainable Development |
| WTO | World Trade Organisation |
| WWF | World Wide Fund for Nature |

# Acknowledgements

This book grew out of my initial interest in the phenomenon of global environmental governance. Puzzled by the immense richness of the scholarly debate and the many different understandings, both with regard to theory and empirical evidence, I started to study the many new mechanisms of governance currently debated. I quickly came to realise that behind the relatively well-known territory of 'non-state actors' in world politics, there lies a vast uncharted area of 'non-state institutions' to be explored. Starting from the notion of private rules and rule making in global environmental and sustainability politics, I attempted to shed some light on the emerging phenomenon of private governance. The research presented in this book is my tentative answer to the question of why private governance emerges in world politics and what the measurable impacts of this transformation are.

However, science is never a monologue, but a broad conversation with past and present ideas and, most importantly, people. Among those who have supported, influenced, criticised and motivated this study, I am particularly indebted to Prof. Frank Biermann and Prof. Bernd Siebenhüner who have supported the project from its very beginning. In addition, I would like to thank my colleagues at the Global Governance Project, with whom it has been an extraordinary pleasure to work. I am particularly indebted to Klaus Dingwerth, who not only shared the work in coordinating the research group MECGLO – *The New Mechanisms of Global Governance*, but also has been a constant source of inspiration developing the notion of private and transnational governance. I also owe my sincere gratitude to Prof. Karl Kaiser for stimulating my interest in International Relations and global environmental politics in the first place.

Next, I am grateful to a number of colleagues for commenting on the manuscript and/or for providing extremely helpful comments on related articles and conference papers. In addition to those mentioned above, I would like to thank Steffen Bauer, Per-Olof Busch, Sabine Campe, Keith Capellini, Lauren Kelly, Hans-Dieter Sohn, Mirreia Tarradell and several anonymous reviewers. Robert Falkner, David Levy and Paul Wapner kindly reserved some of their valuable time for discussing their ideas of private governance with me. I would also like to thank Neil McLean for rigorously proofreading the manuscript and Mathijs Seegers for turning it into a readable manuscript.

Furthermore, I would like to express my gratitude to the many interview partners who shared their valuable time and experience with me, provided numerous documents and constantly responded to my frequent inquiries via the telephone and Internet. In addition, I would like to thank Anna Schreyögg for compiling a number of documents on the FSC from electronic sources.

I am also greatly indebted to the German Environment Foundation (Deutsche Bundesstiftung Umwelt, DBU) and the Volkswagen Foundation for funding the research presented in this book. In particular, I would like to thank Jan Peter Lay for his patience and support throughout the years. In addition, I want to express my gratitude to the Environmental Policy Research Centre (FFU) at the Freie Universität Berlin, the Institute for Environmental Studies (IVM) at the Vrije Universiteit Amsterdam and the Centre for Environmental Policy and Governance (CEPG) at the London School of Economics, where I had the pleasure to pursue research as a visiting fellow. A mobility grant from the GARNET network of excellence is also gratefully acknowledged.

Parts of this book have appeared in the following articles and are reprinted with kind permission: Philipp Pattberg (2005), 'The Institutionalization of Private Governance: How Business and Non-profit Organizations agree on Transnational Rules', *Governance: An International Journal of Policy, Administration, and Institutions*, **18** (4): 589-610 (Blackwell Publishing); Philipp Pattberg (2006), 'The influence of global business regulation: beyond good corporate conduct', *Business and Society Review*, **111** (3): 241-268 (Blackwell Publishing); Philipp Pattberg (2006), 'Private Governance and the South: Lessons from Global Forest Politics', *Third World Quarterly*, **27** (4): 579-593 (Routledge).

Finally, this book would not have been possible without the constant support of a handful of close friends and family. They know that my gratefulness goes far beyond what can be expressed in words.

Amsterdam, December 2006

# 1. Introduction: From Public to Private Governance

The last decade of the 20th century and the early years of the new millennium are repeatedly described as an era of profound transformation (Rosenau 1990, 2003; Gill 1997; Mittelman 1997; Held et al. 1999). The end of the Cold War has altered the international system from bipolar to one of multiple sites of power. Technological developments have changed the ways in which we process and distribute information, while economic globalisation constantly integrates an ever-increasing number of people into the structures of global capitalism. At the same time, it becomes apparent that humankind no longer predominantly alters its local and regional environment, but has entered into a phase of change of a truly planetary dimension. In this context of large-scale transformations, a growing number of scholars are concerned with the perennial question of governance, or in other words, the manifold ways in which humans regulate their affairs to reach common goals and react to a changing environment (Falk 1995; Rosenau 1997b; Cable 1999; Biermann and Bauer 2005a).

As far as governance at the global level is concerned, studies in International Relations (IR) in general and global sustainability politics in particular have focused primarily on international regimes and intergovernmental organisations that have been designed to address transboundary problems. In recent years, a number of scholars have acknowledged the growing importance of transnational non-state actors and their role and function in agenda setting, lobbying governments and implementing international agreements (Risse-Kappen 1995b; Weiss and Gordenker 1996; Raustiala 1997; Keck and Sikkink 1998; Florini 2000; Arts, Noortmann and Reinalda 2001). However, while many authors have written about transnational relations since the late 1960s and early 1970s, the transnational arena is widely regarded as fundamentally anomic, shapeless and unorganised (Djelic and Quack 2003b). In contrast, this book starts from the assumption that the transnational arena is gradually becoming more rule-based and organised. Therefore, considerable attention should be paid to the sources of transnational organisation and the underlying process of institutionalisation.

One remarkable indicator of this emerging transnational sphere is the many novel institutional arrangements that no longer predominantly focus on the international policy cycle, but have begun to develop, implement and monitor their own transnational rules and regulations. Innovative forms of collaboration can be observed in a range of different organisational settings and issue areas. Firms may engage in strategic alliances with suppliers and competitors, develop informal industry norms and practices or even formal private regimes, regulating the behaviour of a wide range of business actors in sectors ranging from chemicals to minerals and mining. International organisations seek the assistance of corporations in implementing universal social and environmental norms or engage in partnership with business actors and non-governmental organisations to introduce globally applicable schemes for sustainable corporate reporting. Civil society representatives take part in deliberations involving corporations, governments and international organisations with a view to establishing a sustainable framework for the planning and operation of large-scale dams. Some forms of institutionalised rule making and implementation even deliberately exclude public authorities and create social obligations that are private in their nature, but transcend national boundaries in issue areas ranging from forestry to organic farming and corporate environmental reporting.

Examples of this novel institutional form of rule making and problem solving include the Forest Stewardship Council (FSC), the Marine Stewardship Council (MSC), the Marine Aquarium Council (MAC), the Coalition for Environmentally Responsible Economies (CERES), but also less known initiatives such as the Rugmark Foundation labelling scheme for carpets produced without child labour, the Earth Island Institute's 'Dolphin Safe' label for tuna, the Common Code for the Coffee Community (4C) or the Mining, Minerals and Sustainable Development (MMSD) initiative are further illustrations of a growing market of non-state processes in which issues are defined, rules are made and compliance with these rules is monitored beyond the control and interest of individual states.

These examples indicate at least three potential shifts in world politics. First, the locus of authoritative problem solving does not rest with governments and international organisations alone. Authority is indeed relocated in many different institutional settings, involving public–private, as well as purely private actor constellations. Second, the predominantly confrontational relations between companies, governments and civil society has been complemented, at least rhetorically, by partnership as one possible mode of interaction. And third, partnerships are becoming more and more institutionalised, resulting in rules, norms and social practices that potentially govern specific issue areas or functional domains. The term *private governance* encapsulates these important shifts within one conceptual framework. It emphasises the role of private actors, both profit and non-profit, in the establishment and maintenance of issue-specific transnational rule systems, in contrast to either private agenda setting and lobbying or international rule making. Therefore, private governance can be understood as a functional equivalent to public forms of global governance involving states and intergovernmental institutions.

As a result of this similarity, key questions with regard to private governance resemble many of the questions posed in international institutional theory. Instead of asking 'What accounts for the emergence of instances of rule-based cooperation in the international system?', 'How do international institutions affect the behaviour of state and non-state actors in the issue areas for which they have been created?' or 'Which factors, be they located within or without the institution, determine the success and the stability of international regimes?' (Hasenclever, Mayer and Rittberger 1997: 1), this book is interested in the institutionalisation of private governance. Understanding the process of institutionalisation as a source of rule-based interactions at the transnational level involves two mutually constitutive analytical steps. First, analysing the institutionalisation of private governance needs to account for the emergence of private rules and the distinct actor constellations making and sustaining them. Second, the analysis of institutionalisation is also interested in the actual influence of private rules on actors and structures, as well as in the recurrent functional pathways leading to observable effects. This dual understanding of the process of institutionalisation is reflected throughout this book as it analyses the emergence and influences of private governance in global sustainability politics.

The concept of private governance is gaining currency within the discipline of IR and International Political Economy (IPE). However, most empirical studies have focused either on relations between economic actors exclusively (Cutler, Haufler and Porter 1999a) or dealt with one specific instrumental approach to private governance (for example certification and labelling). This book approaches private governance from a different perspective. It focuses on the empirical case of business co-regulation, which has been largely neglected in current debates, by comparing two instrumental approaches to private governance, namely certification and corporate reporting. This 'private co-regulation' of global problems, from forestry to marine living resources, sustainable tourism and corporate environmental reporting, describes a phenomenon that is different from forms of industry self-regulation, public–private regulation and international regimes that stood at the centre of most of the previous debates. It involves an institutionalised form of cooperation between two or more actors from the profit and non-profit sector of society with a view to the establishment and maintenance of regulation to cope with a transnational or global problem. Next to its theoretical relevance as a source of increasingly rule-based behaviour at the transnational level, the phenomenon of global business regulation is also of particular empirical relevance in the context of global sustainability politics. As Levy and Newell (2005a: 1) summarise:

> Private firms are engaged, directly or indirectly, in the lion's share of the resource depletion, energy use, and hazardous emissions that generate environmental concerns. ... At the same time, firms can serve as powerful engines of change, who could potentially redirect their substantial financial, technological, and organizational resources toward addressing environmental concerns. The environmental impact of firms' activities makes them central players in societal responses to environmental issues.

In sum, this book explores the empirical phenomenon of business regulation from the theoretical perspective of global governance. It answers the question of why transnational arrangements that combine claims to ethical superiority with economic incentives are institutionalised among a range of private actors including profit and non-profit organisations and how they actually gain influence in world politics. It attempts to advance our theoretical understanding of private governance, while at the same time enhancing the empirical knowledge about the institutional arrangement of private business co-regulation in the area of sustainability politics. Hence, this book combines the two academic debates of global governance and business regulation that have so far been treated rather in isolation. The following analysis is based on the assumption that the current regulatory transformation within and beyond the field of sustainability politics amounts to a new level of transnational organisation, both in quality and quantity. In the words of Djelic and Quack (2003a: 8):

> The transnational level is a space in itself where interactions take place and behavioural patterns get structured. This is particularly true and interactions are particularly dense in periods when cross-border processes of exchange, competition and cooperation intensify. As such, the transnational space is bound to give way to processes of institutionalization or institution building.

The chapter is organised in the following way: the first section provides a brief summary of the research questions posed and the corresponding answers given in this book. The second section briefly sketches the existing research on private governance in IR, IPE and partnership approaches and points to major shortcomings in the literature. In addition, the key concepts of private governance, business co-regulation and global sustainability politics are briefly introduced as the theoretical and empirical vantage points for a reassessment of the current system of world politics. The third section clarifies the methodology applied to study private governance, while the last section gives a summary of the argument and provides a brief outline of the subsequent chapters of this book.

## RESEARCH QUESTIONS AND RESULTS

If some observer had been asked to describe the relationship between corporate actors and civil society organisations in the mid-1990s, he or she could very well have pointed to the Brent Spar conflict between Shell and Greenpeace as a telling example of this complicated relationship. Today, this pattern of conflict can still be observed in a range of issue areas, but it has been accompanied by much more intriguing forms of interaction: business and non-governmental organisations (NGOs) not only cooperate on various occasions, for example through monetary endorsements, strategic alliances or product partnerships, but they increasingly begin to agree upon and implement detailed regulation that is applicable on a global scale and that often goes beyond existing international agreements. What do a logger in the province of British Columbia, a communications expert in an office in Bonn, an indigenous campaigner from Brazil, a forest expert on his trip trough a Malaysian forest plantation, a retail-store manager in Switzerland and his customer have in common? They are all part of, connected to and affected by the Forest Stewardship Council, a private transnational institution in sustainable forestry and a prime example of business co-regulation that brings together actors from the non-profit and the profit-making worlds.

These empirical observations are new for several reasons: first, they involve NGOs and business actors that are generally believed to follow different logics of action in traditional accounts of international politics (Waddell 1999); second, they involve both the ordering elements of markets and norms, combining claims to moral superiority with the incentive of higher profits, enhanced brand reputation and access to new markets; third, they transcend state-centred, territorially-based forms of politics, thereby establishing new spaces of transnational organisation; and fourth, they are highly institutionalised, in the form of rules, standards and regulations, and thus go beyond the cooperation, alliances and partnerships discussed in most previous debates (for example Balling 1997; Hartman and Stafford 1997; Austin 2000).

Next to the empirical novelty of private business co-regulation, four theoretical gaps have motivated this book.[1] First, there is a need for conceptual clarification, both with regard to the concept of global and private governance, because the confusion in current uses puts severe limits on accumulative theory building. Second, existing explanations for the formation of private governance in various issue areas has mainly centred on functional arguments that are neither theoretically convincing nor empirically justified. In this line of reasoning, the formation of novel institutions of governance seems to be a simple correlate of globalisation dynamics. However, it remains largely unclear how demand for private regulation is created and corresponding supply organised and structured to achieve effective solutions. Third, although it is often claimed that institutional arrangements of private governance have some measurable impact on distinct actors and structures, the concrete functional pathways and mechanisms of realising transnational order have rarely been assessed in a systematic manner. And finally, while the institutional literature on international phenomena has produced strong and widely accepted explanations for the effectiveness of public regulatory systems and organisations, no comparable attempt has yet been made with regard to private (co-regulative) institutions that engage in governing a specific issue area or functional domain.

In this context, this book attempts to answer four specific questions:

- What is the nature of private governance beyond the state within the general analytical framework of global governance?
- What explains the emergence of private governance systems in the forest certification and environmental reporting domain?
- What are the influences of private governance systems in global sustainability politics and how are they realised?
- Why do some governance systems have more influence than others?

In relation to these questions, this book presents four main results based on the analysis of private governance in the global forest arena (FSC) and the corporate environmental reporting and management domain (Coalition for Environmentally Responsible Economies, CERES):

(1)   Private governance beyond the state can be understood as a source of transnational organisation. From this perspective, the empirical phenomenon of private business co-regulation is analysed as a distinct arrangement of private governance that institutionalises the behaviour of profit and non-profit actors around a set of consciously devised and relatively specific rules. As a result, next to other sources of private authority, specific private governance systems introduce an ordering element to the transnational arena that has until now been treated as an anomic and shapeless space in many empirical and theoretical accounts of world politics. In contrast, this analysis approaches the transnational realm from an institutional perspective by highlighting the increasing density of rule-based interactions that gradually gives rise to an organisational field of transnational rule making in global governance.[2]

(2)   This book suggests that the explanatory factors for the emergence of private governance institutions in sustainability politics are best thought of as a set of four related conditions, two at a macro- and two at a micro-level of political structures. In this view, macro-systemic transformations, resulting in

the perceived or actual decline of public regulatory power, the emergence of civil society as a legitimate and credible actor and the increased environmental and social impact of corporate players, as well as powerful ideas that serve as common points of reference, constitute the macro-level of necessary conditions. At the micro-level, a specific problem structure of interrelated interests and the available organisational resources of the actors involved constitute the necessary conditions for private regulatory institutions to emerge. Hence, a model that combines macro- and micro-level analysis is able to overcome the shortcomings of existing demand- or supply-side explanations.

In addition, an integrated model, combining the macro- and micro-level of political structures, draws our attention to a variety of inter-linkages between different conditions that would not be observable using a single-factor account. First, the relation between shifts at the macro-level and new resources for organisational actors, leading to new strategic choices, becomes apparent; second, an integrated model draws our attention to the relation between resources and the problem structure, addressing the ability of actors to construct a problem in the first place; and third, it highlights the relation between ideas that emerge and diffuse at the macro-level and the subsequent integration of competing perspectives in the actual negotiations.

(3) The influences of private governance systems in global sustainability politics fall broadly within three categories: first, normative influences that are the result of the regulatory function of FSC and CERES; second, cognitive and discursive influences that result from inter-organisational learning processes and the general function of knowledge-brokering and dialogue-facilitation; and third, structural influences that are mainly the result of the integrative function of private governance systems. The empirical analysis of private forest governance and corporate environmental reporting suggests that private arrangements influence both their direct stakeholders (first-order effects), as well as actors not within their formal reach, such as timber retailers, pension funds, national governments and international organisations (second-order effects). On this account, the analysis provided in this book suggests that in addition to regulatory influences, cognitive/discursive as well as structural influences, such as changes in political or economic incentive structures, are most relevant. In particular, as most research on the effectiveness of private governance in global sustainability politics has mainly focused on the intended consequences measured by standard-uptake and compliance data, this assessment provides an alternative account of influences, paying attention to social dynamics rather than to interest-based processes.

(4) With reference to explanations of the differences in the actual influence of private governance systems, this book engages in a preliminary discussion

of plausible explanatory factors for the influence of private governance. Therefore, this study should be read as a first attempt to generate specific hypotheses about the causal mechanisms through which private governance influences states, international organizations, transnational corporations and social discourse. The analysis suggests that some variables hold promising explanatory power, while others do not.

First, the degree of the formalisation of a private governance system (degree of obligation, precision of rules and delegation) is correlated with the actual influence through its regulatory function. The comparison suggests that a higher degree of institutionalisation leads to a higher level of influence. However, the data is inconclusive about the potential to generalise this finding, because the CERES case lends some credibility to an alternative explanation. In this view, CERES' rather modest influence through its actual regulatory framework was only possible because the rules were rather informal and lacked the precision of other private schemes.

Second, the organisational structure and the quality of the network surrounding a private governance system explain the influence through its cognitive/discursive function. Here the comparison shows that in both cases a diverse network of actors and frequent interactions between them have induced substantial learning processes and discursive changes.

Third, the comparison suggests that the higher the fit with existing transnational norms is, the more influence a private governance system has through its function of downward integration. The reverse trend of upward integration seems to be best explained by existing political interests and contextual factors at the domestic level. Hypotheses based on problem structure and cost structure could not be verified. Here the analysis shows that a benign problem structure is conducive to cooperation in general. Whether it enhances the influence of private governance is unclear. In addition, cost structures do not play a major role in the regulatory effects of private governance. Although corporate environmental reporting is less costly than forest certification, it has shown less influence through its actual rules.

## PRIVATE GOVERNANCE IN WORLD POLITICS: STATE OF THE ART, KEY CONCEPTS AND ACADEMIC CONTEXT

This section reviews the existing literature on the question of private governance in world politics, introduces some conceptual clarifications and finally locates the research questions in the wider context of global governance research and the corresponding puzzle regarding the nature of the contemporary system of world politics.

**From Non-state Actors to Non-state Rules: State of the Art in Private Governance Research**

Research on private governance within the discipline of IR and IPE is still rather limited and fragmented in scope. Some authors use the term to refer to a wide variety of different and often contradictory empirical examples, while others abstain from using the concept of private governance, but still analyse essentially the same empirical phenomena. The purpose of this section is to provide a brief overview of the conceptual and theoretical approaches that have been used to date to assess the phenomenon of private governance. Relevant academic debates touching upon the question of private governance fall within three categories: actor-centred approaches, network theories and institutional perspectives.

It is a generally held view that the discipline of IR is firmly based on a state-centred ontology and predominantly directed towards questions of war, peace and security, the predominant heuristic level of analysis being the relation between similar units. However, this mainstream 'Westphalian' perspective has always been contested. In recent years there has been a resurgence of research on roles and relevance of non-state actors (Higgott, Underhill and Bieler 2000; Arts, Noortmann and Reinalda 2001; Josselin and Wallace 2001; Risse 2002). Non-state actors at the international level are found to be involved, *inter alia*, in agenda setting, decision making, monitoring and reporting, as well as in standard setting and rule implementation. Non-state actors fall into three broad categories: public-interest-oriented non-profit actors, profit-oriented corporate actors and their associations and public intergovernmental organisations (Reinalda, Arts and Noortmann 2001: 1-3). Among those non-state actors that capture the attention of scholars, civil society institutions, transnational business actors, global scientific networks (cf. Biermann 2002), and, more recently, international organisations (Barnett and Finnemore 2004) and intergovernmental bureaucracies (cf. Biermann and Bauer 2005a) are the most prominent. However, research has mainly focused on the influence of private actors on intergovernmental decision making processes as an intervening variable between state interests and international policy outcomes.[3] What is largely missing in current research is attention paid to political processes that are both emanating from, as well as directed towards, private non-state actors.

Newell (2001) comes closest to this conception of private governance in his assessment of novel strategies taken by environmental NGOs to target business actors. From the perspective of IPE strategies of consumer boycotts, shareholder campaigns and the general exposure of corporate misconduct are analysed as instruments of governance because they induce behaviour that is rule-bound and socially regulated (Newell 2001: 89). In addition, studies on the different dimensions of the power of non-state actors have also addressed them as a source of regulation (Arts 2003). However, both approaches do not cover private governance at the global level in its entirety, but rather concentrate on the contribution of organisational actors to the construction of governance. This also holds true for approaches dealing specifically with the role of private organisations in global governance (Ronit and Schneider 1999).

A second literature that has partially contributed to understanding the phenomenon of private governance is the debate on private authority[4] in international affairs (Cutler, Haufler and Porter 1999a). Private authority is theorised as the individual or organisational capacity of private actors to make decisions within a particular issue area that are accepted as legitimate by the addressees of the decisions (Cutler, Haufler and Porter 1999b: 5). Here the empirical focus is on cooperation among economic actors and the resulting impacts on the international political system. Different from actor-based approaches, studies on private authority have paid considerable attention to processes of institutionalisation in the form of informal industry norms and practices, cartels, production alliances and private inter-firm regimes. Other studies have focused on the emergence of private authority in IPE and global governance in general, addressing moral, market-based and illicit forms of authority (Hall and Biersteker 2002) as well as the related phenomenon of governmentality at the transnational level (Lipschutz 2005b). Despite considerable insights into the empirical richness of the phenomenon and the many inter-linkages with the more traditional international system, some empirical manifestations of private governance have been largely omitted. In particular, cases in which market mechanisms and claims to moral superiority work in tandem have rarely found their way into studies of private authority. In this context, this book attempts to close an empirical gap left by the private authority debate by explicitly focusing on instances of private business co-regulation beyond inter-firm regimes.

A third genuine approach to the question of governance by and for private actors can be found in the broad literature on policy partnerships[4] (Heap 1998; Bendell 2000; Glasbergen and Groenenberg 2001). Although this literature is rooted in domestic and comparative politics,[5] it has found its way into the study of IR. However, most attention focuses on partnerships between public and non-state actors, such as corporations and civil society organisations. These public–private partnerships at the international level, sometimes also referred to as global public policy networks (Reinicke and Deng 2000), are active in rule setting, rule implementation and service provision (Börzel and Risse 2005). Research that explicitly deals with partnerships between private actors from a theoretical perspective is, however, rare. Most studies instead address the engagement of private actors from a policy-oriented perspective. One notable exception is the concept of policy arrangements advanced by Arts and Tatenhove (2000). The term policy arrangement 'refers to the temporary stabilisation of the content and organisation of a policy domain', including policy programmes and discourses as content and actors and their coalitions as organisations (Arts 2002: 4). These policy arrangements are influenced by the macro-societal process of modernisation that affects the policy domain at the meso-level and forces actors to adapt to the changed environment. Mirroring the general trend of political modernisation, with its move from static, state-centred forms of governance, to more pluralist and open governance styles, the relationship between the private sector and civil society has developed along roughly the same lines. What is missing from most applications of the concept of policy arrangements is the empirical focus on rule-based behaviour, rather than more strategic forms of interaction such as round tables, research-oriented projects and product-orientated projects.

A fourth perspective on private governance in world politics can be found in the management literature on strategic alliances and partnerships (Hartman and Stafford 1997; Austin 2000). Research on partnership as a business strategy has particularly focused on the many ways in which the new relationship with other non-state actors affects core corporate business goals. Among others, better risk management, cost reduction and productivity gains, the development of new products and the intrusion into new markets, the reorganisation of production chains and the construction of barriers to other companies through ethical distinction are seen as important effects of increased business–NGO collaboration (cf. Waddell 1999). From a more encompassing perspective, the phenomenon of private governance has recently been addressed as a manifestation of corporate social responsibility (CSR). Discussing this potential 'market for virtue' (Vogel 2005), a number of shortcomings such as the risk of window-dressing and imbalanced geographic and sectoral representation have been highlighted. Although I share most of the critical remarks made in this respect, this study starts from the assumption that looking beyond good corporate conduct and the practice of CSR (Pattberg 2006b) will considerably widen our understanding of private governance in world politics.

In addition to the four perspectives on private governance presented above, scholars have attempted to understand the relationship between IR and the concept of private governance with a special view to global environmental politics (cf. Falkner 2003). Although not a genuine approach in its own right, recent research into global environmental politics has contributed to both creating the research agenda and providing a range of preliminary answers. In particular, research on the role of business in global environmental governance, the privatisation of environmental governance and the idea and practice of standard setting and certification has been most influential (Clapp 1998;

Kern et al. 2001; Newell 2001; Jagers and Stripple 2003; Levy and Newell 2005b). Current research on the structure and processes of global environmental politics highlights four empirical trends: first, the growth of both the scale and scope of non-state actors (multiple actors); second, the emergence of governance systems that connect local, regional and global constituencies, such as the global regime to curb greenhouse gas emissions, regional regimes that govern the environmental protection of regional seas or local communities that play a decisive role in politics (multiple levels); third, the growing legalisation surrounding environmental politics and at the same time the segmentation of rule making into different geographical and functional clusters (multiple authorities); and finally, the emergence of new mechanisms of steering detectible at the global level, often in the form of novel institutional arrangements and actor coalitions (multiple mechanisms). Whereas the former two trends have received major attention, the latter two are still nascent.

There is a considerable overlap between the above-mentioned theoretical approaches and literatures and the insights from the environmental field because the environment has served as the prime empirical testing ground for new theoretical and conceptual developments. I will therefore briefly focus on one approach that has been genuinely developed in the area of environmental studies, the concept of non-state, market-driven governance advanced by Benjamin Cashore and colleagues (Cashore 2002; Cashore, Auld and Newsom 2004; Bernstein and Cashore 2004b). Forms of non-state market-driven governance (NSMD) emerge both at national and transnational levels as a result of political trends that have given market-oriented approaches increasing salience (Cashore 2002: 506). The empirical focus of NSMD is more restricted than the focus of private governance because forms of private institutionalisation that do not involve the mechanism of markets are beyond its scope. NSMD is also not identical with the concept of business co-regulation that builds the empirical focus of this book because the former is applied to all forms of market-driven governance including inter-firm and profit/non-profit interactions, while the latter focuses exclusively on those institutions incorporating the divergent and at first sight often contradictory logics of profit and non-profit organisations. In addition, one aspect of this book that departs from studies using the NSMD concept is the broader empirical landscape that includes cases from different problem areas.[6]

To conclude, the assessment of theoretical and conceptual work that is linked to the question of private governance can be grouped into three broad categories, which have received quite uneven attention. First, an actor-based perspective that is rooted in the mainstream of IR, mainly analysing the strategies and influence of different types of private actors towards states and international institutions. Second, a network perspective, focusing on partnership between public and private actors, that includes political science and management approaches. Third, an institutional perspective on the phenomenon of private governance that has predominantly been applied to cases of inter-firm cooperation and the resulting regulation of economic issue areas in the global economy. In sum, most research has hitherto focused on business cooperation in the form of inter-firm regimes, policy-oriented research on the general phenomenon of partnerships in sustainability politics and research within one thematic area, such as forestry, or on related instruments, such as certification. What is still missing is a thorough assessment of private governance through the partnerships of different actors (referred to as business co-regulation as opposed to business self-regulation), including an analysis of key conditions of institutional formation, functional pathways of influence and potential explanations for varying effects.

**Private Governance, Business Co-regulation and Global Sustainability Politics**

A detailed conceptual discussion of private governance from an institutionalist point of view is provided in Chapter 3. Hence, at this point, some brief conceptual clarifications may suffice. Although the intellectual field of private governance is far from being sufficiently mapped and major room exists for contending definitions and understandings, both with regard to theory and empirical phenomena, some basic constitutive elements of private governance as the central theoretical approach to new institutional forms of rule making and implementation beyond the state can be identified. First, private governance centres on rules and regulation, not on spontaneous, uncoordinated behaviour such as market interactions. Second, private governance may contain processes and instances of institutionalisation beyond cooperation between different non-state actors. Finally, private governance potentially organises political spaces equivalent to public steering mechanisms.

As a result, there is growing agreement that private governance emerges next to public and hybrid forms of steering. Private governance 'emerges at the global level where the interactions among private actors ... give rise to institutional arrangements that structure and direct actors' behavior in an issue-specific area' (Falkner 2003: 72-3). The result of this institutionalisation among a wide range of private actors can be understood as a functional equivalent of the public governing functions of states and international organisations. But private governance should not be equated with mere cooperation between various private actors. In the words of Falkner (2003: 73):

Cooperation requires the adjustment of individual behavior to achieve mutual beneficial objectives. ... It is mostly of an *ad hoc* nature with a short lifetime. Governance, however, emerges out of a context of interaction that is institutionalised and of more permanent nature. In a system of governance, individual actors do not constantly decide to be bound by the institutional norms based on a calculation of their interest, but adjust their behavior out of recognition of the legitimacy of the governance system.

Therefore, it seems adequate to analyse private governance as a form of institutionalisation among private actors, including the profit and the non-profit segments of transnational society. Global private governance then could also be understood as the functional outcome of private institutions active in distinct global policy fields, resulting in a functional equivalent to public forms of problem solving beyond the state. Consequently, private governance appears as a result of many different activities and processes. In sum, private governance can be defined as a form of socio-political steering, in which private actors are directly involved in regulating – in the form of standards or more general normative guidance – the behaviour of a distinct group of transnational actors, in most cases corporations and other business actors. Hence, I contend that the phenomenon of business co-regulation can be adequately assessed from the analytical perspective of private governance.

But what precisely is 'business co-regulation'? Regulation can be defined as the 'act or process of controlling by rule or restriction' (Garner 1999: 1289) or, with a focus on the source of regulation, as

> the diverse sets of instruments by which governments set requirements on enterprises and citizens. Regulations include laws, formal and informal orders and subordinate rules issued by all levels of government, and rules issues by non-governmental or self-regulatory bodies to whom governments have delegated regulatory powers. (cited in Richter 2001: 38)

With regard to regulating business actors, regulation shall be defined as limits imposed on the behaviour of economic actors, contained in rules and standards. However, business regulation not only emerges from public sources or is authorised by public actors, but also increasingly comes from non-state sources of authority. Therefore, business regulation is best classified by its source.[7] In simple terms, business regulation can derive from three broad institutional arrangements: first, regulation may derive from public actors and organisations, including national governments and intergovernmental organisations (public regulation); second, regulation may derive from business itself (business self-regulation); and finally, regulation may derive from a partnership of different actors, among them states, international organisations and private non-state actors such as environmental NGOs. The latter type is labelled 'business co-regulation'.

The third term that needs a brief discussion is sustainability politics. It is used in this book to refer to the policy arena that is concerned with sustainable development. In most accounts it includes the agenda of the 1992 United Nations Conference on Environment and Sustainable Development (UNCED) and its follow-up events, the United Nations General Assembly Special Session (UNGASS) in 1997 and the World Summit on Sustainable Development (WSSD) in 2002. In this context, sustainability politics goes beyond environmental politics in that it deliberately combines social well being, economic development and environmental integrity. However, sustainability is one of the most contested ideas in global environmental discourse (cf. Elliott 2004: 157-177). Consequently, the use of the term sustainability politics, instead of the more restricted term environmental politics throughout this book, does not reflect an uncritical approval of the term sustainability. It rather acknowledges that there is a striving discourse utilising the concept for different purposes. What makes it a useful description for a policy arena can be summarised in the following points. First, sustainability politics not only reflects the fact that policy goals have become multidimensional (economic development, social well being, environmental integrity) instead of environment only, but also that interests are diverse. Second, the term sustainability politics pays attention to the fact that actual discursive practices have shifted in many areas (for example, what has been known as corporate environmental reporting is now sustainability reporting). And finally, the term sustainability politics directs our attention to the causes of environmental degradation by incorporating the social and economic dimensions of this development. In sum, sustainability politics is used to denote a policy arena that is considerably wider than the environmental one, both in terms of policy goals and discursive practices.

## A 'Theory of Global Governance in the Making'?

It is often stated that global governance is different from more traditional perspectives on world politics, but the precise nature of how the task of governance is performed in a specific issue area by non-state actors through new institutional arrangements has not been addressed in great detail. In addition, the debate about global governance in world environmental and sustainability politics has largely focused on normative versions of the concept, addressing questions of institutional design, fit and interplay of, in most cases, international cooperation. Although the possibility of institutionalising, for example in the case of a world environmental organisation (Biermann and Bauer 2005b), brings to the table many important issues in governing the unstable relationship between humans and their natural environment, it is the analytical notion of global governance that needs more attention.

Therefore, this study ventures down an exploratory path, paying special attention to the factors that cause a shift in global governance, as well as to the impacts the privatisation of rules has on our understanding of politics. In this sense, theorising about the characteristics of the current structure of global governance, the inherent processes and functional mechanisms, points to the broader debate about the changing nature of the political system. It is precisely in this discourse on 'post-sovereign' structures in world politics that the empirical transformation of global business regulation and global governance as its possible theoretical manifestation meet.

The basic disagreement in contemporary debates about the nature of sovereignty in the international system evolves around the question of whether states are still the primary loci of sovereignty, or if they have been complemented or even supplanted by other structures of authority. Many scholars claim that state sovereignty is eroding (cf. Camilleri and Falk 1992).[8] Liberals, environmentalists and postmodernists 'seem to be unanimous in their expectation of the inevitable demise of the Westphalian state system, in which territoriality counts as the cornerstone' (Staden and Vollaard 2002: 166). If state sovereignty is understood as territorially rooted political authority, or, in the words of Daniel Philpott, as 'supreme authority within a territory' (1997: 19), it is possible to discern five major developments challenging the construct of state sovereignty (Staden and Vollaard 2002: 167-172). First, market integration and the forces of globalisation are believed to be beyond the state's control; second, advancing military technologies permeate the imagined hard shell of the territorial state; third, sovereignty is also questioned from within the territory, especially when competing authorities are strong (for example language, ethnic origin, religion); fourth, the spread of the idea of universal human rights has contributed to the erosion of state sovereignty through its claim of unrestricted validity; and fifth, states can themselves engage in a transfer of sovereignty to other institutions in order to achieve higher leverage vis-à-vis their national constituencies. An additional challenge to state sovereignty is caused by global change, not only because the physical basis of territoriality becomes flux, but also because global environmental changes such as climate change undermine the state's capability to act unilaterally.

What are, in the light of these different tendencies of erosion, the possible alternatives to territorial authority structures? A global governance perspective that is analytical rather than normative in scope may help to identify the novel institutional arrangements and functional mechanisms that increasingly compete with more traditional authority structures. When van Staden and Vollaard hypothesise international regimes and global public policy networks to complement or even supplant territorially defined authority (2002: 174), one may easily add private rule systems as another possible alternative.

Instead of conceptualising world politics in terms of a single structure of authority, we should start thinking of authority in many different forms; territorial as in the state system, personal as in science, structural as in tribalism or functional as in international cooperation. In addition, authority may be private rather than public, as in the case of co-regulation. Global governance is the adequate theoretical vantage point to assess these multiple structures of authority because it has neither a predisposition for one specific outcome, nor for different mechanisms of governing. A more detailed treatment of the current debate about the nature of global governance, its intellectual precursors and its different uses is provided in Chapter 2.

In sum, this study focuses on the nature of private transnational arrangements within the framework of global governance research, but it also points to a broader debate about the nature of current world politics in general. In particular, it attempts to contribute to a 'theory of global governance in the making' that acknowledges the increasingly important status of private forms of governance in establishing flexible but lasting transnational orders.

# METHODOLOGICAL CONSIDERATIONS: CONCEPTS, CASES AND SOCIAL SCIENCE LOGICS

After having described the puzzle, the resulting research questions, our current state of knowledge and the contextual boundaries of inquiry, I now turn to the methodological challenges of such an endeavour. Three choices need to be justified in more detail: first, the use of concepts as basic tools of social science research; second, the application of the qualitative case study approach, including a justification of research design, case selection and data collection; and third, the logic and application of necessary vs. sufficient conditions arguments (in particular in the analysis of private governance formation). Readers less interested in this more general discussion of current social science research methodology may continue on page 26 with a short outline of the argument presented in this book.

## Concepts as Tools

Concepts are one of the most basic tools social science has at its disposal. Consequently, we should be careful in developing and applying them to understand complex social phenomena. Therefore, I first discuss the general usefulness of concepts in social research and how they should be constructed to avoid the major pitfalls often attributed to the lax handling of concepts. This discussion provides the basis for the reconstruction of the global governance concept approached in Chapter 2.

By relating certain phenomena to each other and keeping others apart, concepts fulfil the pivotal function of ordering and structuring our perception of the world. As a result, concepts help us, among other things, to make judgements about the relevance and significance of information, to analyse specific situations and processes, or to create new ideas and theories. Because they allow us to make generalisations, concepts are fundamental to individual as well as collective learning processes (cf. Dingwerth and Pattberg 2006a). Thus, '[w]e might separately learn about tables, chairs, sofas but the process of learning will be facilitated if we arrive at the concept of furniture' (Bélanger 2003).

Charles Ragin has described the process of social research as a constant 'dialogue between ideas and evidence', resulting in the representation of social life as the ultimate outcome of social inquiry (1994: 55). More precisely, representations of social reality 'emerge from the interplay between analytical frames (which are derived from ideas) and images (which are derived from evidence)' (1994: 65). The term analytical frame is used in a similar way as the term concept: 'An analytical frame might be used, for example, to articulate the idea of a table. People can recognize a table when they see one, even though tables differ greatly, because they have an implicit analytic frame for tables' (1994: 65). But whereas in everyday life these mental operations are rather implicit, science must make them explicit. That is why a great deal of time and effort should be dedicated to the appropriate use of concepts in social science, especially when they are derived from ordinary language.

It is important to note that the same empirical phenomenon may be analysed from different conceptual perspectives, depending on the object of study, the researchers interest and the theoretical/meta-theoretical background. What follows from understanding a concept/analytical frame as a way of seeing or a distinct optic is simply that without choosing the appropriate frame for the accomplishment of a certain phenomenon, it will most predictably go unnoticed. A researcher studying environmental treaties and the subsequent regulation at the international/global level will probably fail to recognise private systems of rule, which arguably have a similar outcome, because his or her mental frame does not incorporate non-state sources of authority. In addition, one concept may even refer to different phenomena, depending on the issue area or scholarly tradition. For example, the term 'governance' is invoked in debates about the minimal state, new public management, corporate behaviour, international aid and development and the changing relationship between public and private actors.

Given this state of confusion, how can we know which concept to choose for our analysis and which one to leave aside? Acknowledging the meta-theoretical and ideological reasons for selecting a certain analytical frame, two pitfalls should be avoided when deciding on a concept. First, concepts should, as far as possible, not group objects together that do not share similarities. In other words, a single concept should not be used for phenomena that are essentially different (polysemy). If this basic rule is neglected, the analytical power of the concept in question is diminished by the various meanings of the term and by the additional efforts analysts have to make in determining which of the various meanings is invoked in a specific argument or proposition. In other words: 'Because we cannot achieve a basic level of agreement on the terms by which we analyze the social world, agreement on conclusions is impossible' (Gerring and Barresi 2003: 202). Second, researchers should also refrain from inventing new concepts for every new phenomenon different from a previous one, because ultimately this would lead to the complete reproduction of the empirical world without any ordering function.

One way to avoid these major pitfalls in concept formation and selection is to adhere to a 'min–max strategy' proposed by Gerring and Barresi (2003). Their point of departure is the distinction between general definitions, determining what a word means in a general context of usage (usually a language, language region or culture), and contextual definitions, applicable only in the specific issue area or scholarly community (Gerring and Barresi 2003: 204). The fundamental difference between the two is caused by the inverse relation between contextual range and empirical utility. By increasing the former, a researcher will most likely decrease the latter, and vice versa. A way out of this dilemma is to combine minimal and ideal-type definitions to arrive at the attribute and entity space of a concept. Minimal definitions identify the essential properties of a concept and thereby maximize their phenomenal range. In contrast, ideal-type definitions aim to incorporate the ideal properties of a concept and thereby increase the number of attributes related to it. As a result, this 'min–max strategy', the authors argue, should help to resolve conceptual ambiguities that plague the use of many social science concepts by defining the universe of possible uses more accurately.

## A Qualitative Case Study Approach

The qualitative case study methodology[9] in social science has attracted considerable attention in the last 15 years (Ragin and Becker 1992; Lieberson 1994; Ragin 1994; Yin 1994; Mitchell and Bernauer 1998; Maoz 2002; Gerring 2004), ranging from affirmative to extremely critical. The main advantages attributed to the case study method in comparison to other research approaches include the possibility of undertaking – at a relatively low cost – explanatory research, the ability to carefully link correlating variables via process tracing, and the opportunity to systematically compare processes across cases (Maoz 2002: 162-164). Objections to the case study method in general, and in qualitative research in particular, often centre around a lack of attention given to four important aspects of case study work:[10] first, choosing questions that benefit from applying a case study methodology in comparison to other approaches; second, defining the 'case' in the study, which means identifying the appropriate unit(s) of analysis; third, choosing the most rewarding case study design with respect to the phenomenon under observation, theoretical and meta-theoretical considerations, and financial as well as time constraints; and fourth, selecting cases to avoid selection bias. With a view to avoiding the negative implications that may result from ignoring these issues – from measurement error to endogeneity and incorrect generalisation – I discuss these four themes in some detail with reference to studying the phenomenon of private governance in general and private business co-regulation in particular.

When should an investigator employ a qualitative case study method and when turn to other approaches, such as experimental research, surveys or computer simulations? Yin argues that the choice of research strategy should be based on three conditions: the type of question posed, the extent of control over the actual events under consideration and the degree of focus on contemporary versus historical events (1994: 4). A case study thus seems most rewarding as a research strategy in situations where 'a "how" or "why" question is being asked about a contemporary set of events over which the in-vestigator has little or no control' (1994: 9). Analysing the emergence and influence of private institutions in contemporary sustainability politics at the global level meets the above-mentioned conditions for choosing a case study approach. The key interest here is to understand why antagonistic actors from the profit as well as the non-profit camp engage in the establishment of transnational rules and how these rules gain influence among a wide range of stakeholders.

Whether a researcher uses a qualitative case study approach is largely determined by the questions of interest and the phenomenological situation (historical/contemporary, control vs. no control over events). Defining the case under observation, the unit of analysis involves logical as well as con-ceptual considerations. What is a case study and what constitutes a case? One recent definition argues that a case study is 'an intense study of a single unit for the purpose of understanding a larger class of (similar) units' (Gerring 2004: 342). A case could than simply be understood as an instance of a larger phenomenon, a theoretically defined class of events (Levy 2002: 133). The unit of analysis in case study work depends on the theoretical context and the puzzle the investigator sets out to study. Units of analysis may include individual people, social groups, institutions, political processes, policies, structures or even functional and sociological roles. Within the context of this study, we can easily identify the phenomenon of business co-regulation (private governance systems) to be an instance of the larger class of events labelled private and global governance in global (sustainability) politics and therefore the primary unit of analysis.

Prejudices against the qualitative case study method not only derive from the imprecision in defining a case, but also from a lack of justification of why a possible case study design is given preference over alternatives. Designs frequently distinguished in the literature include explanatory and confirmatory case studies (Maoz 2002), single[11] and multiple case studies (Yin 1994: 18-20), as well as atheoretical, interpretative, hypothesis-generating or deviant case studies (Eckstein 1975; Lijphart 1975; Levy 2002: 134-139). Because design choices in most instances result from the peculiarities of the research question and are not further specified, specific attention should be paid to enhancing the validity of the case study. Four tests have commonly been used to guarantee the quality of empirical research. Construct validity requires that correct operational measures be established to study the central phenomena under observation. This includes accurate definitions of key concepts (for example private governance and business co-regulation) as well as reliable measures for the indicators applied. Internal validity is concerned with correct inference. Therefore, it is important to clearly state the relationship between different variables and consider all possible alternative explanations. The test for external validity deals with the question of whether a conclusion drawn from the case under observation can be generalised to the larger set of phenomena it belongs to. This involves a clarification of the concept of generalisation in qualitative case study research itself.

Whereas some authors believe that valid generalisation rests on the correct sampling of cases with reference to their overall population (Maoz 2002: 166), others contend that generalisation is only possible to a broader theory, as with experimental research, in which the investigator tries to generalise the results to theory and therefore does not try to select 'representative' experiments (Yin 1994: 37). The latter view is especially important in the context of business co-regulation because empirical cases are scarce and only in the process of discovering additional examples can theory be put to a replicated test. The fourth characteristic of qualitative case study work, reliability, is the best known, and demands that a repetition of the research under the same conditions yields the same results. The discussion of the methodological choices and the applied research tools, as provided in this section, is a prerequisite for reliable research results.

Much criticism raised against the qualitative case study method has been targeted specifically towards the selection of cases and the resulting danger of selection bias (King, Keohane and Verba 1994: 107-109). Whereas the logic behind different case selection designs and the corresponding necessary or sufficient condition arguments are discussed in detail in the following section, here I provide only a brief justification of case selection according to the three conditions of availability, variance and policy implications.

One fundamental problem that the researcher necessarily encounters when approaching the population of private systems of rules at the transnational level is that no database has been collected systematically so far and that, as a result, identifying cases depends on chance. For that reason, the first decisive factor in choosing a certain institution as a case to study was availability of data and access to the case in question. In order to avoid bias introduced by the investigator, we must ensure that the selection criterion (availability of data) is not correlated with the dependent variable in our analysis of emergence. The analysis of functions and impacts calls for variation on the dependent variable (private influence) and the corresponding independent variables. Therefore, institutions were chosen that display different values for private influence (its normative, discursive and structural effects), and at the same time differ according to a variety of dimensions, such as institutional design, issue area, duration, geographical location of headquarters, mechanism of compliance management and public awareness about the problem and the institution itself. The third condition on which the case selection in this study is based can be described as the relevance of policy implications. Although the literature raises concerns about selecting cases because of current policy interests (Mitchell and Bernauer 1998: 14), a better understanding of the cases could also contribute to better policy choices in the respective issues areas. Whereas the methodologically correct starting point for research is theory, the output should, in my opinion, allow for better decisions. This is especially true when it comes to the question of private politics; only a thorough assessment of functions, impacts and implications may enable us to devise better institutions in the future.

I have selected FSC and CERES as case studies because they represent two different instrumental approaches to private governance while displaying a number of similarities in their overall structure and operation. They are both early examples of private institutions in global sustainability politics and therefore have served as points of reference in both the academic and policy domain. In addition, although products of the same macro-systemic conditions and actor rationales, the two cases display different degrees of influence and problem-solving success and hence can be used to illustrate a number of preliminary hypotheses on the overall influence of private institutions in global governance.

## Data Collection

The qualitative analysis of two distinct private institutions in global sustainability politics was based on the examination of primary sources, such as internal and published documents from the organisations; accessible websites; secondary sources, such as academic studies and technical reports; a series of interviews and participatory observation gained through field visits to the headquarters of the respective organisations; as well as additional interviews with stakeholders from profit and non-profit organisations. While written documentation and historical accounts naturally played a major role in the analysis of the early formation process of private institutions,[12] the assessment of roles and functions, as well as feedback at different levels of the political process, has primarily been based on interviews and participatory observation.

Naturally, interviews with members of a relatively new type of institution on questions of function, influence and effectiveness pose a special methodological challenge. Particular attention has therefore been paid to the methodological and practical preparation of the field visits to guarantee both the validity and comparability of data from different cases under observation. To improve the comparability of case studies while retaining openness to the respondents' views and expert knowledge, this study employed a half-standardized interview method (Meuser and Nagel 1991). This method includes written interview guidelines that generate comparable data by asking different respondents the same standardized questions, but also permits the investigator to ask additional questions without standardized answer alternatives, such as grand tour questions and prompts (Leech 2002a). This interview method allows for data collection that is both restrictive and open and enables both general and specific conclusions about different cases. In particular, researchers have employed the expert or elite interview technique, where the respondent is addressed as an expert with knowledge about a specific area, incident or process. In the words of Lewis Dexter (cited in Leech 2002b):

> In standardized interviewing ... the investigator defines the question and the problem; he is only looking for answers within the set bound by his presuppositions. In elite interviewing ..., however, the investigator is willing, and often eager to let the interviewee teach him what the problem, the question, the situation is.

This is particularly important when trying to identify and assess complex causal pathways, as in the case of analysing the influence of private governance, an area that has seldom or never been the topic of social science research.

The written questionnaire[13] for the semi-structured interviews included core questions complemented by specific interview modules, which were used only for a sub-set of interviews.[14] In addition, complementary data was sought from specialised experts and stakeholders, such as NGO and company representatives. The selection of the interviewees within an institution was based on in-depth knowledge about the expertise of different employees, gained through participatory observation. Due to reasons of anonymity, names or positions of interviewees are not mentioned in the text.

### Necessary or Sufficient Conditions?

King, Keohane and Verba (1994) paved the way for a better understanding of the logic of social research in their seminal work on qualitative research as a means of social inquiry. But despite their convincing argument about the nature of qualitative research and its close resemblance to quantitative inquiry, they paid no attention to the logical and methodological differences between sufficient and necessary condition arguments in social science research and the corresponding fundamentally different views of causality.[15] It was not until Dion's (1998) article that selecting on the dependent variable became understood as a legitimate operation in qualitative research among a wider range of scholars.

A standard objection against selecting cases according to values of the dependent variable is articulated by Collier and Mahoney (1996: 59): 'The central concern of scholars who have issued warnings about selection bias is that selecting extreme cases on the dependent variable leads the analyst to focus on cases that, in predictable ways, produce biased estimates of causal effects.' In addition, if values of the dependent variable show no variance, inference from proposed causes to outcomes is impossible. In the words of King et al. (1994: 129): 'When observations are selected on the basis of a particular value of the dependent variable, nothing whatsoever can be learned about the causes of the dependent variable without taking into account other instances when the dependent variable takes other values.'

This is true for correlation analysis looking for sufficient conditions, but the rigorous objection against the possibility of gaining valid inferences from cases that have been selected according to similar outcomes does not apply for necessary condition arguments. In its simplest form, a necessary condition can be stated as: Only if Z, then Y. Stated differently, the key property of any necessary condition is that if a necessary condition is absent, the effect does not occur, or formally:

$$\text{if } Z = 0 \quad \text{then} \quad Y = (Z, X) = 0$$

Verbal expression of the idea of a necessary condition is contained in the following sentences (Goertz 2003: 49): (1) if and only if Z is present does Y occur; (2) Z must be there for Y to succeed; (3) Z makes Y possible; and (4) Z is a precondition or prerequisite for Y. A different representation of the necessary condition idea can be found in set theoretic approaches (Most and Starr 2003). If the dependent variable and the necessary condition are conceptualised as sets, then a necessary condition Z/Y is fulfilled if Y, and only if Y, is a subset of Z. Consequently, it follows from the nature of the necessary condition idea that choosing cases according to a similar value of the dependent variable (for example formation of private governance systems = 1) does not introduce bias or lead to undetermined causality.

Although it is claimed that there is a unified approach to qualitative and quantitative research in social science, it is important to note that different views of causality represent different causal universes (Goertz 2003: 48). The logic of correlation is represented in a proposition of the sort 'the more Z, the more likely the outcome Y', whereas in the causal universe of necessary conditions, 'Z makes Y possible'. What separates the two logics can be summarised in three points. First, whereas sufficient, correlational arguments include equally strong claims for the presence and absence of a condition, the necessary approach to causality makes weak claims for the presence of the condition and strong claims for its absence (that is, if, and only if). Second, there is a difference in the breadth of the definition of causality, which means that necessary conditions apply in many instances as special cases of cause. Finally, in contrast to correlation analysis interested in the effect of a certain observation or variable (what is the effect of Z?), the necessary condition view is most interested in the reasons for the occurrence of Y (what is the condition under which Y occurs, dependent on non-Y never occurring together with Z?).

One problem associated with necessary condition arguments is that they are deterministic. What follows is that one observation that disconfirms the hypothesis (non-Z, but Y) will call into question the whole argument of causality in a given case. However, some scholars argue that it is possible to transform a necessary condition into probabilistic language (Goertz 2003: 52-53; Ragin 2003). As a result, it is possible, at least in principle, to state that a condition Z is virtually always, or in nearly all cases, necessary for Y. Formally, a probabilistic view on the necessary conditions argument assumes that the presence of Z in relation to the occurrence of Y can be represented as:

$$P(Y = 1 | Z = 1) > 0 ;$$

the absence of Z in relation to the occurrence of Y can be represented as:

$$P(Y = 1|Z = 0) = 0.$$

Whereas the former is a weak prediction, the latter makes a strong causal claim.

In sum, the idea and logic of necessary condition arguments justifies case selection on the dependent variable. But in contrast to the rather harsh distinction of sufficient and necessary arguments as two different causal universes, I employ both logics as distinct research strategies. Whereas analysing the emergence of private co-regulative arrangements calls for a necessary condition argument, the question of impact and effectiveness is best answered by applying sufficient condition logic and a correlation analysis.

## CONCLUSION: ARGUMENT AND OVERVIEW

The emerging phenomenon of business co-regulation constitutes a distinct form of private governance, a mechanism through which cooperation is institutionalised and maintained at the transnational level. It is defined as cooperation between two or more actors from the profit and non-profit sector of society with a view to establishing and maintaining regulation of a transnational or global problem. The regulation does incorporate explicit as well as implicit rules and norms, typically addressing economic behaviour, but also including non-economic activities. Different from public and public–private forms of regulation, private governance systems neither primarily rely on national or international authority nor address the traditional political system directly. I attempt to answer (a) how we can best conceive the phenomenon of private governance within the academic context of global governance and institutional analysis; (b) why and how private institutions emerge at the transnational level; (c) what function they perform within the larger system of global (sustainability) governance; and (d) why some institutional arrangements are more influential than others. The argument of this book unfolds in three broad steps. First, I engage in a reconstruction of the concept of governance at the transnational level, including the development of a detailed framework of analysis (Chapters 2 and 3). Second, this book provides an empirical analysis of global business regulation, followed by two in-depth case studies on private co-regulation in the field of global sustainability politics (Chapters 4, 5 and 6). Finally, a concluding section emphasises the larger implications of private governance for our understanding of world politics, drawing on a detailed comparison of the two empirical cases (Chapter 7). In more detail, the argument proceeds as follows:

After Chapter 1 has introduced the research question, the research methodology and the general argument, Chapter 2 provides the necessary foundations for the subsequent discussion of private governance and transnational business regulation by reconstructing the contested concept of global governance as an overarching conceptual framework for the analysis of current transformations in world politics. I propose to use global governance as a concept for the assessment of large-scale socio-economic transformation and the resulting reorganisation of the political realm. From this analytical perspective, the concept of global governance focuses on five key characteristics that describe the current nature and transformation of world politics. First, a global governance perspective stipulates no hierarchy between actors; the mode of steering is predominantly non-hierarchical and often based on arguing rather than traditional bargaining. Second, a global governance perspective ascribes a central status to novel forms of political organisation. Hence, new relations between organisational parts of the governance architecture, as well as new relations between the actors of governance, are of central interest. A third key feature is the equivalence of international and transnational decision making procedures, as well as the resulting norms and rules. A fourth key characteristic of the current global governance order is the emergence and persistence of non-territorial, post-sovereign forms of authority. Complementing and sometimes even contradicting well-established systems of rules, such as governments and nation states, new mechanisms for aggregating societal choices emerge that are boundary crossing and highly flexible. Finally fifth, actors are also increasingly flexible in their roles and responsibilities within a distinct governance arrangement, thereby constantly altering the landscape of governance.

Following these more general thoughts, Chapter 3 develops an analytical framework to assess the phenomenon of private governance with regard to its emergence, function and influence. I stipulate that recent forms of environmental co-regulation between business actors and non-profit organisations are going beyond more traditional forms of private involvement in world politics, such as influencing discourse or shaping political decisions at the global level for two reasons. First, private cooperation to solve policy problems is getting more and more institutionalised in very specific rules and regulations. And second, the resulting rules neither emanate from public sources of authority, nor are they primarily directed towards public actors. In sum, this institutionalisation of private policy-making amounts to a new quality of patterned and repetitive behaviour at the global level: transnational organisation. To better analyse the process of institutionalisation and the influence it produces, I describe the empirical phenomenon of private co-regulation as a private system of governance that includes two distinct characteristics: first, norms, rules and procedures as the institutional dimension and second, individual and collective actors within a complex network as the organisational dimension.

The second part of Chapter 3 is concerned with theoretical approaches towards the puzzle of the emergence of private governance systems. Private business co-regulation at the global level is understood to emerge as a consequence of large-scale transformations and its interplay with rather micro-level conditions. Constituting a necessary condition for the formation of private governance systems involving antagonistic actors, four interrelated factors must work together: (1) a lack of adequate public regulation on the issue in question; (2) a strong unifying metaphor, idea or model to bridge the gap between different interests; (3) a problem structure of interrelated interests; and (4) the organisational resources of non-state actors, such as public trust, credibility and environmental impact.

Private governance systems, once established, acquire influence via different functions performed within the global political system, as well as within the actual private network constituted by non-state actors. Among these functions (or functional roles), the following are the most important: (1) making, implementing and enforcing the private regulation (regulatory function); (2) producing and disseminating knowledge, constituting a learning network and early warning system and changing existing discourses (cognitive/discursive function); and (3) transferring standards (both international and private) via different channels to different addressees (integrative function).

With regard to possible explanations for varying influences across the empirical cases, I propose five variables that are put to the test in the concluding chapter: the degree of formalisation (obligation, precision and delegation), the cost of devising and implementing private rules, the problem structure, the quality and organisational structure of the network sustaining the institutions and finally, the degree of authorisation by existing international or transnational norms and rules.

After the analytical framework of global governance in general and private governance in particular has been established, Chapter 4 introduces the phenomenon of global business regulation as the empirical context of this study. I argue that global business regulation, broadly understood as limits imposed on the behaviour of economic actors, contained in rules and standards, is undergoing a profound transformation. International regulatory frameworks are complemented by private institutions spelling out detailed rules and standards for economic behaviour in issue areas ranging from corporate environmental reporting to labour and human rights. Among those transformations, the establishment of co-regulative arrangements between corporations and non-profit organisations rewards further attention. To provide a broad empirical context for the in-depth analysis of two specific co-regulative institutions in global sustainability politics from a governance perspective, I briefly engage in an argument about the need for global business

regulation, possibilities for classification and broad contextual factors
forwarded in the literature.

Based on this empirical overview, Chapter 5 analyses the emergence,
functions and influences of the Forest Stewardship Council as the first in-
depth empirical example of global business co-regulation from a private
governance perspective. In addition, the chapter also critically assesses the
prospect for and limitations on private governance in the global forestry
arena.

Subsequently, Chapter 6 analyses the institutionalisation of private governance in the area of corporate environmental reporting and environmental
management. The Coalition for Environmentally Responsible Economies is
analysed with regard to its emergence, functions and influences, as well as
with a view towards potential shortcomings and limitations.

Finally, Chapter 7 summarises the main findings of this study. In particular, I provide a brief comparison across the cases. Emphasis is laid on identifying shortcomings and failures of private governance, thereby formulating a
working hypothesis about the effectiveness of private forms of governance
within the field of global sustainability politics and beyond. The chapter
concludes with a brief outlook on future research in the field of transnational
organisation.

## NOTES

1.  It is widely acknowledged today that social science research should be theory-driven rather
    than idiographic. But in some instances, starting from an empirical puzzle or an emergent
    phenomenon is the more adequate strategy, especially when the accompanying theory is
    still in the making and the empirical knowledge is scarce. Unfortunately, exploratory work
    is 'quickly dismissed as a matter of guesswork, inspiration, or luck...' (Gerring 2004: 349).
    At the same time, it is widely acknowledged that many seminal works derive their classic
    status from new ideas, perspectives or theoretical propositions that only later are put to
    confirmatory tests.
2.  On the notion of organisational fields, compare DiMaggio and Powell (1983) and Scott
    (1994).
3.  One notable exception is studies addressing forms of private authority beyond the state, in
    which private actors are found to have impacts beyond international decision making, for
    example in the case of bond rating agencies (cf. Sinclair 1999, 2002).
4.  As McQuaid (2000: 10) observes, '(t)he term "partnership" covers greatly differing con-
    cepts and practices and is used to describe a wide variety of types of relationship in a
    myriad of circumstances and locations'. In addition, Richter (2001) has pointed to the fact
    that the term 'partnership' represents a policy paradigm based on the assumption of trust,
    shared benefits and an underlying win–win situation, concealing the fundamentally
    different goals and power resources of the actors involved. Throughout this thesis, the
    concept of partnership is employed as a value neutral term, equivalent with cooperation.
5.  The ongoing debate about partnership must be put into the perspective of the long tradition
    of research on public–private cooperation, especially at the national and local level, on

issues such as urban regeneration and local economic development. See, among others, Harding (1990); Sellgren (1990); Kouwenhoven (1993); Bennet and Krebs (1994).

6.  To my knowledge, the concept of NSMD has so far only been applied to the area of forest politics (Cashore, Auld and Newsom 2004). Key questions addressed within the NSMD concept include the distinct process of granting legitimacy to non-state forms of governance and the underlying causal factors of firm-level choices with regard to competing certification systems (Cashore, Auld, and Newsom 2004: 32-38; Sasser et al. 2004).

7.  Business regulation may also be classified by issue area; among others, typical areas of regulation include anti-trust, anti-corruption, anti-discrimination, corporate taxation, labour, health and safety, consumer protection and environmental protection.

8.  For an elaborate rejection of the 'state sovereignty in crisis hypothesis', see Jänicke (2002). In addition, on the persistence of sovereignty as a key concept in IR, see Krasner (1999, 2001).

9.  Although this book takes a qualitative approach and the case study method is discussed with reference to qualitative data, the method itself should not be equated with qualitative research exclusively. In the words of Yin (1994: 14), 'case studies can include, and even be limited to, quantitative evidence. In fact, the contrast between quantitative and qualitative evidence does not distinguish the various research strategies'.

10. These four aspects are linked to, but should not necessarily be equated with, linear research steps advocated in the literature. See Mitchell and Bernauer (1998: 9-10).

11. Note that a single-case design is not equal to the N = 1 design because the latter is only hypothetical. A single unit observed at a single point in time (N = 1) offers no plausible causal proposition since an indefinite number of lines might be drawn through the single data point (cf. Gerring 2004).

12. To the extent that it is possible, key players from the early partnering process between profit and non-profit organisations have been identified and questioned in in-depth interviews. In addition, documents summarising the early negotiations and subsequent decisions were secured.

13. For a discussion of the functions and benefit of questionnaires in qualitative research, see McCracken (1988: 24-25); Atteslander (2000: 153-155).

14. The core interview module included questions on (1) roles and functions of the institution within the issue-specific as well as the wider political context; (2) historical developments, including possible explanatory factors for the institutions' emergence; (3) decision-making and standard-setting procedures. Specific modules posed questions on (i) financial resources; (ii) the relationship with other actors; (iii) the governance structure; (iv) public relations and information policies.

15. Note that the index of 'Designing Social Inquiry' does not even list the term 'necessary condition'.

# 2. Global Governance: Reconstructing a Contested Concept

> Interesting philosophy is rarely an examination of the pros and cons of a thesis. Usually it is, implicit or explicit, a contest between an entrenched vocabulary which has become a nuisance and a half-formed new vocabulary which vaguely promises great things. ... I am not going to offer arguments against the vocabulary I want to replace. Instead, I am going to try to make the vocabulary I favour look attractive by showing how it may be used to describe a variety of topics. (Rorty 1989: 9)

The previous chapter introduced the research questions and situated them within the larger context of ongoing academic debate on the current nature of world politics. In addition, it introduced the methodological tools that can be applied to reach meaningful conclusions on the issues in question. Following these considerations, this chapter introduces the necessary conceptual clarification to understanding the institutionalisation of private governance within the academic context of International Relations in general and the emerging global governance debate in particular. Hence, this chapter provides the larger conceptual and theoretical context for the analytical framework developed in Chapter 3 and the subsequent empirical case studies. Consequently, it situates the study within the larger realm of global governance research. Paying attention to conceptual issues is of paramount importance, because the global governance debate is still a nascent and highly contested academic field. I argue that it is the analytical understand-ing, as opposed to normative or critical readings of global governance, that is best suited to assess the large-scale transformation in world politics, signified by the institutionalisation of private governance. Firmly embedded within the analytical camp, I propose to understand global governance as a specific set of related observable phenomena – namely the sum of all institutions, processes and interaction between various actors at all levels of the socio-political system that address, in a non-hierarchical manner, a specific transnational or global problem.

The attempt to develop a concept to capture empirical phenomena of trans-sovereign global politics in general and private rules in particular is grounded on conceptual considerations often referred to as 'global governance debate' or even 'global governance theory'. However, the concept has been overloaded with specific connotations and meanings derived from different scholarly traditions and empirical occupations. As Finkelstein (1995: 368) argues, 'we say "governance" because we don't really know what to call what is going on', and that '"Global Governance" appears to be virtually anything'. As a result, a definite and uncontested definition is currently not available. Hence, this chapter attempts to reconstruct global governance as a useful political science concept. To achieve this aim, I first discuss the conceptual confusion generated by the different understandings of both 'global' and 'governance'. Subsequently, I give a brief overview of the academic ideas that constitute the basis on which the current global governance research agenda is erected. The third section analyses three current and often contradictory uses of the term 'global governance'. First, an analytical version that evokes global governance as an integrative term that captures many current transformations in world politics; second, a normative version that uses global governance to denote a political project towards greater multilateralism and international cooperation; and finally, a third version that analyses the current global governance debate as a hegemonic discourse. The subsequent section proposes a definition of global governance based on a triangular understanding of the concept as reflecting structure, process and outcome. In addition, the possible 'geographies' of global governance are discussed as heuristic tools to order the many emerging modes, forms and mechanisms of governance according to their place of origin and effect. The concluding section summarises the main findings and highlights the definition of global governance that provides the broader theoretical and conceptual context of this book.

## WHAT IS 'GLOBAL GOVERNANCE'?

From the influence of civil society on international decision making processes to the role of intergovernmental organisations and transnational corporations (TNCs) in world politics, many different phenomena have recently been addressed as a manifestation of global governance (O'Brien et al. 2000; Biermann and Bauer 2005a; Levy and Newell 2005b). But what precisely is 'governance', and when is it 'global'? The different understandings of 'global governance' in various contexts derive from disagreement about the precise meaning of both the terms 'global' and 'governance'. While the attribute 'global' can at least refer to the top-level scale of human activity or the sum of all scales of activity,[1] the term 'governance' is found to have a minimum of ten separate uses in the literature (Rhodes 1996; Hirst 2000; Kooiman 2002). The first main use of the concept of governance refers to the minimal state, redefining the nature of public responsibilities and private interests in the provision of public goods and services (Rhodes 1997). The second use, closely connected to the first, relates to the emergence of new public management strategies since the early 1980s, which have introduced commercial management practices to the public sector, taking up debates about cost and efficiency in the public domain (Osborne and Gaebler 1992; Peters 1996a). The third use is that of corporate governance, referring to ways large corporations are directed and controlled and including issues of accountability and the transparency of transnational business actors (Tricker 1984). A fourth use can be observed within the field of economic development, focusing on the good governance of administrations as a compliance condition for foreign and international aid, for example in the World Bank context; a fifth use of the term governance relates to qualitatively new processes of coordination and cooperation in decentralised networks, involving a wide variety of actors, from state bureaucracies to regional authorities and firms to advocacy networks and other non-governmental actors (Rhodes 1996). A sixth use of governance is reflected in the body of literature on European Governance with its focus on multi-level governance within the European Union (Börzel 1997; Albert and Kopp-Malek 2002). A seventh use of the term builds on the legacy of Michel Foucault under the heading of governance and governmentality (Hindess 1997). An eighth use is observable in the conception of participatory governance (Grote and Gbikpi 2002), while a ninth refers to governance as socio-cybernetic steering (Kooiman 2003). And finally, governance refers to an international order within the field of international relations, predominantly focusing on international institutions, most often international regimes, which cope with complex transboundary problems.

Etymologically, the term 'governance' derives from the Greek *kybernetes* and *kybernan*, relating to navigation and helmsmanship. The Latin expression *gubernnare* and *regere*, both used to describe the steering of a ship as well as that of the state (Schneider 2004), are also linked to the current English, French and German word for steering: to 'govern', 'gouverner', and 'regieren'. Governance in the social sciences in general is understood to refer to the lasting process of steering a technical or social system through distinct mechanisms and components. In the context of political science, the term governance has risen to prominence in close relation to the – real or perceived – decline in the institutional strength of the modern nation state and the increase in societal interdependencies (Pierre 2000; Kooiman 2002). As a result of this transformation, interests are no longer either public or private, but frequently shared among public authorities of all levels and a wide range of non-state actors. With the dividing lines between public and private sectors becoming increasingly blurred, a growing awareness emerges that governments are only one of the many potential actors active in addressing societal issues. From this perspective, the question of governance centres on 'what new instruments and new forms of exchange between state and society can be developed to ensure political control and societal support' (Pierre 2000: 2). In short, governance is first and foremost a political strategy under the conditions of the ongoing transformation of the liberal state. In a similar vein, the concept of global governance has also developed as a reaction to a fundamental transformation, in this case the restructuring of the Westphalian states system through the process of globalisation (Zacher 1992).

Various authors have defined governance in quite different ways. For Stoker (1998: 17), there exists a baseline agreement that governance 'refers to the development of governing styles in which boundaries between public and private sectors have become blurred'. Specifying these governing styles, Rhodes (1997: 15) refers to 'self-organizing, interorganizational networks characterized by interdependence, resource exchange, rules of the game and significant autonomy from the state'. For Lipschutz (1997: 83), one of the 'central issues facing human civilization at the end of the twentieth century is governance: Who rules? Whose rules? What rules? What kind of rules? At what level? In what form? Who decides? On what basis?', while the perennial question of governance for Reus-Smit is: 'How can human beings organize their social relations to enhance individual and collective security and physical well-being...?' (1998: 3). And in a similar straightforward manner, Kooiman (2002: 73) understands governance simply as 'solving problems and creating opportunities, and the structural and procedural conditions aimed at doing so'. However, three key features that constitute the main characteristics of governance can be identified. First, governance is occupied with rules, organisation and the conditions for order in a broad sense. Second, governance stipulates the existence, to various degrees, of new processes and mechanisms of problem solving. Finally, it describes a qualitatively new relation between public and private actors and a broadening of governing capacities, often in the form of self-organising networks. To conclude, one reason for the current (pre)occupation with governance is its capacity to include a wide range of phenomena within its scope. However, this strength is also a weakness. The governance approach is an intellectual home for many scholars with considerably different research agendas and theoretical occupations. As we will see in the next section, transferring it to the international and global level makes it even more vague.

# HISTORICAL SOURCES OF THE CURRENT GLOBAL GOVERNANCE DEBATE

Recent debates about the growing political influence of non-state actors, multiple interconnected policy levels and new functional mechanisms of steering beyond the nation state can all be subsumed under the headline of global governance. They have opened up space for a fresh perspective on large-scale transformations, which profoundly alter our understanding of 'who is doing what for whom' in world politics. Although there is neither an uncontested definition of global governance, nor a common understanding of what the term refers to in terms of structure and processes, the highly controversial debate highlights some empirical observations that go beyond traditional accounts of international relations. However, the current fashion of global governance research is firmly grounded in older debates within the discipline of political science and IR. In particular, the current convergence towards a global governance paradigm in IR must be seen as a new stage of the oscillation between state-centred and non-state accounts of the political order (cf. Nölke 2003).

Hewson and Sinclair (1999: 5-16) present three literatures that have either served as influential intellectual sources of the concept of global governance or have developed in close relation to it. First, the literature on globalisation and global change that points to transformative processes as one important cause for increasing interest in the socio-political order beyond the state; second, the literature on transnational relations that provides an early non-state heuristic and essentially multi-actor perspective; and finally, the literature on the United Nations (UN) and its organisational reform that acknowledges the need for cooperative and multilateral solutions to a range of accelerating global problems.

Almost any account of the world at the beginning of the 21st century acknowledges that social, political, economic and ecological environments are fundamentally changing. Attempts to grasp the nature of this transformation along with the structures and qualities of the emerging new order make frequent reference to two central concepts: globalisation and global governance (Fuchs 2002: 1). Their relation, however, is less clear. One valuable approach to delineating the relation between the two phenomena understands the process of globalisation as creating the demand for global governance. As a minimum definition, globalisation may be thought of as the 'widening, deepening and speeding up of worldwide interconnectedness in all aspects of contemporary social life, from the cultural to the criminal, the financial to the spiritual' (Held et al. 1999: 2). This interconnectedness is a key reason for government failures. As sovereign borders are getting porous and the frontier between national and transnational phenomena is becoming blurred (Rosenau

1997a), external effects gain a much greater impact on the responsiveness and problem solving capacity of nation states. In this view, global governance has emerged as the social, political and economic reaction to the process of globalisation, incorporating many of its ontological assumptions. In short, global governance is a distinct form of socio-political steering in the era of globalisation. However, the relation between the two concepts is less clear as it may appear at first sight. In particular, assuming a linear relation between globalisation as the cause and global governance as the systemic reaction is misleading for two reasons: first, as a process in flux, globalisation is constantly altering the conditions for effective socio-political response structures and problem solving capabilities. Second, global governance as the task of – at least partially – creating ordered rule at the global level changes the conditions under which globalisation progresses. In fact, critical accounts of globalisation have frequently highlighted the very political nature of the current transformation, in particular the economic policies of the 'Washington Consensus'.

With regard to the academic debate, current global governance approaches resemble much of the key propositions found in the globalisation literature. The concept of globalisation is heralded as a new paradigm in International Relations (Mittelman 2002). Several key assumptions underlying such a paradigm have – on closer inspection – been incorporated into the current global governance debate. First, the appropriate perspective is global rather than inter-national. Second, globalisation constitutes a structural transformation in world order. And third, new ontologies are needed to accommodate the increasing number and qualities of actors in the globalisation process.

A second influential source of the current global governance debate can be found in the transnational relations literature that dates back more than three decades. Not only does politics seem to be a dialectic process, but also academic debate. Whereas the 1990s and the new millennium have brought considerable preoccupation with topics such as the end of the state, the transformation of sovereignty, the emergence of global civil society and governance without government (Rosenau and Czempiel 1992; Ohmae 1995; Sassen 1996; Kaldor 2003), the 1980s were dominated by state-centric approaches, especially Waltzian neo-realism. Turning back another ten years in time, the picture changes again. The 1970s were the time of transnationalism challenging mainstream IR. The two approaches – state-centric inter-governmental relations and transnationalism – represent two distinct heuristics that presuppose many scholarly assumptions about the phenomena being studied. As global governance theory and other trans-sovereign approaches draw heavily on the idea of transnational relations, I will briefly discuss how this stands in opposition to state-centric conceptions of world affairs.

According to Keohane and Nye (1970: xii), the concept of transnational relations refers to 'regular interactions across national boundaries when at least one actor is a non-state agent'. In an early article, Kaiser (1969: 96) highlights three important aspects incorporated in the concept of transnational relations: first, different national societies communicate across national boundaries; second, these interactions lead to changes within a given society; and third, as a result, these changes force governments to react, either towards their own society or towards other governments. Transnational politics can therefore be understood as a system of institutional inter-linkages between societies – including a wide range of non-governmental societal actors – affecting the realm of domestic politics without involving intergovernmental relations. The idea of transnational politics therefore 'transposed pluralist theory to the level of international affairs' (Risse 2002: 258). As a result, research interests shifted from traditional topics of IR, such as democratic peace, non-intervention or cooperation under anarchy to transnational capital flows, coalitions of peace movements and transnational alliances of subnational governments. As early as 1962, Wolfers (1962: 23) noted that 'the United Nations and its agencies, the European Coal and Steel Community, the Afro-Asian bloc, the Arab League, the Vatican, the Arabian-American Oil Company, and a host of other nonstate entities are able on occasion to affect the course of international events'. In addition to a multi-actor perspective, the theory of transnational politics also contested the traditional boundary between domestic and international politics, as well as the resulting demarcation of fields of study. Comparative politics on the one hand deals with national systems and International Relations, on the other, relates to the space between the units.

But the more transnational approaches diverged from traditional approaches, the less meaningful results they generated. As Risse-Kappen notes, '[t]o study the policy impact of transnational relations becomes virtually impossible if the concept is used in such a broad way' (1995a: 8). In addition to its broad conception, three factors further contributed to the quick demise of the transnational relations approach in IR during the 1980s: first, as the transnational relations concept generated few theoretical propositions, meaningful empirical testing proved difficult. Second, while state-centred approaches appealed through their lean methodological design and operated with few basic assumptions, the rather complex transnationalism could not compete. Finally, the fairly bold advocacy of the end of the state by leading transnational relations theorists was defied by most traditionalists as radically overstated. However, transnationalism serves as a central reference point to global governance approaches by providing a transnational heuristic that captures the structure of world politics as being fundamentally shaped by the existence of multiple political actors, rather than by governments alone.

A third source for the current global governance debate is provided by scholarship on the United Nations, multilateralism and its organisational reform. From this perspective, the UN system constitutes the organisational and normative core of any effort 'to bring more orderly and reliable responses to social and political issues that go beyond capacities of states to address individually' (Gordenker and Weiss 1996: 17). Hence, it is analysed as the most ambitious institutional arrangement to date in terms of the multilateral management of global problems (Reus-Smit 1998). For many people, practitioners and scholars alike, the end of the Cold War and the bipolar system it was rooted in signified a profound transformation in the structure of world politics. High expectations have been directed towards the international community for bringing about peace, development and a solution to the environmental crisis of modern societies. The fact that many of them have at least been addressed can be seen in the series of world conferences on issues ranging from the environment and sustainable development to the state and status of women (cf. Messner and Nuscheler 1996). In sum, the concept of global governance is closely related to debates about the UN and its reform for two reasons: first, as the only truly global organisation, including almost every state as a member, the UN commands a significant amount of the organisational resources required to govern world affairs. Second, through its encompassing web of specialised agencies, organisations and commissions it touches on the vast majority of current global problems. As a result of the transformation of the international system in 1989/1991 and the high expectations that were attached to a 'new world order' of cooperation, the early global governance debate consequentially focused on governments as the main actors, while cooperation, regimes, international organisations, in short multilateralism, were considered their main instruments.

Besides the three debates firmly grounded in the IR camp – globalisation, transnationalism and the UN system – the concept of global governance is also linked to renewed discussion of national and sub-national public policy making since the early 1980s, implying new roles for a wide range of private actors in issue areas from urban regeneration to local economic development (Harding 1990; Sellgren 1990; Kouwenhoven 1993). The underlying causes of this state transformation can be attributed both to international and domestic sources. On the one hand, the 1970s world recession, deepening globalisation and the growing authority of the EU have triggered widespread reconstruction of the public domain (Krahmann 2003: 326). On the other hand, it is the unprecedented success of the welfare state itself, incorporating an ever-increasing portion of society within its range, that forces governments to privatise, outsource or co-produce the provision of public goods. In sum, global governance discourse is rooted in domestic debates about new steering instruments and innovative actor constellations, as well as in IR debates, including long-established views such as transnational politics and complex interdependence (Keohane and Nye 1970, 1977) and the more current themes of globalisation and multilateralism.

## ANALYTICAL, NORMATIVE AND DISCURSIVE UNDERSTANDINGS OF GLOBAL GOVERNANCE: ONE PHENOMENON OR MANY?

This section seeks to clarify the different uses and meanings of the term global governance to bring order to a vibrant, but often confusing debate.[2] However, I do not stipulate that any specific reading, meaning or understanding of global governance is better than any other. On this question, I agree with an interpretation of the global governance discourse as an essentially pragmatic undertaking that derives its success and durability from its relative vagueness (Albert and Kopp-Malek 2002).

Three paradigmatic understandings of the concept of global governance can be observed in current academic and policy-oriented debates that differ according to the line of reasoning employed to justify the use of the new concept. The first understanding sees global governance in close relation to the phenomenon of globalisation, but in contrast to a political understanding, it presumes that global governance is an analytical concept to make sense of the current transformations in the socio-political realm. Consequently, it highlights distinct qualities of the governing process, such as non-hierarchical steering modes and the inclusion of private actors within that process. The second understanding focuses on the necessity and adequateness of political answers to the challenge of globalisation. In this perspective, global governance is first and foremost a political programme to regain the necessary (state-based) steering capacity for problem solving in the postmodern age. The third understanding highlights the discursive nature of the current global governance debate and analyses the concept first and foremost as a hegemonic discourse to rhetorically conceal the negative implications of the neo-liberal economic and political agenda. I will discuss each understanding in more detail.

The first understanding is that of global governance as an analytical perspective on the current transformations in political organisation and problem solving at the global level. From this perspective, global governance is generally believed to encompass different systems of rule at different levels of human activity as an organising social principle beyond hierarchical steering and the sovereign authority of nation states. Key features are the non-hierarchical nature of the governing process and the centrality of non-state actors in this process. Although the analytical approach to global governance is hardly monolithic – in fact, it displays considerable theoretical and methodological diversity – a number of central assumptions have emerged that depart from more traditional concepts in IR.[3] Hence, as an analytical tool for making sense of the 'crazy-quilt nature' of world politics (Rosenau 1995: 15) the concept of global governance (1) ascribes special relevance to non-state actors; (2) analyses multiple spatial and functional levels of politics and their interaction; (3) is concerned with new modes and mechanisms of producing and maintaining global public goods; and (4) highlights the establishment of new spheres of authority beyond the nation state and international cooperation.

As we have seen above in the discussion about the intellectual sources of the current global governance 'paradigm', transnationalism has already highlighted the increasing importance of non-state actors in exercising political influence. An analytical understanding of global governance takes this notion further. In search of a new ontology of the current global order, Rosenau (1999: 287) explains: 'A depleted toolshed suggests that understanding is no longer served by clinging to the notion that states and national governments are the essential underpinnings of the world's organization.' In fact, Rosenau counts at least ten new governance actors that are not instruments of states and governments, including transnational lobbies, epistemic communities, sovereignty-free actors and social movements (1999: 298).

The second focus of the analytical global governance perspective is on the multi-level nature of current social interactions and resulting institutions of governance. In this view, the interconnectedness of different levels of the political process, different time frames and different geographical spaces call for a re-conceptualisation of the state-centric, two-level model of traditional international politics. The observation that the separation of domestic and international policy levels should no longer be accorded the central heuristic status it occupied for much of the history of political science, has been most strongly emphasized by Rosenau, who tirelessly notes that 'in a rapidly changing, interdependent world the separation of national and international affairs is problematic'; that 'to probe the domestic as aspects of "comparative politics" and examine the foreign as dimensions of "international politics" is more than arbitrary: it is erroneous'; and that 'we can no longer allow the domestic–foreign boundary to confound our understanding of world affairs' (1997a: 3f). As a consequence, the notion of multi-level governance has gained currency not only among scholars of European governance, but also among academics addressing global governance. Most recently, Hooghe and Marks (2003: 241) have distinguished between two types of multi-level governance – a first type constituted by competencies in jurisdictions at a limited number of territorial levels; and a second type according to which governance is 'splicing the public good provision into a large number of functionally discrete jurisdictions'.

An analytical perspective on global governance allows the third observation that governance beyond the state occurs in multiple modes utilising multiple instruments and logics. As Rosenau (1995: 9) argues,

> [t]here is no single organizing principle on which global governance rests, no emergent order around which communities and nations are likely to converge. Global governance is the sum of myriad – literally millions of – control mechanisms driven by different histories, goals, structures, and processes. … In terms of governance, the world is too disaggregated for grand logics that postulate a measure of global coherence.

However, one central feature of the 'new modes of global governance' researchers have identified is their fundamentally non-hierarchical nature. Unlike governing by governments, who possess, at least in theory, the necessary means of coercion to enforce compliance with existing laws, global governance has to rely exclusively on non-hierarchical modes of steering (cf. Risse 2004).

A fourth characteristic of the analytical global governance paradigm is the emergence, location and persistence of autonomous spheres of authority beyond the states-system (cf. Rosenau 2003: chapter 13). For Krahmann (2003: 323), the key feature of governance is the fragmentation of political authority. Thereby, it is possible to distinguish governance as an ideal type of fragmented authority from government as centralised authority. What follows from this perception is that authority is stripped from its two modern-day characteristics: territoriality and totality. The first characteristic refers to the ability of rule makers (governments) to control a distinct territory within defined boundaries without external interference. The second characteristic describes the ability to control all aspects of economic, social and political life. A global governance perspective, however, analyses emerging spheres of authority as both geographically and functionally fragmented. Such a 'sphere of authority' (Rosenau 2002: 72) defines the range of a formal or informal rule system's capacity 'to generate compliance on the part of those persons towards whom their directives are issued'. As a consequence, and contrary to the preoccupations of much of the traditional IR literature, '[t]he core of the global governance argument concerns the acquisition of authoritative decision-making capacity by non-state and supra-state actors' (Fuchs 2002).

The normative understanding of the term global governance is most visible in its use as referring to a political programme. It is based on the assumption that the plethora of disintegrative processes attributed to globalisation call for a political answer. Global governance is envisaged to bridge the gap between accelerating global transactions in goods, services, capital and people on the one hand and the territorially-bound steering capacity of national governments on the other. This mismatch of political capacity produces not only problems of effectiveness, but also a democratic deficit. As a result, high expectations are placed on new institutional arrangements such as global public policy networks with regards to their democratic legitimacy (for example Reinicke and Deng 2000; Witte, Reinicke and Benner 2000). For example, the Study Commission 'Globalization of the World Economy: Challenges and Answers' of the German Bundestag (Deutscher Bundestag 2002b: 67) states:

> As the world becomes increasingly globalized and economic activities grow beyond national regulatory frameworks, it becomes more necessary to politically shape economic, social and environmental processes on a global scale. How the global challenges can be democratically managed has recently begun to be discussed under the heading of 'global governance'.

In simple terms, 'global governance means to steer the process of globalisation politically' (Deutscher Bundestag 2002a: 415, own translation), and hence refers to the 'orderly management of global affairs' (Held 1995: 91).

Another normative understanding of global governance can be found in the work of the Commission on Global Governance. This group of 28 eminent public figures, mostly former heads of states, international bureaucrats or corporate leaders, emphasises the crucial importance of building and sustaining a global civil ethic based on shared values (Commission on Global Governance 1995: 48-67). However, at this point in time, global governance is still more of a vision than a description of the actual state of the global system (Deutscher Bundestag 2002b: 74).

Nevertheless, a number of key characteristics can be attributed to the normative use of global governance as predominantly describing a political programme to regain at least part of the steering capacity that has been lost after the end of the 'embedded-liberalism compromise' (Ruggie 1982). The first recurring point is that global *governance* is not global *government*. Rather than a world-state, global governance envisages a confederation of independent republics, a vision already developed by Immanuel Kant (Nuscheler 2000: 310). Second, global governance rests on different forms of cooperation, coordination and decision making at different levels of the international system. Third, global governance acknowledges the essential multi-polar structure of world politics. Hence it places considerable emphasis on developments of regionalisation from which strong impulses for further integration and cooperation as the cornerstones of normative global governance arise. Finally, global governance stipulates the incorporation of non-governmental organisations as an important prerequisite for increased democratic legitimacy and effective problem solving in the global arena. In sum, global governance is, in its normative understanding, frequently conceived as a long-term project of global integration that rests on traditional multilateralism, increasing regional cooperation and a multitude of actors.

A third general use of the term global governance refers to it as a hegemonic concept. Global governance, in this view, is a discursive attempt to conceal the nature of the current neo-liberal agenda.[4] In the words of Brand (2003: 205), '[t]he discourse of Global Governance ... serves as a means to deal more effectively with the crisis-prone consequences caused by [post-fordist-neoliberal social transformations]'. This understanding has been developed, in large part, within the theoretical confines of transnational historical materialism.[5] From this perspective, fundamental criticism is in particular raised against normative understandings of global governance (Overbeek 2004: 1). First, global governance appears as a consensual process whose highest purpose is to cooperatively manage common affairs. Secondly, the focus on multiple actors and the resulting plurality of interests conceals the structural nature of social relations and the underlying hierarchical configuration of social power. And thirdly, global governance is criticised for being an ahistorical concept that overlooks the pervasive nature of governance issues in human history. As a consequence, the protagonists of this critical version of global governance perceive the prevailing discourse on global steering mechanisms beyond the state as deeply embedded in a general political trend towards re-regulation of the world economy that conceals the negative tendencies of late capitalism. Consequently, global governance as an attempt to reclaim political influence to reshape the institutional landscape of world politics is not understood as a counterforce to globalisation, but as its ideological companion. In the words of Overbeek (2004: 15):

> The concept of global governance thus has suffered the same fate of other initially progressive normative concepts ...: it has been hijacked by social forces that have emptied it of its counter-hegemonic content and redefined it in such as way that the concept in fact supports the further consolidation of the world-wide rule of capital.

In sum, I argue that the current uses of the term global governance fall within the three broad categories of normative, analytical and discursive/critical understandings. The confusion, however, not only derives from the existence of three different uses, but also from the practice of using them interchangeably within one and the same argument. Hence, different uses should be made explicit and conceptual polysemy (cf. Chapter 1) should be avoided. As neither a commonly accepted definition exists so far, nor seems to be desirable given the many divergent connotations the term governance carries, scholars should at least carefully consider their own understanding of global governance and attempt to communicate it as clearly as possible. Such a commitment to clarity would not only enhance knowledge accumulation within the discipline of IR, but also allow for bridges between the disciplines and between meta-theoretical orientations. The next section tries to deliver what I have just demanded.

## APPROACHING A DEFINITION: STRUCTURE, PROCESS AND OUTCOME OF GLOBAL GOVERNANCE

The following section will approach a definition of global governance as an analytical concept by spelling out its dimensions, its key characteristics and resulting assumptions, as well as its conceptual boundaries.

As we have seen above, the concept of global governance is understood and applied in a range of different manners, from outlining a political programme to re-embed the current global economic structures into a global political architecture to a critical view on global governance as a potentially hegemonic discourse, as well as an analytical perspective on world politics. In line with the latter general understanding of global governance as an analytical concept, I propose to use the term for a specific set of related observable phenomena – namely the sum of all institutions, processes and interaction between various actors at all levels of the socio-political system that address, in a non-hierarchical manner, a specific global problem by describing implicit and explicit norms and rules of behaviour, inducing at least some transnational repercussions. This definition contains five central elements: first, global governance as an observable phenomenon not only contains institutions, but also recurring processes and interaction between a wide variety of actors; second, and specifying the former claim, these actors within global governance are situated at all levels of the socio-political system; third, their relationship is formally non-hierarchical[6] because a central authority is absent on the international as well as at the transnational level; fourth, the purpose of global governance is problem solving and fifth, the means are implicit and explicit norms and rules of behaviour. Finally, the effects of governing global problems are border-spanning and transnational in nature.

This broad definition reflects the premise that global governance is constituted of at least three analytical dimensions: first, the procedural dimension of governance, emphasizing the activities of different actors, the policies pursued and the instruments applied; second, the structural dimension of governance, highlighting the distinct 'architecture' of a governance arrangement, including norms and rules, networks and actor constellations, as well as formal or informal links to other areas of governance; and third, the functional dimension of governance, focusing on the material and ideational outcomes of a governance arrangement as a functional equivalent to other forms of political resource allocation. As a result, global governance as an overarching concept contains approaches that focus on the process of governing and the adequate instruments within that process (for example Lafferty 2004). In addition, other approaches rather focus on the structure and quality of distinct governance arrangements, often under the headline of network studies (for example Betsill and Bulkeley 2004). The third analytical dimension is reflected in approaches that highlight the emergence of autonomous and non-territorial spheres of authority in world politics (for example Biersteker and Hall 2002). Hence, the distinct uses and understandings that fall within the analytical perspective on global governance will greatly depend on the questions a researcher sets out to answer and the empirical terrain he or she approaches.

When turning to the actual empirical phenomena of global governance, scholars often use the term 'governance arrangement' to describe 'how the interaction between various actors pursuing common goals is structured' (Koenig-Archibugi 2002: 50). To classify existing arrangements in global governance and to assess their institutional variation, three core questions can be posed that are in line with the threefold understanding of global governance as process, structure and outcome.

The first question that relates to the process dimension is: Who is participating in global governance? The previous discussion has shown that a global governance perspective highlights the contribution of a wide range of actors to global problem solving and therefore includes 'the activities of governments, but it also includes the many channels through which "commands" flow in the form of goals framed, directives issued, and policies pursued' (Rosenau 1995: 14). What follows from this perception is that there are two different 'geographies' of global governance. One is distinctly wide, encompassing those actions of states and non-state actors at the international level that involve non-hierarchical modes of steering, like intergovernmental or inter-organisational bargaining, and the other is more restricted, only including non-hierarchical modes that involve at least one non-state actor, such as global public policy networks.[7] I take a middle ground, arguing that different modes and actor constellations are positioned along a continuum from more traditional international negotiations, which already involve non-state actors in the process of rule making and the resulting implementation of provisions, to hybrid public–private partnerships and fully private transnational co-operations, institutions and organisations.

The second question with reference to governance arrangements is: How is participation in the arrangement organised and how is the governance task shared among different actors? The main focus here is inclusiveness. In some areas of global governance, there might be a congruence of rule makers and rule takers, while in others decision-making power might be concentrated in a few hands or be exercised by similar and like-minded entities (Koenig-Archibugi 2002: 52). Consequently, global governance arrangements can be classified along a congruence axis that displays both the scale of participation of affected actors and the quality of their inclusion. Examples range from decision making in the UN context (security council resolutions or General Assembly votes) to rule making by non-state actors, either among similar actors (business self-regulation) or between dissimilar actors such as NGOs and transnational corporations (the empirical scope of this book).

Finally, the third question to classify existing governance arrangements in world politics is: What functions do they perform? This perspective is focused on outcome and the related functional pathways of global governance. In general, two broad functions can be attributed to governance arrangements in world politics: first, policy implementation and service provision, and second, rule- and policy-making. Hence, governance arrangements can be situated on a continuum ranging from low autonomy (wherein the governance task is delegated to specific institutions or organisations) to high autonomy (wherein networks and organisations act on their own behalf and not as part of a principal–agent relation). Taken together, the three dimensions of institutional variation provide a descriptive matrix of transnational, socio-political steering. Examples from global sustainability politics are depicted in Table 2.1.

*Table 2.1  Examples of governance arrangements in global sustainability politics according to their actor constellation and governing purpose*

| | Actor Constellation | | |
|---|---|---|---|
| Function | Public | Hybrid | Private |
| Implementation and service provision | Global Environment Facility | Global Network on Energy | Cement Sustainability Initiative |
| Rule making | Johannesburg Summit | World Commission on Dams | Forest Stewardship Council |

In sum, the analytical perspective on global governance is best understood as a three-dimensional concept that includes the procedural, structural and functional dimensions of political steering beyond the state. As we have seen above, distinct governance arrangements can be classified along three broad conceptual continua: the first displays the publicness of governance and ranges from international to transnational and purely private governance. The second continuum displays the congruency of those governed and those governing, while the third continuum focuses on governance functions and ranges from a low degree of autonomy, as in the case of delegation, to a high degree, such as in independent rule making bodies.

## CONCLUSION: TOWARDS CONCEPTUAL CLARITY

In this chapter, I have attempted to reconstruct global governance as a useful scientific concept in the field of IR. Based on an assessment of the current uses of the term governance and some historical remarks on its intellectual precursors, I have identified three broad understandings of the term global governance in the literature. Further clarifying the analytical use, I have consequently spelled out its different conceptual dimensions and the key parameters of institutional variation. Finally, I have argued that the term global governance refers to different 'geographies', depending on the theoretical and practical orientation of the individual researcher.

In more detail, I have proposed to use global governance as a concept for the assessment of large-scale socio-economic transformation and the resulting reorganisation of the political realm. From this analytical perspective the concept of global governance focuses on five key characteristics that describe the current nature and transformation of world politics. First, a global governance perspective stipulates no hierarchy between actors; the mode of steering is predominantly non-hierarchical and often based on arguing rather than traditional bargaining (cf. Risse 2004). Second, a global governance perspective ascribes a central status to novel forms of political organisation. Hence, new relations between organisational parts of the governance architecture as well as new relations between the actors of governance are of central interest. A third key feature is the equivalence of international and transnational decision making procedures as well as the resulting norms and rules. A fourth key characteristic of the current global governance order is the emergence and persistence of non-territorial, post-sovereign forms of authority. Complementing and sometimes even contradicting well-established systems of rules such as governments and nation states, new mechanisms for aggregating societal choices emerge that are boundary crossing and highly flexible. Finally fifth, actors are also increasingly flexible in their roles and responsibilities within a distinct governance arrangement, thereby constantly altering the landscape of governance.

To conclude, the end of the Cold War has not only changed the 'territory' of international relations, but also the 'map' used to make sense of it. The discipline of IR has grappled with profound transformations of the international system and the accompanying reorganisation of the political order (Mittelman 1997; Lawson 2002). However, most of the vocabulary used to describe the process was still rooted in long-established certainties, while the world had become fundamentally more uncertain. Recently, global governance has emerged as an integrative concept that allows many different scholarly traditions and meta-theoretical assumptions to use one general language when it comes to understanding processes of change in world politics. Hence, it could well develop into a new paradigm challenging the more traditional and state-centred mainstream of IR. However, global governance is not a theory in its own right and we should be careful not to overload it with too many expectations. What an analytical understanding of global governance can deliver nonetheless is a fresh view on world politics that is becoming more complex and is changing at an ever-increasing rate.

The following chapters build on this reconstructed understanding of global governance as an analytical concept for the assessment of large-scale transformations in world politics, in particular when I develop an analytical framework to better understand the emergence and influence of private business co-regulation as a prime example of governance arrangements at the transnational level.

## NOTES

1.  In the terms of discourse analysis, 'global' is understood as 'an undetermined phenomenological totality framing everything happening (politically, economically etc.) and all the differences between things happening' (Albert and Kopp-Malek 2002: 456).
2.  For a more detailed account of the different conceptual uses of global governance and the related criticism raised against the concept in general, see Dingwerth and Pattberg (2006a, 2006b).
3.  The distinction between a traditionally state-centric 'inter-national' approach and global governance is naturally an exaggeration for the sake of argumentative clarity. With constructing this differentiation, I do not argue that all IR theories are based on an exclusively state-centric ontology. However, I assume that most 'traditional perspectives within IR' – most notably realism, neorealism and liberal institutionalism – share basic ontological characteristics different from those prevalent in the concept of global governance.
4.  For a detailed theoretical and methodological criticism of the discursive-critical global governance concept, see Weller (2003).
5.  For a discussion of transnational historical materialism as a theoretical approach to international relations, see Gill (1993), Overbeek (2000), Rupert and Smith (2002).
6.  This understanding of relations between actors in global governance as 'non-hierarchical' does not stipulate that governance arrangements are free of conflict or that power might not play a role. However, the lack of formal authority on the global scale, both international and transnational, is a central characteristic of global governance because it explains the demand for organisation and the limits to it.
7.  See Börzel and Risse (2005) for an illustration.

# 3. The Institutionalisation of Private Governance: An Analytical Framework

Many different phenomena in world politics are currently analysed as instances of private governance, from the influence of non-state actors on intergovernmental negotiations to the activities of private organisations such as bond rating agencies to rule making processes beyond the state (Ronit 2001; Biersteker and Hall 2002; Sinclair 2002; Falkner 2003; Jagers and Stripple 2003; Gulbrandsen 2004; Pattberg 2004). Similar to the confusion surrounding the concept of global governance, private governance still lacks the conceptual clarity to be a useful tool for analysing world politics. Disagreement not only exists about the conceptual nature of private governance at the transnational level, but also about causes for its formation and explanations of its varying influence. Hence, this chapter first provides a brief reflection on the conceptual nature of private governance, before it develops an analytical framework for assessing the institutionalisation of private governance, including questions on the emergence and influence of private arrangements in global sustainability politics.

This chapter approaches private governance from an institutional, rule-focused perspective.[1] After defining private governance within the context of institutional analysis, I spell out the meaning of 'private rules' and adequate ways of assessing different institutional arrangements and their operation. The following section searches for common propositions found in the literature with regard to the question of the emergence of private governance and develops an appropriate model for its assessment. Subsequently, I propose a framework of analysis for the discussion of functions and influences of private governance in world politics. The concluding section finally summarises the overall analytical framework of private governance developed in the previous sections.

# AN INSTITUTIONAL PERSPECTIVE ON PRIVATE GOVERNANCE

Students of international organisation try to understand how and when political orders are created, maintained and changed at the international level (March and Olsen 1998). If we accept the claim that next to international order in the form of foreign policy interactions, international organisations and international institutions there exists also political order in the form of transnational organisation, then an institutional perspective on private governance is most adequate. This seems well equipped to contribute to our understanding of change and transformation in world politics because it deliberately closes a research gap in private governance left behind by a predominantly actor-focused approach to transnational order (cf. Chapter 1).[2]

An institutional approach is one 'that emphasizes the role of institutions and institutionalization in the understanding of human actions within an organization, social order, or society' (March and Olsen 1998: 948). However clear-cut this definition may appear at first sight, the term 'institution' points to a range of different phenomena in different contexts. In addition, several institutional approaches, perspectives and theories compete with each other. Peters (1999: 17; 2000: 2) for example, identifies seven varieties of institutional theory. Despite this abundance of theoretical variation, there seems to be a common core that binds all approaches together (Peters 1999: 18). First, institutions are understood as a structural feature of society or societal subsystems. Second, although institutions can be created and may change over time, a certain element of stability is a central element to all institutional approaches. And finally, institutions are thought to affect individual or collective behaviour, that is, they constrain the behaviour of actors within the scope of a particular institution, at least to a certain degree.

In general terms, an institution is referred to as the 'rules of the game', in which a rule can be formal (for example law) or informal (for example social habit) (cf. Rothstein 1996: 145-146). In a narrower sense, political institutions can be defined as 'formal arrangements for aggregating individuals and regulating their behaviour through the use of explicit rules and decision-making processes enforced by an actor or a set of actors formally recognised as possessing such power' (Levi 1990: 405).[3] Transferred to the international level, the term 'institutions' has been used to refer to a broad range of phenomena over the course of the past few decades. Among the most common subjects of scholarly inquiry in IR were intergovernmental organisations and international regimes (Simmons and Martin 2002: 192). Whereas intergovernmental organisations are predominantly perceived as highly institutionalised entities that possess actor quality, regimes are more broadly defined as 'a set of implicit or explicit principles, norms, rules and decision-making procedures around which actors' expectations converge in a given area of international relations' (Krasner 1983: 2). But the term 'regime', originally invented to cover processes of institutionalisation and cooperation among states beyond formal organisations, has become an overloaded concept and is accused of causing so much definitional confusion that scholars in the 1990s have replaced the regime concept with the more general term 'international institution' (Simmons and Martin 2002: 194). The baseline agreement seems to be that international institutions confine the rules meant to govern international behaviour. Applied to the realm of transnational organisation, which includes non-state actors, the term institution refers to the rules that govern the behaviour of private actors. However confusing the different uses of the term 'institution' may appear, they share the concept of 'rules' as a common element (Levi 1990: 403; Burch 2000: 185). As a consequence, institutions can be understood as ensembles of rules, of whatever scope. Therefore, the term institution can refer to relatively stable and robust things such as the Westphalian system of states or highly specialised phenomena, such as private regulations governing the behaviour of chemical firms towards disclosure of environmental information.

The following section first provides a definition of private governance from an institutional perspective. Subsequently, I address the nature of private rules in world politics in more detail, while the concluding section summarises the findings.

**Defining Private Governance**

Private governance offers an overarching conceptual framework for the theoretical analysis of a wide range of phenomena. Within the context of IR, private governance occurs as a transnational, boundary-crossing phenomenon, transcending territorial conceptions of political organisation. We can distinguish between a broad and a more restricted understanding of private governance as a concept and observable phenomenon.

In the broader understanding, private governance includes the full range of ways that non-state actors use to organise their affairs (for example Webb 2004). From this encompassing perspective, both formal arrangements, as well as informal structures that actors perceive to be in their interest, fall within the scope of private governance. Broad conceptions of private governance also include more traditional activities of private actors directed towards states, such as lobbying governments in international negotiations or implementing the resulting international accords. In addition, interactions between private actors on the one hand and state actors on the other may also be included in an assessment of private governance at the transnational level.

However, this encompassing perspective is contested. A more restricted understanding includes only those interactions between private actors that give rise to institutionalised behaviour. In the words of Falkner (2003: 72-73), private governance emerges 'at the global level where the interactions among private actors ... give rise to institutional arrangements that structure and direct actors' behavior in an issue-specific area'. In effect, private governance is understood as a functional equivalent to the structuring effects of international treaties, international organisations and the broader international regimes containing them.

From my perspective and with a view to the questions underlying this study, the latter understanding of private governance is more adequate. There are three basic characteristics that need to be distinguished. First, private governance centres around rules and regulation, not around spontaneous, uncoordinated behaviour such as market interactions.[4] Second, private governance contains processes and instances of institutionalisation beyond cooperation between different actors.[5] Third, private governance potentially organises political spaces equivalent to the effects that public steering mechanisms have. What follows from these basic characteristics are two fundamental definitional elements of private governance that are mutually constitutive. First, to qualify as private governance, a phenomenon must include institutionalised and rule-based behaviour. Second, private governance must include institutional constraints in the form of rules, standards or norms directed towards specific actors. Private governance without institutional constraints would amount to spontaneous organisation and processes of diffusion and convergence. Private governance without institutionalised behaviour would not appear as governance because there is no measurable effect. In sum, private governance can be defined as a form of socio-political steering, in which private actors are directly involved in regulating – in the form of standards or more general normative guidance – the behaviour of a distinct group of transnational actors, including business and, in a wider understanding, also public actors such as states.

**Private Rules in World Politics**

The idea of rules seems self-evident in most domestic and international contexts, but if we talk about rules and rule making by private actors at the transnational level, what do we refer to? In abstract terms, rules are statements that forbid, require or permit particular kinds of action (Ostrom 1990: 139). In the context of private governance, rules emanate from private sources and are conceptualised as 'consciously devised and relatively specific commands for behavior whose normative authority is such that a certain level of compliance can reasonably be expected' (Dingwerth 2005a: 70).

From the perspective of institutional theory, rules occur as four different types: (1) principles (beliefs of fact and causation); (2) norms (rights and obligations); (3) regulations (pre- or proscriptions for action); and (4) procedures (decision making rules) (Krasner 1983). However, disagreement exists about the nature of these rules. Krasner (1983: 3) argues that '[a] fundamental distinction must be made between principles and norms on the one hand, and rules and procedures on the other'. Principles and norms provide the basic characteristics of an institution, whereas regulations and procedures may change without altering the substantial content of a regime. To capture this important difference, scholars have argued to distinguish between *constitutive* rules on the one hand, and *regulative* rules on the other (Giddens 1984).[6] Constitutive rules prestructure domains of action in which specific social behaviour occurs. Regulative rules convey concrete standards of conduct.[7] As a result, a change in the constitutive rules is understood to alter the institution as a whole, whereas a change in the regulative rules only implies a transformation of existing procedural, structural or substantive rules, such as a tightening of certain product standards or introducing additional aspects of environmental management into an already existing management scheme.[8]

Within the context of private business co-regulation as the empirical focus of this book, constitutive rules refer to shared norms and beliefs, fundamental institutional goals and basic rules of procedure such as voting rights and dispute settlement mechanisms. Regulative rules on the other hand refer to concrete behavioural constraints that limit the choices of actors. Following from these considerations, standard setting – as the most common example of private rule making – is conceptualised as the act of agreeing on regulative rules which, although being voluntary in nature, require some degree of compliance to qualify as private governance. Standard setting, as opposed to the more general process of establishing and maintaining constitutive regulations, is consequently defined as the making of voluntary, expertise-based structural, procedural or substantive regulation (Kerwer 2002: 297-298).

If we accept an institutional perspective towards the phenomenon of private governance and its primary occupation with rules and regulations, we have to face a fundamental theoretical problem of institutional analysis in general: the 'paradox of constraint' (Grafstein 1992; Peters 1996b: 213). Institutional theories contend that institutions impose constraints on the behaviour of their members. However, institutions are also the products of human choices and therefore behavioural constraints are more closely linked to purposeful decisions than to rules. The pragmatic question that results from this paradox is how to understand the relation between individual and organisational behaviour, and between actors and rules. Scholars associated with the sociological and historical tenets of institutionalism have approached this problem by arguing that consciously devised institutions emerge in 'a world already replete with institutions' (Hall and Taylor 1996: 953). In a similar vein, but from the perspective of institutional economics, Williamson (1996: 4-5) argues that there is a difference in intentionality between the level of the institutional environment, the so-called 'rules of the game', and a micro-analytical level of the 'institutions of governance'. Whereas the latter are understood as the concrete mechanisms of political steering, the former largely constrain their environment. In sum, specific and consciously devised governance systems are embedded within a larger institutional environment.

In the context of business co-regulation, a private governance system[9] contains both *constitutive* and *regulative* rules, whereby roles and responsibilities of distinct actors are defined and constraints are imposed on their behaviour. With reference to institutional arrangements in general, von Prittwitz (2000: 23) has identified four definitional elements that also apply to private governance systems. First, they are consciously devised institutions or, more precisely, systems of rules that have some permanence. Second, systems are institutionalised as the result of interactions between at least two private actors not associated with states, international organisations or other public non-state actors. These interactions possibly contain characteristics of negotiation, argumentation and learning processes. Third, private governance systems are accepted as legitimate by their addressees and are thereby influential, at least to a certain extent. However, formal rules and actual behavioural practice may differ considerably from case to case. And fourth, private governance systems are flexible arrangements and thus can adequately react to changes within their environment.

In sum, within a private governance system, actors are bound together by roles and responsibilities that have a degree of permanence but can, at least in principle, be altered. Consequently, a private governance system can be described as a systemic interaction of actors through rules within a given field (in our case: global sustainability politics). This twofold understanding of a private governance system as a set of rules and a network of actors is in line with the distinction made in institutional theories between 'institutions without actors' and 'institutions with actors' (Göhler 1994: 22-23). In the first case, the institution is a normative framework, in which validity is not dependent on any distinct actor, such as in the case of a written constitution. In the second case, however, the institution is also an organisation that depends on identifiable actors such as staff, members or supporters, as in the case of parliaments. The latter point is of particular importance in the context of private governance for three reasons. First, the institutionalisation processes, which are an inherent characteristic of private governance systems, often lead to an organisational core in the form of a secretariat comparable to those established by international treaties. Second, the identification of such an organisational core makes it possible to better demarcate the boundaries of a governance system with respect to its environment, especially when it comes to assessing the actual influence of private regulation on its stakeholders. And finally, focusing on private governance systems as the systemic interaction of actors through rules, roles and responsibilities avoids fruitless debates about the agent–structure problem embedded in any institutional analysis.

The institutional approach to private governance allows us to analyse distinct governance systems, that is the rules and actors sustaining them, as mechanisms of transnational organisation. Through the operation of such governance arrangements, more precisely through the institutionalisation of regulatory practices among a range of private non-state actors, private governance as a functional equivalent to international regulation is established. Mechanisms in the social sciences are understood to represent a set of 'recurrent processes that link specified initial conditions and a specific outcome' (Mayntz 2002: 3). As such, mechanisms are a subtype of the category 'process'. However, unlike a 'process' that can be unique in its appearance, mechanisms represent causal relations that are open for generalisation. As we will see in the empirical case studies, several functional pathways can be identified as mechanisms through which the governance task is fulfilled and hence a relatively stable structure of transnational organisation is established.

## Summary

The preceding sections were concerned with developing a coherent analytical framework to capture the ongoing transformation from public to private forms of governance in world politics from a rules-focused, institutional perspective. The adequacy of such a perspective, I argue, derives from the prevalent focus on actors in global governance and the corresponding neglect of rules as an explanatory factor for transnational organisation. In this context, private governance is understood as the result of institutionalisation processes and institutional constraints. However, private governance as a functional equivalent to public forms of socio-political steering cannot be fully comprehended without paying considerable attention to the specific arrangements of governance, understood as the systemic interaction of actors bound together by constitutive as well as regulative rules that prescribe detailed roles and responsibilities within a specific issue area. Consequently, these private institutional arrangements have some degree of permanence, but are the result of the conscious decisions of actors and thus can adapt to changes within their economic and political environment.

To conclude, governance describes rule-based behaviour and the implications of this behaviour within a defined system. From an institutional perspective, private governance is both concerned with processes of emergence and the institutional constraints of certain rules on certain actors. To better understand this institutionalisation of private governance, the following sections address possible explanations for the formation of novel institutional arrangements in global sustainability politics, as well as possible ways to analyse their influence on world politics.

## THE EMERGENCE OF PRIVATE GOVERNANCE: IN SEARCH OF COMMON PROPOSITIONS

The emergence of private governance and its theoretical implications is evolving into a prominent field within the study of IR in general and global sustainability politics in particular. Different theoretical approaches and single or comparative case studies offer promising explanations for the formation of private institutions that regulate business activities on the global and transnational scale. However, the problem seems to be that most theoretical approaches are not specifically tailored to the newly emerging phenomena and that empirical studies that address them tend to isolate causal factors or at least fail to specify their relationship and the causal pathways operating in the process of institutional formation. One common assumption, for example, is that private rules to regulate business have emerged as a reaction to increased capital flows across borders and the assumed decline in the regulatory capacity of states (Evans 1997; Haufler 2003). This functional causality is hardly convincing because the need for new institutions becomes their sole explanation. Other theoretical approaches either highlight transaction costs and changing market dynamics (North 1990) or the fundamentally political nature of institution building in the global economy (Fligstein 1996). However, most explanations fail to account for the interaction of larger systemic transformations and the decisive conditions at the organisational level.

Therefore, this section proposes a framework of analysis integrating different assumption into one heuristic model. Hence, it should become possible to understand the precise relationship between the different factors and the causal pathways connecting them to produce the result of institutionalisation. Possible explanations are clustered around macro- and micro-levels of analysis, the former being concerned with systemic transformations and developments, the latter with factors that arise from the individual actors and contexts involved. Consequently, this section discusses different theory-based approaches to the puzzle of the emergence of private institutional arrangements in search of common propositions. The focus is on three literatures that are related to the problem of private institutionalisation, but represent three different theoretical backgrounds: first, the concept of private inter-firm regimes that is building on general regime literature and institutional theories; second, the more policy-oriented literature on partnership and collaboration between different actors and third, the critical theory debate about large-scale transformations in the context of globalisation.

**Regime Literature**

Regime literature is interested, among other questions, in explaining the formation of 'normative institutions' that are 'based on a persistent and connected set of rules' (Mayer, Rittberger and Zürn 1993: 393). The object of regime analysis is 'voluntarily agreed-upon, issue-area specific normative institutions created by states and other international actors, which are studied as the mainstay of establishing intentional social order by self-regulation in international relations' (Mayer, Rittberger and Zürn 1993: 393). Therefore, as Haufler (1993: 96) argues, 'neither the common definition of "regime" nor the fundamental assumptions made about regimes suggest that there can be no such thing as a purely private regime'. Consequently, the regime literature is a valuable starting point for theorising about the possible causes and conditions of the emergence of private regulatory institutions.

The question of regime formation has been explored along three lines of argumentation (Hasenclever, Mayer and Rittberger 1997). Power-based explanations highlight the importance of power resources, both in monetary and non-monetary terms, in bringing about cooperation. The basic premise is that institutions are structured by and reflect the distribution of power within a given social system, be it international and public or transnational and private. Interest-based explanations focus on the interactions of self-interested parties coordinating their behaviour to reap joint gains. What follows as the basic premise is that in order to reach cooperation there must be a zone of agreement or contract, a possible realm of joint gains for all the participants. The third line of argumentation is labelled knowledge-based and revolves around the importance of ideas, arguments and social identities. The basic premise holds that the different interest determining a specific zone of agreement is not exogenously given, but subject to cognitive processes and developments, such as scientific information and the convergence or general framing of issues.

Case studies on private authority, especially on inter-firm cooperation and institutionalisation, have revealed three possible explanations for the emergence of private inter-firm regimes. Contextual factors and systemic changes are identified to have a major influence on private institutionalisation. Haufler (2000: 122) for example argues that the globalisation of economic activities has resulted in 'a mis-match between markets and politics in terms of governance'. Consequently, the 'demand for rules to govern commerce has given rise to a variety of sources of supply, and one of the most significant ... is the private sector itself' (Haufler 2000: 121). But the growing private institutionalisation of rule making can not only be explained in terms of macro-systemic transformations, discernible in the recurrent failure of governments worldwide to cope with transboundary problems, but also by applying rationalistic approaches that focus on utility-maximising actors as the fundamental heuristic units. Efficiency gains approaches analyse cooperation and subsequent institutionalisation in terms of a possible reduction of transaction costs (Cutler, Haufler and Porter 1999c: 338). In this view, inter-firm regimes and other forms of cooperation among business actors may reduce costs associated with information and uncertainty, costs related to negotiations and consensus-seeking and costs related to the enforcement of regulations.[10] A second type of rationalistic explanation centres on the factor of power. From this perspective, institutions are predominantly established because they enhance the capacity of some actors to exercise power over others in a given field of competition. These considerations seem to substantiate the propositions discussed under the framework of international regimes. But although rationalistic and contextual explanations seem to have some merits in the case of private institutions, even leading scholars in the field suggest that 'it is not always possible to disentangle them in practice' (Cutler, Haufler and Porter 1999c: 338). Therefore, an integrated approach to the emergence of private institutions may prove superior to single-factor accounts of formation (Efinger, Mayer and Schwarzer 1993: 272-274).

With a particular view to multi-stakeholder approaches and forms of self-regulation in the global forest arena, Haufler has proposed the following line of reasoning. Novel forms of business regulation such as industry self-regulation and multi-stakeholderism are becoming more common at the global level for two reasons: first, forces that have changed the structure of both markets and politics; and second, changes in the strategies of actors operating within those structures (Haufler 2003: 239). The structure of markets has changed significantly through increased economic integration. Corporations that are linked in border-spanning networks of production, research and development and investment are competing for market access and market share, while countries, on the other hand, compete for investment. Changes in the international political system are characterised by the growing failure of intergovernmental problem solving under pressure from global environmental change and rapid social transformations, while at the same time transnational forms of organisation gain currency (Haufler 2003: 240). These macro-systemic conditions have spurred new strategies within both the profit and non-profit camps. Activists have begun to organise themselves in transnational networks using high profile campaigns and boycotts against transnational corporations and their public counterparts (cf. Keck and Sikkink 1998). Business actors have also responded to changing macro-systemic conditions by paying growing attention to demands from civil society. Their major rationale has been to pre-empt a resurgence of tight public regulation by engaging in voluntary dialogues with their critics. In addition, growing concern about brand reputation damage has played a role.

What can be learned from the general regime literature and the more specific debate about private inter-firm regimes for our puzzle of emerging private governance systems? Looking from a single-factor perspective, we can assume distinct empirical observations to substantiate the individual propositions. For power-based hypotheses to be true, we would expect to find strong leaders in each network, influencing the outcome of the negotiations to their own benefit, or at least a group of actors having considerably more power than others in shaping the outcome of the cooperation, in most cases the rules governing their own behaviour. For the interest-based and efficiency gains approach to prove valid, one would expect to observe reduced transaction costs, better positions in the market and reputation gains. These objectives should be identified by the partnering organisations prior to the establishment of the institution and not just occur as the unintended result of cooperation. Furthermore, a possible zone of agreement should be imaginable for all the participants of the arrangement prior to the actual institutionalisation. For contextual factors to be decisive, one would assume that evidence for large-scale transformation or eruptive events within a given policy field exists. Observations could include a new influential discourse, absence or inadequacy of governmental and intergovernmental regulation, the emergence of new scientific knowledge or an environmental catastrophe.

Although regime theory provides us with a range of possible propositions, it should be evident that a simple application of findings from either the international regimes literature or the inter-firm and business regimes perspective to the case of private business co-regulation is problematic. At least three caveats must be considered. First, the literature on international regimes considers states to be fundamentally similar (at least in theory), while the dissimilarity of profit and non-profit actors is the case in point in our examples. Second, in contrast to international cooperation, private institutions may develop under a shadow of hierarchy that is not easy to detect in each case. Third, private regimes among firms and business units constitute a different case compared to business co-regulation, because the former involve organisationally similar actors, while the latter do not. There are at least two factors that make institutionalisation easier in the case of private industry regimes: a similar language and cognitive framework, including recognisable roles and responsibilities as well as mutual 'rules of the game', and often long-standing personal relations among Chief Executive Officers (CEO).

**Partnership Politics**

A second approach to the question of private institutionalisation can be found in the growing literature on 'partnership politics' (Eisler 1996: 565). Next to studies on public–private partnerships and inter-organisational collaboration, researchers started to address business–NGO partnerships in the mid-1990s. This research strategy is action-orientated, but nevertheless provides useful insights into the specific types and rationales of business–NGO partnerships (Long and Arnold 1995; Murphy and Bendell 1997; Heap 1998). The existing policy-orientated studies on partnerships identify four preconditions for business actors and NGOs to engage in cooperation. The first is the perceived or actual decline in the effectiveness of state regulation with regard to the enforcement of environmental and social regulation, both at national and international levels. Secondly, there is acknowledgement on the part of NGOs that large transnational corporations are both cause and possible solution to global problems. The third area is the impact of new NGO campaigning strategies that focus on corporate brand reputation and thus threaten their market position. And fourth is the recognition on the part of companies that NGOs have acquired power and legitimacy as agents of social change, thus presenting themselves as potential partners for solving pressing business problems.

An alternative approach that falls into the category of partnership approaches is inter-organisational collaboration. Gray (1989: 5) defines collaboration as a process 'through which parties who see different aspects of a problem can constructively explore their differences and search for solutions that go beyond their own limited vision of what is possible'. Collaboration involves a dynamic process of joint decision making among the key stakeholders of a given problem field. The central characteristics of this process are the interdependence of the actors, the joint ownership of decisions and the resulting collective responsibility for the future of the collaboration. The emergence of the collaborative process that gives rise to a new negotiated order among the key stakeholders is contingent on specific attributes of the problems to be addressed. Typical problems show the following characteristics: they are ill or controversially defined; stakeholders are interdependent and have vested interests in the problem; resources for dealing with a given problem are distributed unequally; problems are characterised by technical complexity and scientific uncertainty, and at the same time stakeholders have different levels of expertise and different access to information about the problem. Furthermore, differing perspectives on the problem lead to adversarial relationships among stakeholders and, as a result, unilateral approaches to dealing with the problem often produce sub-optimal outcomes (Gray 1989: 10).

In sum, the research on business–NGO partnerships and collaboration highlights the importance of two sets of conditions. The first is macro-trends, such as globalisation, resulting in the perceived or actual decline of state capacity to regulate complex problems, the growing impact of business actors on the natural environment and the corresponding new role of civil society. Secondly, there are the conditions that depend on the specific case and actors in question, such as problem characteristics and organisational resources. Although the partnership debate offers valuable propositions in the context of private governance and some generalisations may be possible, it should be noted that conditions underlying the emergence of private governance systems are harder to find than those necessary for partnership and collaboration.

**Global Political Economy**

The third broad theoretical approach considered here focuses on the global political economy as an explanatory factor for large-scale transformations. The debate about globalisation and the changing role of the nation state in addressing transboundary problems provides a vantage point for the discussion of the possible causes for the emergence of private governance. Falkner (2003: 74) identifies three claims that address the relation between globalisation and the rise of private forms of global governance.

The first claim stresses the relationship between globalisation and the perceived decline of the nation state system. From this perspective, private governance is an indicator for a long-term shift in the locus of authority, especially within the realm of the global economy. Private actors have become the 'real players' in issue areas ranging from financial stability and foreign investment (for example bond-rating agencies) to industrial standard setting (for example the International Organization for Standardization, ISO). As a result, 'the powers of most states have declined still further, so that their authority over the people and their activities inside their territorial boundaries has weakened' (Strange 1996: xi).

The second claim addresses the hypothetical link between the growth of civil society and the emergence of private governance. In this view, civil society pressure exerted on corporations, accompanied by far-reaching media coverage, is seen as a main driver for the emergence of institutionalised responses to the growing demand for corporate social and environmental accountability (Wapner 1997).

The third claim is closely related to the work of Antonio Gramsci. In this view, new partnerships between states, business actors, international organisations and civil society institutions signify a shift from more traditional forms of environmental politics to market-oriented, corporate-sponsored environmental regimes that benefit corporate interests (Falkner 2003: 75). The applicability of this concept to the realm of private governance stems from the particular importance of business and civil society as central categories within the framework of the institutionalisation of private governance. Neo-Gramscian theory seems capable of explaining the current grand transformation of the economic arena, which is driven by a hegemonic bloc of business and society elites, resulting in a new approach to regulation, such as market-driven self-regulation. From this perspective, the concept of hegemony refers to the stabilisation of a specific ensemble of discursive and economic relations. Within this institutional setting, a managerial elite from multinational corporations, professionals from transnational NGOs, academia and governmental agencies comprise a transnational historical bloc, exercising leadership as a consequence of individual and collective human acts (Cox 1987; Pijl 1997; Germain and Kenny 1998: 6). In this view, NGOs are not natural adversaries of business interests, but play a dual role as 'arenas of cultural and ideological struggle, and also as key allies in securing hegemonic stability' (Levy and Newell 2002: 90).

**Summary**

The aforementioned three broad theoretical approaches towards the phenomenon of private institutionalisation in global governance – regime theory, partnership politics and studies in global political economy – contain valuable propositions with regard to the emergence of private governance arrangements. Four recurrent aspects seem to be important, although they receive different degrees of attention in the three literatures: (1) macro-systemic transformations, such as globalisation or hegemonic reconfiguration, as well as contextual factors at the macro-level; (2) problem structure, characterised by interdependent interests as well as different levels of information and knowledge; (3) organisational resources that enable actors to reduce transaction costs or improve their strategic position; and finally (4) ideas and models that allow actors to agree on a common framework for their collaboration. For analytical purposes, these aspects can be grouped into two broad categories, one containing the micro-level conditions, the other those observable at the macro-level. Micro-level conditions contain the problem structure and organisational resources because these are dependent on the specific issue area and the actors involved. Macro-level conditions relate to large-scale transformations in the structure of the international system, as well as to the emergence and dissemination of ideas and knowledge.

The two condition sets are supposed to be interconnected and form an integrated model that describes the emergence of private governance because distinct variables are systematically interacting with each other and thus jointly produce a certain result (Efinger, Mayer and Schwarzer 1993: 273). This approach is helpful because it draws attention to a variety of inter-linkages between different conditions that would not be observable using a single-factor account. First, the relation between shifts at the macro-level and new resources for organisational actors, leading to new strategic choices; second, the relation between resources and the problem structure, addressing the ability of actors to construct a problem in the first place; and third, the relation between ideas that emerge and diffuse at the macro-level and the subsequent integration of competing perspectives in the actual negotiations. It is further assumed that the distinct interplay between the macro- and the micro-level of conditions creates a window of opportunity for the emergence of private rules.

Based on the review of different literatures related to private governance and the question of emergence, and applying the analytical distinction between micro- and macro-systemic factors, the following assumptions will guide the empirical analysis of the formation of private governance systems throughout Chapters 5 and 6.

First, I assume that a lack of effective public regulation at the domestic or international level forces non-state actors to address problems bilaterally. Public regulation does not necessarily have to be completely absent, but rather inadequate in terms of scope, precision or timeliness. Second, I assume that civil society pressure creates demand for regulation that is not adequately addressed by public sources. Therefore, emphasis is laid on the political process of transforming an uncontested issue into a business case, instead of assuming that a demand for coordination and cooperation simply exists. Third, the general idea of cooperation and partnership embodied in the concept of sustainable development and other macro-level discourses has facilitated seemingly unlikely alliances between formerly antagonistic actors. And finally, changes in the relations between state and non-state sources of authority have led to new or more effective strategies towards regulation and novel organisational resources, both within the profit and the non-profit sector.

## THE INFLUENCE OF PRIVATE GOVERNANCE: DO SYSTEMS OF RULES MATTER IN WORLD POLITICS?

It is not only the emergence of novel institutional arrangements, combining divergent actors from all sectors of transnational society, that poses questions to the investigator of private governance, but also the distinct causal pathways by which they acquire authority and thus matter in world politics. The analysis of the influence of private governance includes three major sub-questions: first, how can we assess the effects induced by a private governance system and thus claim that it matters in world politics? To answer this part of the puzzle, the following section will discuss the possibility of measuring the influence of private governance systems. The second question refers to the different ways in which a private governance system realises its influences and policy tasks, in short: How does it work? To answer this specific question, I propose three hypothetical functions along which the actual influences of private institutional arrangements can be examined in the empirical case studies. Subsequently, I propose five variables that might explain differences in the observed influence of private governance arrangements.

### Assessing the Influence of Private Governance Systems

This section develops an analytical framework to assess and analyse the influence of private rules in global sustainability politics. In simple terms, the judgement 'something is effective/has influence' refers to the situation that some organisation, policy or institution is performing some generic function that can be assessed against some point of reference involving some metric of measurement. The task of analysing the influence of private governance systems therefore involves three analytical steps: first, defining the object to be evaluated, that is, the dependent variable of the measurement; second, introducing an appropriate standard against which the object can be evaluated; and finally, defining the appropriate measurement and metric. Before I propose my own answer to these questions, let me briefly argue why I prefer the term influence to the more widely used term effectiveness.

The term influence is given preference over other terms used to describe behavioural changes resulting from specific activities or structures such as power or authority for several reasons. Power carries strong connotations of force, whereas authority often invokes the association of either formal legitimization (as in the case of a public authority) or informal authorisation through knowledge or belief systems (as in the case of teachers and priests). The term influence is more neutral in this respect, defined as 'the act or power of producing an effect without apparent exertion of force or direct exercise of command' (*Longman Dictionary of the English Language* 1984: 754). Consequently, the sum of all effects, according to *Webster's* (1976: 724), something that is 'produced by an operating agent or cause; the event which follows immediately from an antecedent, called the cause; the result, consequence, or outcome', is considered influence. In addition, the term influence is also given preference over the frequently used term effectiveness for two reasons. First, effectiveness is a restrictive concept when it comes to the direction of effects, because it limits the scope of analysis to those observations that contribute to goal attainment and problem solving.[11] Effects that display no link to addressing the principle goal of the respective institution, or are counterproductive, cannot be measured within the framework of effectiveness. This is of particular importance when it comes to analysing the effects on non-state actors. Consider for example a firm that, through the effects of a given institution, raises its profit margins. As increases in profits are not linked to the primary goal of the institution under consideration (for example a private institution addressing the problem of child labour), the observed effect would not count as effectiveness. The second reason for using influence as the more encompassing and neutral term instead of effectiveness is the comparative notion embedded in the latter term. Effectiveness is a relational concept; its meaning is linked to a specific point of reference, whether this point is reaching its organisational goal or reaching its organisational goal to a higher degree than a comparable case. Therefore, instead of using the term effectiveness, I prefer influence as a generic term.

Scholars studying the effects of international regimes, and recently also international bureaucracies, as well as scholars in the field of policy analysis agree, although in different terminology, that there are three different objects of measurement when it comes to analysing influence (Easton 1965; Underdal 2002; Biermann and Bauer 2005a). First, *output*, referring to the actual activity of organisations and institutions such as agreeing on regulations, producing reports, conducting research or organising meetings or simply agreeing on certain rules; second, *outcome*, understood as observable changes in the behaviour of those actors targeted by international regimes, public policies or international bureaucracies; and third, *impact*, defined as changes in economic, social or environmental parameters such as gross domestic product (GDP), literacy rate or atmospheric carbon dioxide concentrations.[12]

In addition to this basic understanding, most scholars agree that, while focusing on outcome exclusively would be too unambitious as the primary level of analysis, measuring impact seems at least difficult for several reasons. First, as there is a plethora of institutions, organisations, policies and structural factors influencing a specific issue area, it is quite impossible to disentangle this background noise from the effects under consideration. This is particularly the case with rules and regulations that are embedded in a broader set of institutional practices or prone to changes in the general political or economic context. And second, the more complex the affected system is, the more difficult it will be to assess the actual impact of any given influence on this particular system. This is most evident in the case of organisations and institutions targeting environmental problems. For example, how could we practically assess the influence of national and international fishery policies on the state of the world's fisheries as a whole, given the fact that many of the ecological interactions between fish stocks, marine environment, climate change and pollution from land-based sources are not fully understood? As a result, most scholars agree that outcome, indicating actual behavioural changes of the actors targeted or affected by a specific policy, organisation or institution, is the most appropriate level for measuring their overall influence.

What follows from this concentration on a behavioural indicator is the particular attention paid to problems of identifying an adequate point of reference for the assessment of influence. Against what standard should relative changes in the behaviour of actors be assessed? This intricate question has recently been discussed with regard to the effectiveness of international regimes, particularly in the field of environmental politics (Bernauer 1995; Jakobeit 1998; Victor, Raustiala and Skolnikoff 1998; Young, Levy, and Osherenko 1999; Helm and Sprinz 2000; Mitchell 2002a). Three quite different approaches have been described in some detail: first, measuring behavioural changes against the institutional goals under consideration; second, an economic concept of optimal solutions; and third, counterfactual reasoning assessing relative changes against a hypothetical state of 'absence of effects'. However, they all include three logical steps towards measuring effects. According to Mitchell (2002b: 508), '[t]o determine how much movement towards some goal a policy induced involves three tasks: identifying an appropriate goal, an appropriate metric of movement and an appropriate indicator of the share of that movement to attribute to the policy'.

With reference to private governance this approach translates into the following analytical steps. First, identifying the institutional goals of private governance systems as relative changes in the behaviour of actors (for example improvements in forestry practices or corporate environmental reporting). In addition, I also consider the unintended side effects of institutionalisation. Second, measuring the direction of changes, both in quantity and quality (for example more reporting companies, more complete reports); and third establishing the link between observed changes and the actual rules by applying counterfactual reasoning (for example how would forest practices within a distinct area look like in the absence of private regulation?). This procedure avoids both the problem of endogeneity and the problem of accounting for effects that are not caused by the governance system, but by larger structural or discursive developments.

Based on this brief discussion of the term 'influence', possible points of reference, and different levels of analysis frequently referred to in the literature, how can the influence of private governance systems within world politics be understood? Two complementary views can be distinguished. The first approach is to consider the influence of any private governance system to be the aggregate of two different orders of effects. First-order effects are direct effects that can be traced to the specific rules of the institution under analysis. We can measure these direct effects by looking for behavioural changes in those actors that are within the scope of the rules (in our empirical cases: forest operations, supply chain firms and companies providing environmental reports). Indicators include standard uptake, compliance, corrective action undertaken by the actors and the general tendency in the number of regulated actors. Taken together, these measurements can tell us how far the rules of an institution change the behaviour of those actors that fall under the regulatory scope of this very institution.

Indirect effects constitute the second order of effects. These effects should be understood as effects that are induced by the rule system as a whole and have an impact on those actors not under the direct scope of private regulation. Consider for example large retailers in the case of private forest governance (cf. Chapter 5). These economic actors, often TNCs, participate in governing the institution as members, but are not regulated by the distinct rules describing sustainable forestry practices on the ground. Nevertheless, retailers may change their behaviour as a consequence of indirect effects of the governance system. Possible indirect effects include endorsement of the governance system by non-regulated parties, the incorporation of private rules in other existing regulatory systems, political incentives directed towards the private rule system and the organisational diffusion of a specific private arrangement to other geographical or issue areas. In addition, the creation, deepening and widening of markets for environmentally sound products can also be considered an indirect effect of private governance systems. In sum, the second-order effects are constituted by the behavioural changes of the non-regulated actors connected with the private governance scheme in a broader sense.

The second approach towards categorising the influence of private rules in world politics is analysing the distinct characteristics of effects. First, private rules can be expected to have normative effects resulting from the concrete rules and standards, if they become socially binding to a certain extent. Second, private rules can have discursive effects. In this case, private rules and procedures become a point of reference in transnational debates that can only be omitted while also accepting high reputation costs and other strategic disadvantages. And finally, private rules are expected to have structural effects such as shifts in markets or power relations. In addition to first- and second-order effects and the three broad characteristics, influence can be observed at the national, international and transnational levels of the political system.

In sum, assessing the influence of private governance systems necessitates three basic justifications: the object of evaluation, the standard of evaluation and an appropriate metric of measurement. With reference to the first task, I have argued that the outcome dimension of behavioural changes is the most adequate object of evaluation, because output criteria easily become tautological and impact is hard to determine in environmental politics due to long cycles of cause and relation, incomplete scientific knowledge and the complexity of the institutional environment. With reference to the second task, I have argued that applying a counterfactual reasoning in linking observed effects with a specific institution is theoretically adequate. Finally, with reference to the third task, I have proposed an understanding of the effects induced by a private governance system by order and characteristics at the international, national and transnational level of the political system.

## Analysing the Functions of Private Governance Systems

Private governance and other forms of transnational organization are increasingly invoked as manifestations of a larger transformation of the political arena. A number of theoretical approaches, from institutional to critical theory, today acknowledge that the structure, process and actors of world politics have changed profoundly in the last thirty years, often referring to the larger debate about global governance. However, while most research has paid considerable attention to conceptual debates and the larger picture of post-international politics, few studies have attempted to devise detailed hypotheses that can be put to empirical tests. This is particularly true for the important question of influence and effectiveness of private and transnational governance. Those studies that have looked at the influence of private forms of political steering mainly focused on the questions of standard uptake, rule implementation, compliance with private policies or the institutional complementarities between international and domestic settings of private governance (Kollman and Prakash 2001; Mattli and Büthe 2003).

Resembling many of the assumptions frequently encountered in the international regimes literature on effectiveness and the debate about compliance (Bernauer 1995; Chayes and Chayes 1995; Miles et al. 2002), targeting issues of rule implementation and rule following seems to be a justified and straightforward approach. However, this strategy may not be sufficient for several reasons. First, the focus on the direct influences deriving from private rules and standards potentially overlooks substantial influences that are normative, discursive and structural and go significantly beyond rule implementation and compliance issues. Second, as a result of this blind spot, scholars may systematically underestimate the importance of private governance arrangements in world politics.[13] And finally, as a consequence of this narrow view, the question of variance in influence and effectiveness has largely been confined to the question of firm-level choices in accounting for different standard uptakes and growth rates. To overcome this state of affairs, this study introduces a wider understanding of influence and possible ways of assessing it. Consequently, I propose five variables that account for varying degrees of influence within each functional arena.

Having discussed the possibility of assessing the influence of private governance systems, this section approaches the question of how private arrangements realise their influence. With reference to international environmental regimes, Keohane, Haas and Levy (1993: 21) argue that actor behaviour, in this case that of states, is affected by the three functional 'Cs': raising concern, creating a contractual environment and increasing capacity for environmental protection. In a similar vein, I assume that the behaviour of stakeholders is affected by three broad functions of private governance systems. In this perspective, function is used as a heuristic term that describes the abstract influence of a social phenomenon, acknowledging that it is the product of a number of specific processes and mechanisms.

Starting with the most evident, I assume that behavioural changes result from the *regulatory* function of private governance. In this view, behavioural changes can be attributed to the standards and regulations emanating from a governance system that are directed towards business actors. Possible indicators may include the rate of standard uptake, actual implementation and compliance, changes in markets and economic incentive structures, environmental improvements or deterioration and impacts on social parameters such as working conditions and labour rights. Therefore, an analysis of the regulatory function will most likely focus on the process of standard development and the different approaches taken towards putting them into practice. However, next to direct influences deriving from the concrete rules, indirect influences may also occur, for example changing roles of economic actors not within the direct reach of private standards.

Next to regulation, private governance is also achieved through a *cognitive/discursive* function. Private governance systems in the area of global sustainability politics operate within the complex environment of scientific uncertainty. The development of adequate standards for sustainable forestry, for example, will depend on expertise in issue areas ranging from biodiversity conservation to the global timber trade and consumer preferences. Brokering knowledge and organising effective learning processes among different stakeholders is therefore key to influencing the behaviour of relevant actors. In this view, knowledge is produced and disseminated through a network of actors bound together by the constitutive rules of the institution. In addition, learning processes may occur that enable actors to fulfil new roles and take over new responsibilities. The cognitive/discursive function of private institutions might also lead to discursive changes within a specific policy community and beyond.

The third function through which private governance is thought to occur is *integration*. By this I refer to potential spillover processes, wherein several directions of influence should be observable: first, international norms that are already embodied in international treaties may be partially integrated into the private governance system and thus influence actors that are not directly targeted by the international norm. This is also true for standards that emanate from public–private institutions such as regulations by the ISO. Second, private governance systems may serve as a model for other issue areas or even be replicated within the same issue area. In addition, a particular model of private governance may serve as the organisational model for governance that is not exclusively private but incorporates public actors. And third, the direction of influence may well be focused on public actors or political systems through the endorsement of private governance, as a whole or in parts. From this perspective, behavioural changes that occur as a result of the integrative function of private governance may include public policies at national and international levels, as well as instances of endorsement or emulation of private governance by other actors of the political system such as states or international organisations.

In sum, while the actual influence of private governance can be assessed at different levels of the political system (national, international, transnational), it is constituted by different orders of effects (first and second), and produces different outcomes (normative, discursive, structural), the regulatory, cognitive/discursive and integrative functions of private governance systems should explain in detail how these behavioural effects are realised.

**Explaining the Varying Influence of Private Governance Systems**

Following the discussion about influence and the different functional pathways through which private governance is constructed, how can we hypothesise possible explanations for variance on the output dimension, that is, the influence of private governance systems in global sustainability politics? Literature that offers plausible and tested hypotheses on variations in the influence of private governance is largely missing. The few existing studies have mainly compared institutions within an issue area (for example forest certification) and largely focused on explaining firm-level choices, rather than overall influence (Sasser et al. 2004). Therefore, I propose an initial set of hypotheses to explain the variance in influence of two cases of private institutionalisation in sustainability politics involving the profit and the non-profit segment of transnational society. I assume that influence will vary within each of the three functional areas identified in the section above. As a consequence, I introduce five explanatory variables that relate to three functional pathways of private governance systems. They are derived from key explanatory figures frequently used throughout much of the international regimes literature, namely the problem structure (Miles et al. 2002), the political economy surrounding the problem to be regulated (Barrett 1999), the institutional design and organisational structure (Mitchell 1994) and the degree of cooperation and institutionalisation (Underdal 2002).

The relevance of the problem structure for the effectiveness of international accords is one robust finding of the regime literature. Following Underdal (2002: 13-23), the problem structure underlying an international regime can be benign (characterised by coordination, symmetry or indeterminate distribution and crosscutting cleavages), or malign (characterised by incongruity, asymmetry and cumulative cleavages). As a result, the political malignity of a problem is understood to be correlated with the possibility of achieving an effective cooperative solution. Similar arguments have been made with reference to the economic costs of problem solving (or inaction for that matter). Barrett (1999: 193), for example, argues that differences in effective problem solving in the ozone and climate cases can be explained by the specific costs and benefits of action. However, as the costs of providing a global public good are largely given, institutional and organisational design of agreements can make a difference. Following this line of argumentation, a range of studies have engaged in spelling out appropriate design choices for international institutions. In addition, a fourth line of thought has highlighted the importance of cooperation and institutionalisation for effective problem solving, although in most cases this factor has been treated as an intervening variable (Underdal 2002: 7).

The first hypothesis with regard to the regulatory function of private governance systems is that the degree of formalisation determines regulatory effects. I assume that the higher the degree of formalisation existing within a private governance system is, the more influence the arrangement will have through its regulatory function (predominantly normative effects). But how could such an assumption be empirically verified, and hence, how could appropriate indicators for the degree of formalisation be constructed?

To answer this question, I briefly refer to the debate about the 'legalisation' of world politics that has become one of the most prominent debates in IR (Goldstein et al. 2001). Legalisation is understood as a particular form of international institutionalisation characterised by three components that are conceptually independent. *Obligation* refers to the observation that states or other actors are bound by rules and obligations. In the context of international legalisation, this means that actors are legally bound 'in the sense that their behaviour thereunder is subject to scrutiny under the general rules, procedures, and discourse of international law, and often domestic law as well' (Abbott et al. 2000: 401). *Precision* means that the rules and obligations describing specific conduct are unambiguous and clear. In this sense, rules are 'determinate' (Frank 1990), leaving little room for reasonable interpretation. *Delegation* finally refers to the empirical observation that third parties have been granted authority to implement, monitor and change the rules.

Following Zangl and Zürn (2004), the concept of legalisation can be transferred, at least to a certain extent, to the transnational realm. The process of transnational legalisation (for example the private Lex Mercatoria) goes beyond a simple growth in the number of rules and regulations targeting transnational private actors. Legalisation means that processes of rule making, rule implementation and rule interpretation are gradually becoming more law-like. In the context of rule making, this could mean that the process of agreeing on certain regulations reflects the requirements of procedural justice such as openness, transparency and deliberativeness. With regard to rule implementation, legalisation could refer to processes in which compliance is reported independently of those under regulation and, as a result, sanctions cannot be circumvented by those in breach of the rules. The most advanced form of legalisation in the transnational realm would be the establishment of quasi-courts and appellative bodies. What comes closest to such processes is complaint procedures that are open to all parties. In sum, if we follow the basic assumption of this debate, namely that legalisation is a specific form of institutionalisation, we can assess the degree of formalisation of private governance arrangements by addressing their degree of obligation (sanctions), precision (scope of the rules) and delegation (complaint procedures).

The second hypothesis with regard to the regulatory function of private governance systems is that the costs of devising and implementing private rules determine their regulatory effects. I assume that the higher the costs of devising and implementing the specific standards are, the less influence they will have on the behaviour of targeted stakeholders. Hence, governance systems that rely on more costly instruments such as certification (that might involve fundamental changes to existing production processes) are expected to be less influential through their regulatory function than those that rely on less costly approaches such as environmental reporting (wherein fundamental changes to production and management processes are only long-term goals).

The third hypothesis with regard to the regulatory function of private governance systems is that the problem structure determines the influence.

However, taking a closer look at the existing literature on problem structure and institutional effectiveness, it becomes evident that rather than stipulating a causal relation between the benignity/malignity of a problem and the scale and scope of the regulatory effects, there seems to be a relation between the problem structure and the degree of cooperation. Hence, I hypothesize that a benign problem structure will result in more cooperative and institutionalised relations among actors than a malign problem will eventually produce.

Turning to the cognitive/discursive function of private governance systems and the resulting outcomes, organisational design features warrant closer attention. I assume that the quality and scope of the supporting network determines influence through learning and other cognitive processes. The production and dissemination of knowledge, the facilitation of problem solving and learning processes, as well as the diffusion of regulatory models is contingent on the qualities of actors involved in a private governance system and adequate organisational procedures and structures defining their interaction. Two possible relations emerge. First, the more diversified in terms of expertise and experience a network is, the greater the cognitive influence of private governance that can be expected. And second, the more the relationship between individual organisations in the network is clearly organised, the greater the cognitive influences that can be expected.

Finally, with regard to influence through integration, I assume that fit and congruence with international, transnational and domestic norms explains the variance in observed outcomes. As private regulatory systems are voluntary in nature, they use a variety of strategies to gain authority vis-à-vis their stakeholders (cf. Cashore, Auld and Newsom 2004). One obvious strategy is relating their own standards to widely accepted norms that exist at the international or transnational levels. Hence, I assume that the more a private governance system matches existing norms and rules for external authorisation, the higher the influence through its integrative function will be.

In sum, the aforementioned hypotheses are of rather preliminary nature and are put to the empirical test in a comparative perspective in the concluding chapter of this study. Rather than providing a final answer to the puzzle of the varying degrees of influence of private governance systems in global sustainability politics, these broad hypotheses provide the basis for establishing the plausibility of causal relations and thus developing better explanation for future research. Table 3.1 summarises the hypotheses and variables.

*Table 3.1   Variables and hypotheses on varying degrees of influence of private governance systems*

| Variable | Hypothesis | Explanandum |
|---|---|---|
| Degree of formalisation | The higher the degree of formalisation existing within a private governance system, the more influence the arrangement will have through its regulatory function. | Regulatory influence |
| Costs | The higher the costs of devising and implementing the specific standards are, the less influence they will have on the behaviour of targeted stakeholders. | Regulatory influence |
| Malignity/benignity of problem structure | A benign problem structure will result in more cooperative and institutionalised relations among actors than a malign problem will eventually produce. | Regulatory influence |
| Quality and scope of network | a) The more diversified in terms of expertise and experience a network, the greater the cognitive influence of private governance that can be expected. b) The more the relationship between individual organisations in the network is clearly organised, the greater the cognitive influences that can be expected. | Cognitive/discursive influence |
| Fit with existing normative structures | The more a private governance system matches existing norms and rules for external authorisation, the higher the influence through its integrative function will be. | Integrative influence |

## CONCLUSION: UNDERSTANDING THE INSTITUTIONALISATION OF PRIVATE GOVERNANCE

This chapter is based on the premise that the institutionalisation of private governance – its emergence, its functions and its influence in world politics – has been treated only on the margins of the discipline of International Relations. Although the concept of transnationalism and the roles and influence of non-state actors have featured prominently in recent debates about transformations in the global political system, and despite the central role of regime theory within the study of IR, private institutional arrangements and their governing function have largely been excluded from systematic evaluations. In particular, when cooperative rule making and the subsequent implementation of these rules by profit and non-profit actors is at the centre of interest.

Therefore, this chapter approaches private governance from an institutional perspective and subsequently defines it as a form of socio-political steering in which private actors are directly involved in regulating – in the form of rules, standards or more general normative guidance – the behaviour of a distinct group of stakeholders, including business and, in a wider understanding, also public actors such as states. I have argued that we can best understand the emergence of private governance along two interrelated levels of analysis, one focusing on the macro-systematic conditions, the other focusing on factors identifiable at the level of the individual problem, the actors involved and their strategies pursued.

I argue further that assessing the influence of private governance is best approached by measuring behavioural changes (outcomes) of relevant actors, observed against some counterfactual state of affairs. However, unlike studies on international institutions and their impact, analysing the influence of private governance institutions has to acknowledge two distinct orders of effects in addition to different political levels on which effects could possibly manifest themselves. First-order effects refer to the direct effects of rules and regulations directed towards actors within the institutional framework under analysis. Second-order effects are indirect effects, influencing actors that are grouped around the institution in a wider sense. Next to the distinct order of effects, influence can also be categorised by its characteristics. In this context, I argue that influence predominantly occurs as normative, discursive and structural influence.

In addition to theoretical considerations about the emergence and influence of private governance, this chapter has briefly engaged in a discussion of possible explanatory factors for hypothetical variations in the influence of distinct private governance systems. Based on four broadly accepted theoretical positions, five variables are of particular importance: first, the degree of formalisation understood as the precision of the rules and the degree of both obligation and delegation; second, the costs underlying cooperative action, including the establishment and implementation of appropriate standards; third, the political malignity of the problem creating the demand for private regulation; fourth, the quality of the network supporting the institution including the organisational provisions spelling out their precise mutual relationship; and finally, the degree of authorisation through reference to widely accepted international or transnational norms.

## NOTES

1.  An alternative perspective on private governance, which has been applied more frequently than the institutional approach, is provided by network analysis and its focus on actors and their interests in a given policy field (for example Keck and Sikkink 1998; Ottaway 2001; Betsill and Bulkeley 2004). For a critical view on networks as a form of governance, see Nölke (2000).
2.  However, for a contradicting position, excluding rules, norms and institutions from the realm of governance, see Smouts (1998).
3.  See also Göhler (1994: 22) for a similar definition of political institutions as sets of rules for aggregating and legitimising binding and societally relevant choices.
4.  This deliberate exclusion of spontaneous organisation from the realm of private governance does not preclude the question of whether institutions are the products of deliberate design or result from structural developments. On this debate, see Onuf (2002).
5.  This understanding of private governance is in line with Kooiman's understanding of governance as an inter-organisational phenomenon analysed in terms of 'co-management', 'co-steering' and 'co-guidance' (1993; 2003: 96-114).
6.  An alternative conceptualisation has emerged from the Institutional Analysis and Development (IAD) approach (Kiser and Ostrom 1982; Ostrom 1999). It distinguishes between seven types of rules: entry and exit rules (for example describing rules for participation); position rules (for example describing how roles and responsibilities can change); scope rules (who is doing what and where); authority rules (for example spelling out basic norms); aggregation rules (for example voting rights and procedures); information rules (who is entitled to know what); pay-off rules (for example sanctions). However, this conceptualisation appears to be over-complex while a clear distinction between types is often hard to make (for example an information rule describing what has to stay behind closed doors could also be understood as an authoritative rule, a 'norm of secrecy').
7.  A lively debate has focused around the question of how behaviour follows from rules. March and Olsen (1998: 949-954) have highlighted the intrinsic difference between a 'logic of consequence' and a 'logic of appropriateness' when it comes to explaining actors' behaviour. A consequential approach understands political order as arising from the interactions of rational actors pursuing interests and calculating pay-offs deriving from social 'contracts'. In contrast, a 'logic of appropriateness' sees actions as rule-based, constraint by particular roles and identities.
8.  This dualistic understanding of rules as regulative and constitutive is also reflected in Hart's (1961: 79) definition of legal systems as the conjunction of primary and secondary rules. Primary rules are rules of obligation that prescribe the behaviour of actors. Secondary rules, by contrast, are 'rules about rules'.
9.  Young (1994: 26) defines a governance system as 'an institution that specialises in making collective choices on matters of common concern to the members of a distinct group'. In a similar vein, Koenig-Archibugi (2002: 50) refers to the term 'governance arrangement' to

describe 'how the interaction between various actors pursuing common goals is structured'. In accordance with these definitions, I use both expressions, private governance system and private governance arrangement, synonymously.

10. For a more general discussion of the transaction cost approach within the larger framework of new institutional economics, see North (1990).

11. In addition, the analytical category 'problem solving' is based on normative and practical considerations that may introduce a much higher or lower threshold for effectiveness. Consider for example the Forest Stewardship Council. If 'problem solving' refers to the global forest crisis, effectiveness measures may be poor. However, if 'problem solving' refers to creating demand for and supply of some amount of certified timber, effectiveness measures are comparatively high.

12. With reference to the environmental regime literature, there is an agreement that the three objects of assessment constitute distinct phases in the life of a regime, wherein output relates to the early phase of regime formation and the establishment of the international accord, outcome relates to the phase of regime implementation and impact refers to the phase of natural responses as a result of changes in human behaviour (Underdal 2002: 6).

13. The counter argument has been, for example, provided by Drezner (2004), who argues that states have consciously delegated problem-solving authority to non-state actors rather than being weakened by globalization in general. This argument holds true for a number of issue areas; however, it seems not equipped to explain the emergence and persistence of a number of private regulatory systems for at least three reasons: first, in the area of forest governance, states were unable or unwilling to come to an international solution. Rather than delegating authority, they have only reacted to private systems when domestic economic interests were at stake. Second, in the issue area of corporate environmental reporting, states have simply overlooked the emergence of private regulatory systems up to the point when actors started to scale up their efforts to the global level. And finally, private arrangements have also emerged in areas where public regulation is dense but inadequate for private interests, such as in the fisheries case.

# 4. Global Business Regulation in World Politics: An Empirical Perspective

The last three decades have seen a substantial proliferation of global business regulation, loosely defined as limits imposed on the behaviour of economic actors, contained in rules and standards. Today there is a vast number of different codes of conduct, management standards, certification schemes, reporting guidelines, eco-labels or more general behavioural norms applicable at the global level. Regulations are targeted towards TNCs,[1] but in many cases also influence smaller enterprises further along the production chain. Some forms of business regulation emanate from individual firms or business associations, others are institutionalised among a greater number of actors, often including NGOs and public agencies. A recent study of the Organisation for Economic Cooperation and Development (OECD) directorate for financial, fiscal and enterprise affairs surveys 246 codes of conduct, defined as 'commitments voluntarily made by the companies, associations or other entities, which put forth standards and principles for conduct of business activities in the marketplace' (OECD 2001: 3). Existing codes cover a wide variety of issue areas, including labour standards, environmental stewardship, consumer protection and information disclosure. A majority of codes are issued by companies (48 per cent) and business associations (37 per cent), but a substantive number already derive from a partnership of stakeholders (13 per cent) (OECD 2001: 5).

Attempts to regulate the activities of corporations have significantly changed in the context of increasing economic integration since 1970. International regulatory approaches have been complemented and in many cases substituted by transnational institutions. Next to intergovernmental treaties that regulate business activities and norms emanating from international organisations, there exist a number of new modes of regulation that have emerged during the last two decades. Some have already been at the centre of research, such as specific forms of global public policy networks (Witte, Reinicke and Benner 2000; Ruggie 2001) or private inter-firm regimes (Cutler, Haufler and Porter 1999a; Haufler 2000), while others have remained largely outside scholarly interest. The empirical focus of this study is on cooperative approaches to global business regulation, referred to as co-regulation or multi-stakeholder approaches,[2] involving both transnational business actors, as well as their non-profit civil society counterparts. This 'social regulation of the market' (Haufler 2003: 237) constitutes a novel form of private governance within the sustainability arena and beyond.

Within the larger development of deepening and widening global business regulation, it is precisely this observation that calls for closer attention, both in theoretical as well as empirical terms. The roles of business actors and NGOs are no longer limited to shaping the traditional policy cycle.[3] Next to agenda setting, influencing decision making processes, implementing commitments and monitoring state compliance, private actors increasingly begin to establish, maintain, verify and monitor their own private regulations beyond the international arena. These new private rule systems constitute a decisive institutional arrangement of global governance. They differ from ad-hoc partnership or strategic alliances between NGOs and companies because they involve the notion of shared norms and principles, as well as the prescription of new roles and responsibilities that shape the behaviour of organisational and individual actors. In sum, the co-regulation of economic behaviour constitutes a novel mechanism of private governance.

The preceding chapters were concerned with situating the research question in the larger theoretical perspective of global governance research in general (Chapter 2) and private governance in particular (Chapter 3). This chapter starts from the empirical side of matters. I consider global business regulation to be an integral part of transnational organisation. Consequently, I apply a private governance perspective and ask: If private business regulation on the global scale is understood to be a rule-based functional equivalent of international public regulations and standards, what then are the concrete institutional forms in which it occurs? How did they develop? What are the contextual factors of this development? How could different forms of global business regulation be classified? The chapter develops its argument in three stages. First, I discuss the meta-discourse underlying questions of global business regulation, namely the relation between public sources of authority in the form of states and governments and the market as the prime source of private authority. Second, I develop a classification of global business regulation. And finally, I provide a brief history of the last three decades of global business regulation and the contextual factors involved in the current transformation from international to transnational self-regulatory and co-regulatory approaches. This general discussion of the transformation of global business regulation provides the background for the analysis of the formation, influence and functions of private governance systems in forest certification and environmental reporting conducted in Chapters 5 and 6.

## STRONG BUSINESS, WEAK STATES?

The necessity to regulate the behaviour of TNCs has grown with the scale and scope of economic globalisation. The global economy is increasingly organised in cross-border networks and value chains largely beyond the control of public actors. In contrast to economic organisation in the era of 'embedded liberalism' (Ruggie 1982), where capital was predominantly national in terms of ownership and management and integrated into a historic social compromise, the current economic order is largely organised around transnational capital in terms of ownership, management, exchange and relevant stakeholders such as shareholders, suppliers and consumers. Correspondingly, TNCs have emerged as the new powerful actors in the era of globalisation, largely unrestrained by domestic regulation.

The empirical evidence supporting the assumption of the increasing influence of business actors in world politics falls roughly into three categories. First, statistics on foreign direct investment (FDI) are a good indicator of the increase in economic activities taken by large TNCs. Between 1981 and 1985, annual FDI flows equalled $50 billion on average, by 1990 they had reached over $240 billion, and continued to rise steadily to a new peak of $612 billion in 2004. As a consequence, the stock of FDI in relation to world GDP doubled from 4.9 per cent to 9.7 per cent between 1980 and 1994. The actual importance of transnational corporations in the world economy is even greater than these figures indicate, because FDI accounts for approximately 25 per cent of total investment in international production. Foreign affiliates often finance their expansion through retained profits and borrowing on domestic or international capital markets (Held et al. 1999: 246). A second indicator is the substantial increase of TNCs. Their number has risen from 7,000 in 1970 to over 40,000 in 1995 (Karliner 1997: 5). Already in 2001, the number of transnationals peaked at 63,312, controlling 821,818 affiliates abroad (United Nations Conference on Trade and Development (UNCTAD) 2001: 242). A third indicator for the increasing impact of corporations in world politics is the sheer size of their operations. For example, the annual sales of General Motors (GM) exceed the GDP of industrialised states such as Norway, Finland and Israel (Love, Hensman and Rodrigues 2000: 255). In addition, the $5 trillion sales annually generated by the TNC's foreign affiliates exceed the total volume of international trade. Consequently, only 49 of the largest 100 economies are states (Love and Love 2003: 98). What is most interesting in this context is the geographical and economic concentration. Roughly 90 per cent of all TNCs are based in North America, Europe and Japan. Moreover, the top 300 global firms account for one-quarter of the world's productive assets.

But the influence of TNCs on world politics is not only reflected in abstract terms, but also manifests itself on a very practical level. Consider for example the ecological footprint of TNCs.[4] Companies consume huge quantities of resources such as water, energy and raw materials and produce enormous quantities of waste; they transform the environment through resource extraction and the introduction of new materials, substances and species. Through their boundary-spanning activities, TNCs institutionalise unsustainable routines such as long distance air transport and replace deeply rooted cultural routines with new and often unsustainable ones. As Rowlands (2001: 133) notes, '[i]f we did not have TNCs spreading new forms of resource extraction, production and technological development around the world, then we could well not have many of the global environmental problems that we are experiencing today'. Indeed, international political analysis has to acknowledge that environmental risks and potentials are not predominantly produced, accumulated and regulated by public actors, but by private ones (Saurin 2001: 80).

In sum, TNCs can be considered central players in determining economic policies and transforming ecological and social structures. Reasons for the growing influence TNCs exercise in world politics range from the general spread of free-market economic systems after the end of the bipolar bloc confrontation, to specific economic events such as the debt crisis of the 1980s, in which large banks gained considerable leverage over states, to the logic of intensified economic integration that forces states to compete for FDI through fiscal policies and other (de)regulations favouring TNCs. Within this context of intensifying globalisation, business actors have surely acquired novel mechanisms of influence. But do corporations really rule the world, as Korten (1995) contends?

Implicit in the majority of literature on globalisation is the notion that the state has lost most of its regulatory power vis-à-vis non-state economic actors, at least in many areas of the world (Schlichte and Wilke 2000; Strange 1996, 1998). The standard argument holds that a globalising economy integrated only by the market and transnational capital is eroding the power of nation states to adequately address problems of public concern. In this view, both the theoretical and practical claims to the concept of sovereignty and the resulting 'national' economic policies are being undermined. In the words of Ohmae (1995: 78): '[Nation states] have become unnatural – even dysfunctional – as actors in a global economy … They are no longer meaningful units in which to think about economic activity.' However, critics of this scholarly 'state denial' (Weiss 1998: 2) argue that states do possess the capacity for domestic transformative strategies and therefore can adapt to changing economic circumstances (Boyer and Drache 1996; Scott 1997; Bernauer 2000).

In the light of these arguments, what is the precise relationship between transnationally operating business actors and nationally confined states? My tentative answer is that although the balance between states and transnational economic actors has shifted considerably, states still hold fundamental powers to restrain business activities. What has changed is the leverage that corporations hold vis-à-vis states that is created by the free-market environment, de-regulatory state policies, welfare state dysfunctionalities and the power structure within the inter-state system.[5] In sum, the picture is one of many shades of grey rather than black and white. In the words of Fuchs (2004: 27), referring to her recent study on the different dimensions of power that business actors possess in the global economy,

> claims of a lack of business influence on politics or severe limits to such an influence, which are still raised by a small group of scholars and practitioners, should be met with scepticism. At the same time, however, the analysis has demonstrated that undifferentiated claims of a global political rule of corporations ... do not capture the complexities of current developments in the political role of business.

Within the context of a widening – perceived or real – governance gap between a transnational economy and a territorially-based political system, the issue of regulating business activities has become a central theme of practical as well as theoretical considerations within the discipline of IR and IPE. It is through the process of globalisation that regulatory demand and regulatory supply are increasingly mismatched. States, in the organisational form of government, are less and less capable of regulating the activities of business actors within their territory due to processes of de-nationalisation and de-territorialisation (Beisheim et al. 1999). Consequently, we can broadly conceive of the globalisation of business regulation 'as the globalization of the norms, standards, principles and rules that govern commerce and the globalization of their enforcement' (Braithwaite and Drahos 2000: 10). This regulatory globalisation is connected with globalisation of firms and markets. Global firms originate within a specific territory, but spread their operations to other territories through foreign production facilities, franchises, joint ventures and other corporate structures. The globalisation of markets refers to the theoretical possibility that any one buyer or seller from any territory can meet with a buyer or seller from any other territory to conduct economic transactions.

The vast majority of norms, rules and principles that constitute the regulation of business activities at the global level have developed since 1970 (Braithwaite and Drahos 2000: 3). However, regulation has a long history.[6] As early as Roman times, people collectively regulated the activities associated with trade, production and distribution of goods and consequently laid the conceptual foundations of globalised business regulation. The second paramount historical episode in the globalisation of regulation is the development of the law merchant starting in the Middle Ages. For most of history, regulation originated from a web of competing sources. Only through the formation of the early-modern state did regulation slowly fall into the sole responsibility of a unified organisational structure (cf. Opello and Rosow 2004).

What follows from this 'historicity' of global business regulation are substantially different regulatory dynamics across different issue areas within the global economy. Given the different starting-points, contextual environments and divergent actor constellations within each arena, this is not particularly striking. In their broad study on global business regulation, Braithwaite and Drahos (2000: 5) find that

> regulation of the environment, safety and financial security have ratcheted up more than they have been driven down by globalisation. ... While ratcheting-up is more common than race-to-the-bottom in the regulation of safety and environment, the opposite is true of economic regulation. In domains of economic regulation beyond those that anchor financial security (e.g. capital adequacy standards for banks), we find that ratcheting-down has been the dominant dynamic – globalizing deregulation.

In sum, the interpretation of global business regulation as a central phenomenon in world politics will depend on the perspective one adopts towards the question of state–market relations and the social forces therein. As we have seen in the section above, the necessity to regulate corporate behaviour at the global level is a result of political decisions that have produced a mismatch between regulatory capacity and demand. Ironically, attempts to address this problem have largely followed the same logic of privatisation, soft law and blurred political responsibilities that are characteristics of the general process of economic globalisation. The following sections will first propose a classification of business regulation and subsequently address the process of transationalisation of business regulation in more detail.

## A CLASSIFICATION OF GLOBAL BUSINESS REGULATION

To cope with the empirical richness of global business regulation, a plethora of terms has been proposed to classify the phenomenon, such as the 'voluntary codes phenomenon' (Webb 2004), 'voluntary environmental agreements' (Brink 2002), 'certification regimes' (Haufler 2003) or simply 'global standards' (Nadvi and Wältring 2002). There are three different common approaches in the literature used to distinguish between different types of business regulation. The corresponding questions are: Who makes the rules? What is the content of the regulation? How are the commitments verified and what compliance mechanisms exist?

In the general context of global business regulation, rule systems can be discussed with reference to their level of state centrality. Three broad categories can be distinguished:[7] first, traditional forms of public regulation emanating from governments (national regulation) or international treaties and intergovernmental organisations (international regulation). The second is hybrid forms of regulation, involving individual governments, intergovernmental organisations, corporations and non-governmental organisations. The third category is constituted by forms of business regulation that display a maximum distance from public actors. In addition, limiting our view to forms of global business regulation that are clearly located in the realm of private governance, we can make a distinction between self-regulation and multi-stakeholder approaches in the form of co-regulation. Self-regulation refers to arrangements where individual firms or business associations set their own rules of behaviour in the form of codes of conduct, corporate governance guidelines or mission statements (Richter 2001: 40). In contrast, co-regulation refers to regulatory arrangements, wherein at least one actor is not a profit-making entity and therefore conflicts of interests and conflicts of values have to be bridged in order to institutionalise the cooperation and reap joint gains.

Next to distinguishing different types of code-issuers along an imaginary line of state-centrality, the abstract content of the rule can be used for a typology. Here we distinguish between product and process standards. Traditionally, standards focused on technical characteristics of a product such as size, composition or function. Originally confined to the national arena, standards began to be internationalised in the 1950s through the process of regional economic integration. In addition, the liberalisation of international trade induced harmonisation within and across economic sectors. Different from product standards, process standards focus on the actual management practices in the production process. Most standards that include ethical, environmental and social measurements are process standards. However, the distinction is becoming increasingly blurred because a range of product qualities can be linked to corresponding production processes, for example in the case of organic foods, where threshold levels of pesticides are linked to production methods (Nadvi and Wältring 2002: 7).

A third possible category for classification is verification procedures and compliance management of global business regulation. A straightforward distinction is between first, second and independent third party certification, in different terminology also known as 'reporting'. The term 'certification' in general refers to the process of certifying compliance with the basic management or output standards agreed upon. In particular, first party certification includes forms of business regulation wherein the code issuer and the actor monitoring and reporting on (non-)compliance are identical. Second party certification refers to instances of regulation where standard making and compliance management are separated, but still rely on information given by the regulated parties themselves. Third party certification involves a clear-cut separation between rule making and reporting compliance or noncompliance with the distinct standards. This is realised through the involvement of independent organisations (certifiers; certification organisations) that monitor the implementation of regulation on the spot and subsequently issue a certificate of compliance, in most cases in the form of a label recognisable to consumers. The rules and procedures specifying who is eligible to become a certifier and how the certification process is conducted are issued by the rule-making party. In principle, there also exists a fourth category of certification wherein public actors monitor compliance with standards. However, this possibility has so far been limited to the traditional form of global business regulation through intergovernmental organisations.

In addition to classifying global business regulation according to its source of authority, the abstract content of regulation and the applied verification procedures, forms of regulation can also be analysed with reference to their specific content, such as environmental, labour or human rights standards. What becomes apparent is that the transformation not only includes new actor constellations, but also a convergence of content towards issues of sustainability rather than stand-alone economic regulation. Table 4.1 classifies global business regulation according to the source of regulation (issuer of code) and the applied procedures for compliance and verification of commitments (mode of verification).

# THE TRANSFORMATION OF GLOBAL BUSINESS REGULATION

The institutional forms of business regulation have shifted considerably in the last three decades. This shift is often analysed as a transition from state-led mandatory regulation in the 1960s and 1970s, both at national and international levels, to corporate self-regulation in the 1980s and early 1990s, to cooperative rule making between NGOs and business actors, the phenomenon of co-regulation, in the last ten years (Utting 2004). In the realm of transnational business regulation, 'co-regulation arises when two or more actors or "stakeholders" are involved in the design and implementation of norms and instruments that attempt to improve the social and environmental

Table 4.1 Examples of Global Business Regulation

| Mode of Verification | Code Issuer | | | | |
| --- | --- | --- | --- | --- | --- |
| | Government; International Organisations | Firms | Business Associations | Civil Society | Multi-stakeholder Partnerships |
| First party 'self-reporting' | | Nike and Reebok codes of conduct | | | |
| Second party reporting | FAO code of conduct for responsible fisheries | | Responsible Care; CRT Business Principles | WWF Code of Conduct for Arctic Tourism | CERES; GRI; UN Global Compact |
| Third Party 'Certification' | | | Worldwide Responsible Apparel Production (WRAP) | Dolphin-Safe | FSC; FLA, International Cyanide Mining Code |

performance of firms' (Utting 2002: 65). Co-regulation as a novel mechanism of private governance particularly emerges at the intersection of two recent developments in world politics. First, the shift from private policy shaping to private policy making, exemplified in the growing number of industry self-regulation and standard-setting schemes (Gibson 1999; Garcia-Johnson 2001; Brink 2002; Bartley 2003). Second, the predominantly confrontational relation between companies and civil society has been complemented, at least rhetorically, by partnership as one possible mode of interaction. Antagonistic actors, representing the different organisational logics of business (transactions) and non-governmental organisations (values),[8] engage in the development and subsequent implementation of voluntary regulation on a global scale (Hartman and Stafford 1997; Gereffi, Garcia-Johnson and Sasser 2001; Arts 2002). The combination of these two trends amounts to a new quality of private governance, distancing it from mere coordination or cooperation between private actors. Table 4.2 gives a schematic representation of the four possible arenas shaped by the two trends towards private policy-making and private partnership in world politics.

*Table 4.2 Schematic representation of private governance in world politics along a rules and partnership axis*

|  | Organisational individualism | Partnership |
| --- | --- | --- |
| Policy shaping | NGO and business lobbying, monitoring or implementation of public policies | Strategic alliances, product development, communication partnerships, licensing |
| Policy making | Business self-regulation, NGO norms and standards | Co-regulation (institutionalised rule making), multi-stakeholder institutions |

Both developments are best considered as a continuum. On the partnership axis, empirical examples range from individual organisations that rely exclusively on their own resources to institutionalised partnerships that incorporate a wide range of actors within their scope. On the policy axis, empirical examples include lobbying international negotiations, implementing international regulations, monitoring public commitments, as well as setting and maintaining independent norms and standards beyond the international arena. Currently, we are witnessing a shift from the upper left to the lower right field. To place this transformation of business co-regulation as a form of private governance in historical perspective, the central phases in the history of global business regulation are briefly discussed below.

### From Public to Private Forms of Global Business Regulation

The trend towards voluntary codes, standards and general behavioural norms for TNCs as complementary instruments next to compulsory regulation at the global level is a mirror image of changes in national regulatory policies. In the words of Koenig-Archibugi (2004: 246):

> In most countries, heavy regulation until the 1970s has been supplanted by deregulatory policies during the 1980s. Similarly, the emphasis of the international debate in the 1970s was mainly on the creation of mandatory frameworks for TNC regulation, whereas the debates of the 1980s and 1990s were mostly about corporate self-regulation.

The earliest intergovernmental attempt after the Second World War to exercise some influence on the behaviour of corporations can be found in the Havana Charter of the International Trade Organisation (ITO) from 1948. This document includes provisions on the policies of governments towards TNCs, as well as towards the conduct of TNCs themselves. But the United States' withdrawal from the process in 1950 and their support for an alternative General Agreement on Tariffs and Trade (GATT) halted this early regulatory initiative (Bendell 2004). Only in the 1960s did the debate about international regulation of TNCs resurge again (Koenig-Archibugi 2004: 247). This development was partly triggered by the newly won independence of many developing countries and their resulting interest in maintaining control over foreign investment and the actual behaviour of foreign companies while at the same time exploiting the economic benefits of foreign capital and innovations. The related debate on a New International Economic Order (NIEO) and the resulting declaration that was adopted in 1974 by the UN General Assembly paved the way for a renewed discussion on regulating TNCs (United Nations 1974).

From the 1970s, a few international institutions emerged from these debates: in 1974, the United Nations Economic and Social Council (ECOSOC) established a Commission on Transnational Corporations and the UN Centre on Transnational Corporations (UNCTC) as its permanent research body; the OECD established a set of voluntary Guidelines for Multinational Enterprises in 1976; in the same year, the International Labour Organisation (ILO) produced the Tripartite Declaration of Principles Concerning Multinational Enterprises and Social Policy; and in late 1980, the UN General Assembly adopted a Code on Restrictive Business Practices drafted by the United Nations Conference on Trade and Development (UNCTAD) (Abrahams

2004: 5; Koenig-Archibugi 2004: 247). In sum, these regulatory initiatives mark the peak of international approaches to establish binding behavioural norms for transnational business actors. However, voluntarism has its first appearance. The OECD Guidelines 'were used to forestall the compulsory control being sought through the UN. The year 1976 thus marks the entrance of the voluntary code of conduct into business's strategic repertoire' (Rowe 2005: 137).

By the early 1980s, these modest regulatory initiatives were already in retreat. One possible explanation for this development is the substantial shift in international economic policy making that accompanied the election of Margaret Thatcher in the UK and Ronald Reagan in the USA. Classical economic liberalism highlights the unrestricted market as a mechanism to most efficiently govern international trade and investment. Consequently, regulating economic behaviour of companies was seen as a severe disruption of market equilibria and therefore disapproved of by economists and policy-makers. Consequently, the trio of liberalisation, de-regulation and pri-vatisation – known as the 'Washington Consensus' – marked the low end of the regulatory continuum. During the 1980s, only a few of the international codes envisaged in the previous decade could be implemented (Richter 2001: 10) and by 1992, the UNCTC failed to incorporate its draft on environmental regulations for TNCs in Agenda 21, the blueprint for sustainable devel-opment in the 21st century. On the contrary, most language on business roles and responsibilities adopted during UNCED was drafted by the newly founded Business Council for Sustainable Development (BCSD) (Richter 2001: 11). Many observers interpret the later dismantling of the UNCTC and the transfer of its responsibilities to the UNCTAD Commission on In-vestment, Technology and Enterprise Development in 1993 as the end of international and mandatory regulation.

Yet a parallel development was well under way in the late 1980s and early 1990s. Triggered by several social and environmental catastrophes such as the Bhopal accident and the Exxon Valdez oil spill, and supported by the economic orthodoxy of neo-liberalism, companies and business associations began to devise and implement a range of self-regulatory systems to reassure the public of their social responsibility. Responsible Care (RC), the chemical industry's international programme on environmental, health and safety standards, is an example of such a self-regulatory system. Since its inception in Canada in 1985, RC has developed into a global initiative, covering more than 85 per cent of the world's chemical production in 47 countries (European Chemical Industry Council 2002: i). However, it was not until 1996 that the International Council of Chemical Associations (ICCA), which has overseen RC since 1992, established a common procedure for verifying individual company's compliance with the agreed management practices. But

still, the day-to-day operation, implementation and monitoring is the responsibility of regional and national associations. As a result, the status of the
Responsible Care programme differs considerably in different countries and
regions.

It was precisely this vagueness and ambiguity that stirred protest against
forms of self-regulation that were essentially perceived as a window-dressing
and green-washing exercise.[9] Criticism addressed the ad hoc and piecemeal
nature of most corporate self-regulation initiatives, as well as their often
weak implementation and compliance procedures. CorpWatch for example, a
non-profit advocacy group, issued 'greenwash awards' to companies such as
BP, Shell, Monsanto and Ford for not meeting their self-set standards (Utting
2004: 103). As a result, by the mid-1990s, the tide had turned again. Private
regulation became institutionalised between a range of divergent and
antagonistic actors, including transnational business and their civil society
counterparts. This new mode of co-regulation has attracted considerable
attention over recent years, especially from a policy-oriented point of view
(Murphy and Bendell 1999; Hemmati et al. 2002). Although no reliable
figures on the overall population of co-regulative initiatives are currently
available, the general trend is evident. Figure 4.1 gives a graphic representation of the total number of co-regulatory initiatives, as well as the
annual increase from 1989 to 2002. The data is drawn from an extensive review of secondary literature on global business regulation[10] and extensive
web research that has fed into a research database on transnational rules
(Dingwerth and Pattberg forthcoming).

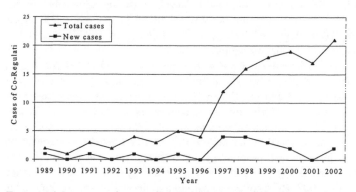

*Figure 4.1 Increase of co-regulatory arrangements in global business
regulation*

**The Rise of Business Co-regulation: Discourse, Politics and Public Opinion**

Various contextual factors are generally believed to have contributed to the emergence of private transnational co-regulation and multi-stakeholder initiatives as novel institutional arrangements for global business regulation. A combination of structural changes of both markets and politics, as well as the changing strategies of those actors operating within the structural limitations constitute the contextual environment of private governance in general and private co-regulation in particular. In more detail, these changes have been attributed to a transformation of the discursive field, a restructuring of the political environment and the correlation of social forces therein as well as a growing public criticism against forms of corporate self-regulation (Utting 2004: 99). I discuss these claims in some detail below.

Several emerging discourses have influenced the transformation of the transnational regulatory environment. First, there is the discourse of corporate social responsibility and corporate citizenship, which highlights ethical corporate behaviour and profits as being mutually supportive. Although the terms vary in their precise connotation, they are often used interchangeably.[11] Most definitions describe CSR as 'a concept whereby companies integrate social and environmental concerns in their business operations and in their interactions with their stakeholders on a voluntary basis' (Commission of the European Communities 2001: 6). Another definition by the corporate-funded non-profit Business for Social Responsibility (BSR) states that CSR is about 'achieving commercial success in ways that honor ethical values and respect people, communities, and the natural environment' (Business for Social Responsibility 2003). The underlying assumption of the CSR discourse is that the relationship between business and society at large should be guided by ethical considerations on the part of companies. From this perspective, not only shareholders, but also the larger community of stakeholders have a legitimate interest in the activities and impacts of business actors. Therefore, companies in response should be concerned not only with profits – the 'bottom line' – but also with a 'triple bottom line' of social and environmental goals next to profitability.[12] Also embedded within the discourse of CSR lies the notion of strategic and economic benefits that result from responsible behaviour towards society, or at least from communicating responsibility towards society. Utting (2002: 68) argues that within the corporate responsibility discourse, companies are believed to engage proactively with the demands from activists and society at large. This would

> allow business to not only deflect or dilute certain pressure but also be in the driving seat to ensure that change took place on terms favourable to business. At the more micro level, so-called "win–win" arguments suggested that corporate

social and environmental responsibility made good business sense by boosting a firm's competitive advantage, creating new markets and, in some instances, even reducing costs.

A second influential discourse that considerably lowered the companies' reluctance to engage in partnerships with civil society can be found in the predominantly academic debate on organisational learning (Senge 1990; Dodgson 1993; Fiol and Lyles 1995) and the more practically oriented debate on stakeholder involvement (Freeman 1984). Both approaches stress the importance of cooperation and social learning as mechanisms through which business actors can adapt to an increasingly risky environment. From this perspective, the knowledge, values and competencies of NGOs are crucial resources for companies to tap in order to gain competitive advantages over other corporate actors. Closely connected to this discourse are arguments that highlight the crucial importance of knowledge under the complex constraints of economic and social globalisation. In this view, governing complex problems in the era of globalisation requires the involvement of both business and civil society, because the problem solving capacity of nation states has declined considerably. The Commission on Global Governance, for example, contends in its final report that the skills and resources of a diversity of people are needed to cope with global problems. Consequently, the discourse on stakeholder involvement stresses the need to 'build partnerships – networks of institutions and processes – that enable global actors to pool information, knowledge and capacities and to develop joint policies and practices on issues of common concern' (Commission on Global Governance 1995: 6).

The third broad discourse that provided a contextual framework for the emergence of novel regulatory institutions is the discourse of sustainable development. Although there are many often contradictory definitions of the term (for example Brown et al. 1987; Dixon and Fallon 1989; Redclift 1992; Toman 1992; Mitcham 1995), it is now widely acknowledged that sustainable development should meet 'the needs of the present without compromising the ability of future generations to meet their own needs' (World Commission on Environment and Development 1987: 43) and incorporate environmental, social and economic concerns within its scope. However, the political implications are highly contested (cf. Luke 1995).

The origins of the sustainability discourse can be traced back at least to the early 1970s when several publications (Goldsmith 1972; Meadows et al. 1972) and the first United Nations Conference on the Human Environment began to investigate the relationship between human development and the natural environment. Other important contributions to the debate came from the World Conservation Strategy (WCS) and the World Commission on Environment and Development (WCED). The WCS, issued by The World Conservation Union (IUCN), the United Nations Environment Program (UNEP) and the World Wide Fund for Nature (WWF) in 1980, contained a systematic approach to development focused on ecological management of living resources to ensure the continuity of life and biodiversity for the satisfaction of human needs now and in the future. The WCED was formed in 1983 to tackle critical issues that the WCS did not address, notably the causes of environmental overexploitation and degradation, and the failure of development policies to alleviate poverty and hunger. Headed by Gro Harlem Brundtland, the WCED was mandated to define a shared perception of the most pressing environmental issues and to develop a long-term strategy for achieving sustainable development by the year 2000 and beyond. The final report *Our Common Future*, better known as the Brundtland Report, substantially shaped the following international debates and finally led to the 1992 Rio summit.

It was during UNCED that business actors seized this opportunity and influenced the emerging global agenda in their interests. It is no coincidence that the year 1992 marks both the founding of the Business Council for Sustainable Development (later to become the WBCSD) and the publication of *Changing Course* (Schmidheiny 1992), an elaborate outline of the role of business in sustainable development. It is noteworthy that it was Canadian businessman Maurice Strong, in his personal capacity as Secretary General to the Rio summit, who recruited Stephan Schmidheiny as the coordinator of the business input to the summit. As a result, corporations became accepted as legitimate actors within the sustainability discourse. Rather than being analysed as part of the problem, business was increasingly perceived as part of the solution by the early 1990s. In the words of Livio De Simone, chairman of the WBCSD in 1997, '[b]usiness used to be depicted as a primary source of the world's environmental problems. Today it is increasingly viewed as a vital contributor to solving those problems and securing a sustainable future for the planet' (cited in Karliner 1997: 31).

Discursive changes were accompanied by changes in the political environment and the correlation of social forces therein. A number of transformations left business and civil society in new positions. The weakening of national governments and the limitations of public intervention due to processes of globalisation and de-regulation strengthened transnational corporations vis-à-vis states. As business actors became more visible in the policy process, civil society organisations turned their regulatory demands towards them instead of governments. Throughout the 1990s, a growing number of organisations and networks began to pressure business directly. Although varying according to goals and approaches, a corporate accountability movement was on the rise (Broad and Cavanagh 1999; Bendell 2004) that forced companies to react to societal demands. As a result, TNCs and business associations sought to enter into various forms of partnership with environmental and social NGOs. Both sides increasingly began to appraise the partnership idea as appropriate to their strategic considerations.

A number of scholars observe the 'greening of the firm', a process in which business actors are moving from perceiving environmental goals as a threat to profits to perceiving them as an opportunity for growth (Prakash 2000; Usui 2002). Corporate environmentalism developed through different phases, from industrial environmentalism in the 1960s to strategic environmentalism in the 1990s (Hoffman 1997: 12-13). This transition is embedded in the broader process of ecological modernisation and the tendency towards market environmentalism. Ecological modernisation refers to a macroeconomic transformation of production via the development and application of more sophisticated technologies. In the words of Gouldson and Murphy (1997: 75), 'ecological modernisation seeks structural change at the macroeconomic level. It looks for industrial sectors which combine higher levels of economic development with lower levels of environmental impact'. Whereas modernisation of economic sectors and the accompanying institutions is primarily a state-led intervention, market environmentalism draws on deregulation and the decline of state intervention. As a political project, it adopts 'the principles of ecological modernisation but seeks to incorporate, and ultimately subordinate, these concerns within the broader project of governance by and through the market' (Stewart 2001: 210).

As a consequence, the older view that there exists a cost–benefit trade-off between ecology and economy has been challenged (Hartman and Stafford 1997: 187). For companies, market environmentalism has at least three basic advantages: first, reducing waste and maximising resource efficiency has a direct influence on the company's bottom line. Second, differentiation advantages allow firms to enter, and in some instances even create, new markets. And third, early-mover advantages occur for companies that invest in ecological modernisation before their competitors do. Engaging in partnerships with social and environmental organisations allows corporations to establish or regain public credibility, to minimise and manage risk, to use expert knowledge for product and process development, to build entry barriers for competitors and finally to avoid binding regulations. In addition, companies may also benefit from cooperation with civil society from an organisational perspective. In this view, the positive image of the partnering organisation increases the company's appeal to actual and potential employees, thus providing a better and more efficient working environment.

Companies are not only positively affected by partnerships, but also increasingly make a business out of them. PricewaterhouseCoopers (PwC) has developed into the world's largest service provider for companies seeking assistance in the complex corporate social responsibility world. PwC does not only conduct factory audits on environmental and social performance for companies such as Nike, The Gap and Walmart, as well as for private regulatory systems such as the Fair Labor Association (FLA) or the WRAP,[13] but it also offers services like reputation assurance and brand protection. In the words of PwC (1995),

> CEOs and boards are finding that public relations efforts alone are not enough to satisfy the market. Rather, corporate leaders are discovering that by engaging stakeholders, adopting rigorous business strategies, and implementing reputation management systems, they can more effectively establish trust with stakeholders, gain a competitive advantage, mitigate the impact of crises, and preserve a company's most important asset – its reputation.

NGOs have adjusted their position towards business too. Recent surveys suggest that NGOs increasingly analyse their relationship with companies as cooperative rather than confrontational (Enderle and Peters 1998; Sustain-Ability 2004). This transformation, of course, should not be overestimated. Civil society actors have not fundamentally changed their strategies, but rather enriched their toolkit by the 'carrot' of partnership, while holding the 'stick' of public campaigns and boycotts quite visibly in their hands (Heap 2000: 55). What then are the benefits NGOs perceive from cooperation with business actors? First, NGOs gain technical and organisational knowledge from partnerships with corporations, knowledge that is helpful in direct communication with firms, but can also be applied to future campaigns. Second, with the state's regulatory influence being divided among a wider range of actors, NGOs realise that partnering with companies can increase their direct impact on environmental and social performance criteria. Third, corporations provide open doors and influential networks, not only to policy makers, but also to other business actors and their associations. And finally, partnering firms may provide additional financial resources, especially in times of severe public budget constraints.[14]

These strategic reconfigurations were accompanied by political support for voluntary and cooperative approaches. The Clinton administration for example developed considerable activism on voluntary environmental and social regulation. In 1996, the US Government put pressure on US apparel companies to engage in the multi-stakeholder Apparel Industry Partnership (AIP) together with trade unions and NGOs. As a result, the partners agreed on a code of conduct defining nine conditions for decent and humane work.[15] Support for voluntary approaches to CSR has also come from the UK Government. In March 2000, the Blair Government appointed a Minister for Corporate Social Responsibility. In addition, the administration has also been active in supporting multi-stakeholder initiatives in the UK such as the Ethical Trading Initiative (ETI).

The third development that triggered the emergence of co-regulatory approaches in business regulation was the growing perception of self-regulation as 'window-dressing'. It became increasingly apparent that while corporations started to talk 'green' they continued using their unsustainable business practices. It was not only civil society organisations and consumers that were reluctant to buy the message of greener and cleaner corporations. Also business actors began to perceive an array of non-binding and self-reported commitments as a hindrance rather than a support. Too many different standards would raise transaction costs and minimise the reputation-related benefits gained from voluntary regulation. As a result, a growing number of companies realised the strategic benefits that would result from joint standard setting and monitored implementation of rules and regulations.

All three contextual factors, the changing discursive environment, new correlation of social forces and the public perception of self-regulation as a profit-driven window-dressing exercise, seem relevant in the context of emerging novel institutional arrangements in private governance. However, they fall short of providing a substantial explanation because most evidence coincides with early manifestations of the phenomenon, but does not pre-date it. The FSC and CERES for example both took shape before and around the time the major discursive changes occurred, societal forces were reconfigured and self-regulation had been publicly contested in the early 1990s. Therefore, it also seems plausible to contend that early examples of co-regulation have stimulated larger transformations, at least partially. Rather than providing an explanation, the three transformations constitute the ideational background upon which the analysis of private governance in global sustainability politics can take shape.

## CONCLUSION: GLOBAL BUSINESS REGULATION AS GOVERNANCE

In sum, the transformation of global business regulation is a reality in world politics. Public regulation at the international level is increasingly complemented by private transnational rules that address the behaviour of economic actors in the global economy. The recent empirical phenomenon of co-regulation, involving civil society organisations and business interests in the creation, implementation and monitoring of various rules and standards, is best analysed in theoretical terms as one mechanism of private governance. The frequent use of the terms corporate social responsibility, business ethics or corporate citizenship overlooks the fact that many of these phenomena have a regulatory impact and thus should be analysed in terms of governance instead of voluntary regulation. This is not to deny that business regulation beyond the state has a voluntary element. However, the institutionalised character and the precision of rules for compliance and monitoring (through certification and reporting) add a definite element of compulsion.

This chapter has approached the question of private governance from an empirical perspective. I argue that global business regulation has undergone a fundamental transformation. Traditional forms of state-centric regulation have been complemented by private, non-state arrangements. The most recent and far-reaching transformation can be observed in cooperative arrangements between profit and non-profit actors agreeing on a wide variety of transnational rules. This 'co-regulation', as one institutional form of global business regulation, is situated at the intersection of two substantial shifts in governance in general: first, the transfer of governance tasks from public to private actors across a wide range of issue areas and institutional settings; and second, the strategic relocation of business and civil society towards partnership, cooperation and compromise. Together, both trends amount to a new quality of private governance, both empirically and theoretically.

To support the argument of a transformation of global business regulation and the corresponding emergence of private governance, I have first discussed the necessity of regulating business behaviour by focusing on arguments about the relation between organised social power in the form of governments and markets. After proposing a classification of global business regulation according to the source of authority, the general content of regulation and the applied instruments for verification of compliance, I have focused on the contextual factors behind this intriguing shift from public to private forms of business regulation.

The next part of the study will address two specific examples of business co-regulation from the analytical perspective of private governance. Questions addressed concern the precise process of emergence, measurable effects and functional pathways of private governance systems. Whereas this chapter has focused on the general empirical trends in global business regulation, the next chapters will take a closer look at two institutions that have developed within the sustainability arena, more precisely in the domain of forest politics and corporate environmental reporting.

# NOTES

1. A transnational corporation shall be defined broadly as 'a firm which has the power to coordinate and control operations in more than one country, even if it does not own them' (Dicken 1998: 8).
2. The term 'business co-regulation' is given preference over the alternative term 'civil regulation' proposed by Bendell (2000).

3.  For a good discussion of more traditional forms of policy-making by non-state actors in the field of global environmental politics, see Rowlands (2001) on business actors and Raustiala (1997) on NGOs.

4.  On the ecological footprint of nations, see Wackernagel et al. (1997).

5.  Gilpin notes that '[j]ust as the Pax Britannica provided a favorable international environment for the overseas expansion of British firms and investors in the late nineteenth century, so American leadership following World War II provided a similar favourable international environment for the overseas expansion of American and other capitalist firms in the post-World War II era' (2001: 288). In addition, Doremus et al. (1998) argue that TNCs heavily depend on their respective home economies and, consequently, that the 'global corporation' in fact is a myth.

6.  See Oliviero and Simmons (2002) for concrete historical examples.

7.  For a similar approach, distinguishing between unilateral approaches, public voluntary schemes and negotiated agreements, see Lévêque (1996).

8.  For a detailed discussion of the different organisational logics of business, non-governmental organisations and states, see Waddell (1999).

9.  For a detailed account of corporate environmentalism and 'green-washing', see Greer and Bruno (1996).

10. Important studies that attempt to assess, at least partially, the overall universe of transnational business regulation include: Gordon and Miyake (1999); Kolk et al. (1999); Jenkins (2001); Hemmati et al. (2002); Nadvi and Wältring (2002); Utting (2002); Dankers (2003); Eritja (2004); and Abrahams (2004).

11. In addition, sometimes the term 'corporate social accountability' (CSA) is used in the same context. However, proponents of the CSA debate have a markedly different agenda compared to those engaged in CSR. In the words of Friends of the Earth (FoE) (2002), 'accountability requires going beyond voluntary approaches and establishing mechanisms which provide adequate legal and financial incentives for compliance. It must also empower stakeholders to challenge corporations'.

12. For a critical discussion of the 'triple bottom line' as an economic concept, see Norman and MacDonald (2004). For a critical discussion of the 'homo economicus' underlying most standard business theory, see Siebenhüner (2001).

13. In 1999 alone PwC conducted over 6,000 factory audits world wide. For a critical assessment of PwC's auditing methods, see O'Rourke (2000).

14. However, it is not only companies that have started to make a business out off the partnership paradigm, also a growing number of NGOs and activist groups have begun to reorganise themselves into more business-friendly service providers. In addition, several environmental campaigners and activists have become environmental consultants, advocating a 'new radical', cooperative approach to realising environmental goals.

15. The partnership later developed into the independent Fair Labor Association. Since 1999, 12 major brand-name companies from the apparel industry, NGOs and universities work together to promote adherence to international labour standards and to improve working conditions worldwide.

# 5. The Forest Stewardship Council

This chapter analyses the institutionalisation of private governance in the forestry sector. The case study takes a detailed look at the most prominent and well-established example of co-regulation in global forest politics, the Forest Stewardship Council (FSC). The FSC has been analysed, from different theoretical perspectives and with regard to a range of different questions, as, *inter alia*, a non-profit organisation, a certification institution, a private policy approach, a rule-making process, a form of business regulation via multi-stakeholder processes or simply a huge act of symbolic politics. From the analytical perspective of governance, however, the FSC is a system of rules through which sustainable forest practices and products emanating from them are certified by accredited organisations and made recognisable to consumers.[1] The rules also define roles and responsibilities and thereby structure and organise the network of actors sustaining and supporting the FSC as a mechanism of governance within global sustainability politics.

Based on the analytical framework outlined in Chapter 3, this chapter will address the following questions: first, how does the FSC operate as a private governance system? Second, why have private rules emerged in the global forestry arena that are endorsed by both profit and the non-profit actors in the field? Third, what influence do these private rules have on global forest politics and beyond? Fourth, what functions do private governance systems in forestry perform to realise their organisational goals and policy tasks? And finally fifth, what risks and potential can be observed with regard to private governance as an adequate answer to global change? I will approach these questions in the following way: the next section briefly reviews the economic, environmental and social importance of the forestry sector to subsequently discuss the failure of an international binding agreement for the world's forest ecosystems. Based on this short contextual assessment, the second section analyses the emergence of the FSC with reference to the theoretical propositions advanced in Chapter 3. Subsequently, the third section briefly assesses the degree of institutionalisation with a specific focus on the constitutive rules, as well as the roles and responsibilities of actors constituting the FSC, followed by a detailed analysis of the influence of the FSC as one example of private governance in forestry along its regulatory, cognitive/discursive and integrative functions. The subsequent section addresses the limitations to private governance in global forestry and outlines a number of internal as well as structural constraints. Finally, I summarise the key findings.

## GLOBAL FOREST POLITICS AND THE INTERNATIONAL FOREST 'NON-REGIME'

This section explores the state of the world's forest, its relevance for economic prosperity, ecological integrity and social stability, as well as causes for the ongoing pressure on forest ecosystems. In addition, I will briefly sketch the political responses to the forest crisis as they emerged in the 1980s and early 1990s. A particular focus is on the reasons for the failure of a binding agreement on forestry at UNCED in Rio de Janeiro and the corresponding discursive struggle about whether the forest problem constitutes a global issue or falls within the confines of national sovereignty.

### The State of the World's Forests: Values under Pressure

The global forest ecosystems are an integral part of the world's biotic community and serve many vital functions both for humans and for the biosphere as a whole. In addition to their significant contribution to the carbon cycle and the world's climate, forests contain over 80 per cent of the terrestrial genetic resources, stabilise local and regional water cycles, protect land against soil erosion and offer many economic and social services that benefit humans, from firewood to foodstuff and medical substances to paper products. As the dominant land-based form of vegetation, forests not only fulfil crucial ecological functions, but also maintain a central role in the daily life of hundreds of millions of people worldwide, both economically and spiritually. But despite these facts, forests are constantly under pressure. Causes and effects may differ from region to region and between boreal, temperate and tropical forests, but there can be no doubt that the degradation and deforestation of large parts of the world's forest ecosystems has a serious impact, both on the state of our global environment and on the social development of our world.

Forests[2] cover 3.9 billion hectares (ha) worldwide, roughly one-third of the land surface (Deutscher Bundestag 1994: 345; Food and Agriculture Organisation of the United Nations 2001: 5).[3] The annual rate of deforestation between 1990 and 2000 is estimated as 14.6 million ha. This figure represents the annual loss of natural forests (16.1 million ha per year) minus the area of natural forests converted to plantations (1.5 million ha per year). On the other side of the balance, the worldwide gain in forests totalled 5.2 million ha per year, representing the sum of afforestation (1.6 million ha per year) and the natural expansion of forests (3.6 million ha per year). As a result, the net global loss in forest cover between 1990 and 2000 is estimated as 9.4 million ha per year, an area about the size of Portugal. The total forest cover lost in the last decade thus stands at 94 million ha – an area larger than Venezuela (Food and Agriculture Organisation of the United Nations 2001: xxii-xxiii).

But scientists are not only concerned about continuing deforestation – the conversion of forests into other forms of land use through total destruction of forest cover – but also about forest degradation, the decreasing quality of forest ecosystems. Latest surveys on forest quality in Europe indicate that roughly 22 per cent of all trees are substantially damaged, 39 per cent are at a level of serious concern, while only 36 per cent remain in a healthy state (UNECE/FAO 2003).

Forest degradation and deforestation have causes and effects at local, regional and global levels, involving the interests of many different stakeholders such as local communities, national and sub-national governmental authorities, multinational companies, professional interest groups and international organisations at the regional and word level. The forest problem is a global environmental issue in the sense that it is caused by global economic–ecological interdependencies and that it has effects that are thought to be addressed best by international cooperation (Simonis 1995: 127).

The complexity of the forest problem results from the different interests, different perceptions and the geographically differing causes and effects of forest destruction in the tropical, temperate and boreal forests of the world. There are three dimensions that define the forest problem and thus help to understand why a coherent and generally accepted formulation of the problem is largely absent (Humphreys 1996: 22-28). The causal dimension refers to deforestation as a global phenomenon and the 'incongruence between the international economic system, composed of a diversity of actors, and the dominant international political system, composed of governments' (Humphreys 1996: 22). The institutional dimension of the forest problem is constituted by the fact that international institutions have failed to solve the problem so far. It is argued that international approaches have not been able to integrate the views of local inhabitants, such as indigenous people, villagers and local community groups. Finally, the proprietorial dimension refers to the question of who owns the forest and whether it should be viewed as a global common, a national or a local resource. It is important to note that the formal principle of state sovereignty is conflicting with the necessity for global cooperation on the one hand and local autonomy on the other (Sowers, Kholi and Sørensen 2000).

What follows from the above assessment is that important forest values are increasingly under pressure and the prospects for remedying the deterioration in the state of the world's forests are dim. The values and benefits that complex forest ecosystems offer to humankind and the biosphere as a whole can be systemised as the ecological, socio-economic and cultural forest-functions.

From an ecological viewpoint, it is the forests' central role in the global carbon cycle that attracts major attention. Through the process of photosynthesis, forests extract carbon dioxide from the earth's atmosphere to build up their organic substances, thus storing approximately 1200 billion tons of the 1800 billion tons of land-based carbon dioxide. Deforestation contributes to approximately 15–20 per cent of the additional human induced greenhouse effect (Deutscher Bundestag 1994: 359). Furthermore, forests influence local and regional climates and are 'the habitat of a large proportion of the earth's plant and animal species, providing the basis for the biodiversity which is essential for the biosphere's future' (Soussan and Millington 1992: 79).

The economic dimension of forest functions is constituted by the fact that forest ecosystems provide a wide array of material values, ranging from raw material to foodstuff to secondary wood products, such as rubber, oil, resin and medical plants. In 1997, the value of forest products entering international trade was over $135 billion (Food and Agriculture Organisation of the United Nations 1999). In addition, forests provide livelihood to over 500 million people. This includes various groups of people with various degrees of dependency such as forest workers, indigenous people, local community members or farmers (Bowling 2000). Besides these economic values, there are other benefits that are immaterial and indirect, including protection against soil erosion, avalanches and storms, as well as maintaining local ground water and surface water supplies. Furthermore, forests possess a high aesthetic and ethical value that is impossible to determine in monetary terms. They also play a central role in religious ceremonies and the traditions of tribal societies, as well as in the mythologies of our western civilisation (cf. Hartenstein and Schmidt 1996).

**Political Responses to the Global Forest Problem: the International Forest 'Non-regime'**

Concern over the substantial degradation and destruction of forests had grown to become a major issue of the public environmental debate by the mid-1980s. The Food and Agriculture Organisation of the United Nations estimates that during the 1980s, 8.1 per cent of all tropical forests were lost, an increase of deforestation from 11.3 million ha per year during the 1970s to an annual rate of 15.4 million ha between 1980 and 1989 (1993). Especially old-growth rainforests in the Amazon, and to a lesser extent in Africa and South-East Asia, were at the centre of public campaigns that increasingly started to address companies and their particular involvement in the destruction of valuable forests and violations of the fundamental rights of affected people. However, negotiations on a binding agreement on the protection of worldwide forests failed, despite strong and explicit public concern that was effectively organised at the transnational level. After the *Non-legally Binding Authoritative Statement of Principles for a Global Consensus on the Management, Conservation and Sustainable Development of All Types of Forests* (United Nations 1993: 480-486) had been concluded in Rio in 1992, a plethora of negotiation rounds emerged at the international level with very little tangible effect.[4]

Despite the complex nature of global forest politics, the failure to reach an international agreement at the time can be attributed to some major causes. The principles underlying global forestry today have emerged, at least to a great extent, in the context of European state formation (cf. Opello and Rosow 2004) and then spread through the European colonial territories to the rest of the world. As a result, forest management techniques were intended for the purpose of commodification and high yield, rather than for preservation, because states depended on forests for financial revenues and raw material for construction, especially in the fast-growing military sector. The parallel development of state formation and forestry practices largely explains the strong perception of forests as a national resource. However, in practice most forestlands are treated as private property, the economic value of which can be exploited. This structure results in a political environment in which 'economic stakes and the maintenance of national control of forests far outweigh the diffuse and scattered interest that the world might have in the secondary benefits of sustainable forests' (Lipschutz 2005b: 99).

A complementary explanation for the failure of international forest politics can also be found in the distinct problem structure. International regulation is most likely to occur in cases where cost structures favour a public solution and when there is already in place an institutional framework or template, within which a new issue can be addressed (Lipschutz 2005b: 102). In many cases, such as the Basel Convention, the Washington Convention on International Trade in Endangered Species of Wild Flora and Fauna (CITES), the Montreal Protocol on Substances that Deplete the Ozone Layer and the Convention on Biological Diversity (CBD), this framework has been the regulatory environment of 'free trade'. As a result, 'those bads for whose substance or effects are transmitted through international commerce are also those for which global regulation seems to be most easily achieved' (Lipschutz 2005b: 102). If we accept this analysis, it becomes clearer why the early approaches to regulation of global forestry, at least partially, have relied on the mechanism of free trade.

International attempts to regulate the sensitive issue of deforestation, especially in the tropics, began to take shape in the early 1980s. In 1983, timber producing and consuming countries agreed on the International Tropical Timber Agreement (ITTA), which was negotiated in Geneva under the auspices of the United Nations Conference on Trade and Development (UNCTAD) and entered into force in 1985, originally representing 36 producer and 34 consumer countries. The agreement also called for an International Tropical Timber Organization (ITTO), which became operational in 1986. The ITTA's objective is to promote the expansion and diversification of international trade in tropical timber, while at the same time encouraging member states to develop and implement appropriate forest management systems with a view to the conservation of tropical forests. The original agreement was renegotiated in 1994 and a considerable controversy broke out over whether the original scope should be expanded to cover all timber trade or remain as limited as it was. In the end, consumer countries successfully avoided an expansion of the ITTA's mandate and scope by simply committing themselves to implement similar sustainable forest management obligations for their forests in an appendix to the formal agreement (Tarasofsky and Downes 1999: 98).

The second influential international instrument in forest politics devised during the 1980s is the Tropical Forestry Action Plan (TFAP), which is based on previous work by the FAO, the World Resources Institute (WRI), World Bank and UNEP. Operational since 1987, the TFAP acts as a framework for the development of national forest programmes for developing countries, on which further development assistance for the forest sector is contingent.

Despite these early approaches, the international community failed to agree on a common framework for the protection and sustainable use of forests in the run-up to the Rio summit in 1992. Developing and developed countries found themselves in a considerable deadlock that centred on the adequate scope of a future binding agreement. While the industrial nations, led by the US and Canada, argued for a global responsibility, developing states vigorously favoured an approach based on national sovereignty. As a result, the negotiations were deadlocked by North–South debates, where developing countries remained cautious of Northern intentions and refused to even consider a binding agreement without financial compensation (cf. Bernstein and Cashore 2004a). In this deadlock, the FSC appeared a possible solution to all those that favoured a quick response, rather than long-term debates. As Gulbrandsen (2004: 76) summarises it, in parallel with the difficult negotiations at Rio, 'and much as a result of the states' failure to produce a binding global forest instrument and inaction on forest products ecolabeling, nonstate forest certification schemes have emerged in the shape of powerful market-driven governance and rule-making systems'. However, the FSC is not the first certification and labelling approach in forestry. As early as 1989, Friends of the Earth England and Wales proposed a certification scheme to the ITTO, but met fierce resistance to the plan (Poore 2003: 69). In addition, the New York-based NGO Rainforest Alliance (RA) established its own SmartWood programme to conduct forest management and chain of custody certification in 1989. In the following year, SmartWood issued the first certificate to a forest operation in Java, Indonesia. In sum, the FSC was not the first, but the first successfully implemented certification scheme that won the support of both environmentalists and business actors. The following section will address the conditions for the formation of the FSC in more detail.

# THE EMERGENCE OF PRIVATE FOREST GOVERNANCE: BUSINESS AT RISK

What are the enabling factors for the institutionalisation of private regulation involving companies and civil society organisations in the forestry sector? I assess the conditions for institutionalisation along the four recurrent themes identified in Chapter 3 – macro-systemic transformations, the problem structure, organisational resources and the discursive environment of ideas and models – starting with the demand side (that is: What is the distinct problem structure and how has it evolved?), followed by the supply side (that is: What regulation exists at the international level? What are the decisive resources organisations hold to solve the problem?).

**Making the Global Forest Crisis a Business Case**

In March 1990, a group of timber users, traders and representatives of social and environmental organisations convened in California to discuss the need for a credible system for identifying well-managed forests as an acceptable resource of forest products (FSC and WWF-Germany 2002: 6). One year later, the WWF had teamed up with major retailers in the UK to form the UK Forest and Trade Network. And already in October 1993, the FSC held its first general assembly after an intense 18-month consultation period in ten countries, including the US, Canada, Sweden and Peru. The FSC was formed as the first private regulatory scheme in the forestry sector with an explicit global focus and a broad membership base.[5]

Several distinct features characterise the problem structure that underlay this process of institutionalisation. Media coverage on tropical deforestation and related social issues, such as the Amazonian rubber tappers' protest against illegal logging and the subsequent investment in cattle, quickly turned the word tropical timber into a synonym for environmental degradation and human exploitation (Bass 2002: 3). Buying mahogany furniture had become a critical issue among northern consumers by the late 1980s. At the same time, many environmental NGOs working on forestry issues strongly felt that both the TFAP and the ITTO had failed to halt tropical deforestation. Timber boycotts and fake 'chainsaw massacres' in front of well-known retail stores soon became the strategies of choice in many industrialised countries (Bass et al. 2001: 23).[6]

With environmental organisations increasingly relying on boycotts against tropical timber retailers, and some governments discussing the possibility of banning timber imports, companies were looking for new ways to protect their markets. Major business players quickly realised that in fact they could not account for the origin and nature of their raw materials. This created a need for transparent product labels, which were nonexistent at that time. A report commissioned by WWF-UK in 1991 found that the vast majority of tropical timber firms' sustainability statements that had been developed as a response to increasing civil society pressure could in no way be substantiated (World Wildlife Fund United Kingdom, 1991). As one representative of B&Q, the world's third largest do-it-yourself (DIY) retailer, recalls in 1996,

> [f]ive years ago, we were asked how much tropical timber we were selling and from which countries we buy it. We realized that we could not accurately answer the question. In fact, we couldn't answer it at all. In public relations terms, if you don't know, you don't care. (cited in Viana et al. 1996: 207)

On the other hand, environmental organisations found themselves in heated debates about the adequacy of tropical timber boycotts. It became increasingly apparent that boycotts potentially increased the pressure on tropical forests because diminishing returns from timber harvesting made other land use forms, in particular the total conversion of forests into grazing land, economically viable. The consequence for environmental NGOs was a severe loss of credibility among concerned consumers and the general public. As a result, some NGOs realised the limitations of a debate focusing only on timber boycotts, which WWF in particular saw as counterproductive. Instead, WWF-UK conducted a seminar on the forest problem, entitled 'Forests Are Your Business', resulting in the WWF 95 group. Ten major DIY and furniture companies agreed to phase out, by 1995, the purchase and sale of nonsustainable wood and wood products (Bendell and Murphy 2000: 70).

This event reflects the strategic reconfiguration that occurred within parts of the NGO scene around this time. In the light of international controversies and the negative environmental impacts of consumer boycotts, the NGOs were seeking new strategies beyond boycotts. In short, whereas the more traditional strategies had been based on the ability to influence the behaviour of public actors, NGOs increasingly developed and implemented their own policies, in collaboration with governments and business actors. Next to the failure and negative externalities of boycotts, the changing global economic context also played a role in the reassessment of NGO approaches towards forestry. As a consequence of an increasingly integrated and borderless global economy, many NGOs shifted their focus from governments and international accords to markets and the private sector (Domask 2003: 167). In addition, while earlier attempts had focused on the lower end of the production chain, where a wide range of companies are producing, processing and trading timber products, the new strategies targeted the higher end of the chain, those companies with strong brands and a high recognition with consumers.

But not only was protest against tropical timber originating in the North key to making forestry a risk to exporters and retailers, also widespread protest in the South itself has been identified as a key condition. As Bendell and Murphy conclude (2000: 68) with reference to the civil society protests in the Amazon throughout the 1980s,

> grass-roots action by Southern unions backed up by international concern did bring some specific successes. Indeed the combined protests of civil society groups in the tropical forests of Africa, South-East Asia and Latin America in the 1980s began to shape a new international policy debate.

In addition to the pressure from NGOs, public authorities also became crucial drivers of change. The constant public protest against unsustainable practices in tropical forestry led a range of municipal governments in Germany, the Netherlands, the United Kingdom and the United States to consider the arguments brought forward by environmental organisations. As a result, bans on the use of tropical timber for publicly funded projects were implemented (Domask 2003: 160). In addition to impacts at the municipal level, both the governments of Austria (1992) and the Netherlands (1994) enacted laws that would ban timber from non-sustainable sources. Although these policies were heavily contested within the framework of free trade (for example GATT), government bans and NGO-led boycotts effectively reduced the imports of tropical timber to Western industrialised countries in the early 1990s, putting additional pressure on the forest industry.

A second argument that made governments more sensitive to public demands concerning the regulation of the global forest arena was the central role forests play in the global carbon cycle. European policy makers in particular were increasingly concerned about the issue of deforestation when it became apparent that forests play a major role in the global carbon cycle and therefore tropical deforestation, in fact any kind of conversion of forest land into other land use forms, contributes to the greenhouse effect and thus may become a direct threat to industrialised countries (Burger 2000: 178).

The competing needs of the major stakeholders became evident at this point. An increasingly competitive global market for timber products drove large transnational corporations, while at the same time brand reputation became a major topic of concern. Small forest owners wanted their share of the market, but to maintain independence, communities in developing countries relied on forests to finance community infrastructure, indigenous people demanded the recognition of fundamental rights, while workers sought to secure employment and fundamental labour standards. Environmental organisations in their term focused on protecting and preserving the integrity of the forest ecosystems. In this context, the formation of the FSC offered something for everyone. It was able to create sensible social and environmental standards that were supported by a wide range of NGOs, which would help wood producing, processing and importing companies keep out of the firing line. In the words of one observer organisation (Rainforest Information Centre 1998):

> There is huge public concern about the destruction of the world's forests. More and more people demand products that come from well-managed forests. This demand has led to many different labels on forest products, making claims such as 'for every tree felled at least two are planted'. Many of these claims are irrelevant or misleading. ... FSC aims to clear up the confusion by providing a truly independent, international and credible labelling scheme on timber and timber products. This will provide the consumer with a guarantee that the product has come from a forest, which has been evaluated and certified as being managed according to agreed social, economic and environmental standards.

In sum, the increasing demand for a private approach towards sustainable forestry must be seen in the context of widespread boycotts against leading retailers in the US and European countries and the support those strategies could muster with consumers and the larger public. Environmental campaigns and boycotts forced exporting companies and, to a lesser extent exporting countries, to secure adequate supplies of sustainable timber. It was the success of this new strategy that turned the global forest problem into a business issue. However, the growing number of self-labelling and 'greenwashing' that occurred as a response to boycotts and import bans, as well as the sustained criticism towards the strategy of boycotts within the NGO camp, led leading environmental organisations to reassess their strategy. FoE UK developed the Good Wood Seal of Approval and the first Good Wood Guide for consumers, but discontinued the certification in 1990 due to problems in credibility. In addition to the idea of certification, NGOs also teamed up with companies directly in so-called buyers groups that were thought to create the initial demand for certified products on a larger and long-term scale. As two observers conclude (Councell and Loraas 2002: 12),

> the FSC was founded on the basis of mass consumer movements, which had been used by environmental pressure groups to bring commercial interests to the negotiation table. They, along with a small number of progressive companies that had specifically positioned themselves as responding to ecologically minded consumers, formed the basis of the informal groups that eventually evolved into the FSC's founding membership.

After considering the factors that created the demand for private governance in the global forestry arena, I now turn to the supply factors, both at the systemic and organisational level.

## Towards a Private Global Forest Convention

Although UNCED was unable to deliver a binding agreement on the world's forests, it nevertheless provided important guidance for the FSC process. The Rio conference was the place where the concept of sustainability gained its greatest appreciation. Based on the 1987 Brundtland Report (cf. World Commission on Environment and Development 1987), UNCED agreed on Agenda 21 as the blueprint for sustainability in the 21st century (cf. United Nations 1993). The document calls on governments to identify appropriate national strategies for the sustainable use of forest resources, acknowledging the crucial contribution of non-governmental actors and business interests. One could argue that the FSC was deliberatively built around the principles of sustainable development as they emerged around 1992, both in terms of organisation and decision making (cf. Bass 2002). For Peter Prokosch, CEO of WWF-Germany in 2002, the FSC constitutes the 'archetype of the participatory process envisioned by Agenda 21' (FSC and WWF-Germany 2002: 3). The idea of participation and equal representation based on the general assumption of the sustainability discourse that environmental, social and economic interests are of the same value has been an important prerequisite for cooperation between the different stakeholders involved in setting up the FSC.

In particular, the unique tripartite governance structure, which gives all interests the same voting power, has served as an early point of reference and a common ground for future negotiations.[7] From an NGO perspective, the FSC as a model provided the solution to the stalemate in forest politics, because there was no conservative majority but an equal representation of interests within the newly emerging institution. In this line of argumentation, the adequateness of the FSC as an alternative instrument in global forest politics derives from the unique governing and decision making structure that centres on consensus rather than conflict. The FSC provides a platform for bargaining and arguing because every member has the same power to be heard in the debate and no one is excluded from the beginning. Although there may be strong arguments about the interests involved in the FSC, the unique structure allows not only for compromise, but also for mutual understanding. As one observer notes, most NGOs feel well represented in FSC because interests have the same status and economic actors are not more powerful per se.[8]

In addition, individual commitment, although hard to measure, seems to have played a decisive role in the emergence of the FSC. Substantial individual political interests derived from the success of the tropical timber boycotts enacted in the early 1990s, which were beginning to bite many forest actors, became so strong that both NGOs and companies were willing to change their behaviour.[9] As interviews with current staff members of the FSC indicate, special credit for getting the FSC started is given to individuals at WWF who approached British companies with a view to partnership and not conflict.

Next to the sustainability paradigm that gained currency around the Rio summit in 1992 and the corresponding focus on the contributions that private actors were able to offer, the idea of forest certification itself played a decisive role in the emergence of the FSC. Certification as an idea developed in advanced industrial societies, particularly in the United States. Reasons can be found in the general mistrust of governmental intervention and the strong position of the consumer. However, business and NGOs were 'taking their US-based certification solutions global' (Gereffi, Garcia-Johnson and Sasser 2001: 58). In the words of Maser and Smith (2001: 83), '[t]he idea of forest certification (or an incentive-based tool for conservation) began with several organizations in the conservation movement and the wood industry nearly at the same moment in time during the 1980s'. Early examples include the Good Wood guide issued by the Rainforest Action Network that listed 'good' and 'bad' companies as a decision making blueprint for consumers and the SmartWood programme that was started in 1989 by the Rainforest Alliance. A particular institutional model was provided by the certification movement in organically grown foods such as the International Federation of Organic Agriculture Movements (IFOAM) that dates back to 1972. RA decided to transfer the certification idea to the forestry sector. After approximately a year of discussions and programme design, the very first forest certification took place when SmartWood certified the Perum Perhutani reforestation programme on the island of Java in Indonesia (Maser and Smith 2001: 84).

Environmental organisations quickly took up the idea of forest certification to the most influential international process in forestry up to this time, the ITTO. However, the plan that was proposed to the International Timber Trade Council (ITTC) in 1989 met fierce resistance and was finally downgraded into a general study on the incentives for sustainable forest management (cf. Councell and Loraas 2002: 11). At the 7th session of the ITTC in November 1989 in Yokohama, the UK delegation, in collaboration with FoE UK, introduced a proposal for a global labelling scheme for the promotion of tropical timber from sustainable sources. Subject to intense debates in the official forum and the corridors, producer countries vehemently rejected this proposal. As Poore (2003: 69) recalls, the 'producers were privately alarmed that it would be difficult for them to provide such label for *any* timber that they marketed. Publicly, they voiced many reservations and objections of variable force and validity'. As a result, the main objective of the proposal had to abandoned and the NGOs took this defeat as proof of the inadequateness of international processes. Poore concludes that this occasion was 'perhaps the first of several occasions on which the Council failed to show the necessary resolution and courage to provide leadership to the international community on an issue of great importance' (2003: 70). In sum, similar to UNCED, the ITTO failed to provide an adequate global response to the forest crisis, pushing the establishment of such an instrument even further into the future.[10]

In sum, the early motivations of the actors involved in forest certification can be summarised as follows: NGOs were motivated by the prospects of converting bad forestry into good practices by using the innovative instrument of certification. In addition, NGOs wanted to explore ways to inform consumers about the impact of their choices building on the experience, but avoiding the problems of the early SmartWood approach offered by the Rainforest Alliance in 1989. Business actors, especially forest producers and retailers, on the other hand, were largely motivated by the prospects of exploring alternatives to timber boycotts and thereby answering the growing concerns of consumers. In particular, the expectations centred on premium prices, reducing risk to brand reputation and maintaining and increasing market share (Bass et al. 2001: 31). As Mark Eisen, Director of Environmental Marketing, The Home Depot, summarises the company's position on the newly emerging private policy (cited in Viana et al. 1996: 201),

> [c]ertification by an independent third-party scientific organization continues to be the foundation upon which The Home Depot is successfully building its environmental franchise with the customer and through which it is aggressively pursuing the interrelated goals of promoting alternative merchandise and delivering environmental information.

IKEA, the world's largest home furnishing retailer, goes even further when stating that '[t]he FSC basic Principles and Criteria, at least presently, appear to be the only available alternative for a world standard for sustainable forest management' (cited in Viana et al. 1996: 206).[11]

In addition, the idea of independent certification and non-discrimination of all stakeholders was not only appealing to NGOs and business actors, but also to governments that found themselves caught between environmental demands and economic necessities in the context of a heated sustainable development discourse. It is therefore not surprising to find the governments of Austria and the Netherlands among the early financial supporters of the FSC.[12]

With the idea of forest certification neglected by the ITTO and ISO and the prospects for a binding agreement to protect the world's forest already becoming doubtful, a group of timber users, traders and representatives of environmental and human-rights organisations met in California (USA) in 1990 to discuss how they could combine their interests in improving forest conservation and reducing deforestation. Their meeting confirmed the need for an honest and credible system for identifying well-managed forests as acceptable sources of forest products. Between July 1990 and October 1993, seven consecutive drafts of what later would become the FSC Standards and Principles were prepared. In March 1992 the FSC founding group elected an interim board and agreed on a draft FSC mission statement.[13] Throughout 1992, the FSC draft Principles and Criteria were field tested in ten countries and tentatively adopted (FSC 2004b). In 1993, the founding board of directors was elected by the first general assembly in Toronto, Canada. One year later, a definitive set of Principles and Criteria, together with the Statutes for the Council was agreed and approved by the votes of the Founding Members. The by-laws were ratified and the FSC began operations in Oaxaca, Mexico (Meridian Institute 2001: 2-3). In sum, as one observer recalls in colourful terms (Elliott 2004),

> in 1993 an, at that time, improbable group gathered in a stuffy meeting room in Toronto, Canada, to discuss setting up the world's first forest certification organisation, a credible system to ensure environmentally responsible, socially beneficial, and economically viable management of forests.

At this point in time, it became apparent that states favoured private voluntary approaches over mandatory ones because the latter were increasingly seen as being in contradiction to the free trade agenda and the rules of the GATT. Austria for example had to reframe a law that banned non-labelled timber altogether in 1993 due to pressure from other governments based on the GATT rules. As a consequence, Austria channelled the money that was originally allocated for its timber labelling project to the emerging FSC (Bartley 2003: 447-448). In addition to governments favouring private solutions, NGOs began to view such approaches in a much more positive light.

The reasons were the major failures at the international level to influence and craft appropriate agreements. In particular, the failure of a certification programme with the ITTO and the minimal consensus of Rio in 1992 convinced many environmental organisations to seek solutions beyond the international realm.

Next to the missing supply of adequate international solutions and the institutional context of free trade, a third explanatory factor can be found at the macro-level. From this perspective, the formation of the FSC as a prime example for the phenomenon of private, market-driven governance can be attributed to economic and political trends in the last decade that 'have given market-oriented policy instruments increasing salience' (Cashore 2002: 506), both at the national and international level. Among those trends, the partial retreat of the state and the accompanying neoliberal economic theories are of particular interest (Elliott 1996: 83; Bartley 2003). Similar to developments in the social field, where companies, predominantly in the US, began to devise their own policies on issues such as the employment of minorities or investments in South Africa independently of the government, business increasingly addressed environmental issues on its own. As a result, the norm complex of 'liberal environmentalism' (Bernstein 2001) has become a dominant approach in environmental politics, nationally and internationally.

After the discussion of the distinct problem structure that has emerged in global forest politics, largely as a result of effective boycott campaigns, and the existing macro-systemic trends, including dominant discourses and policy paradigms, the analysis now turns to the role individual organisational resources may have played in the process of private governance formation. One important observation is that available organisational resources played a greater role in the process of institutionalisation than strategic reduction of transaction costs. Although companies were able to minimise costs, based on information they obtained through the cooperation with environmental NGOs, for example by eliminating intermediate traders, this has been an unintended consequence rather than a clear strategic vision on the part of companies.[14]

More decisive was the fact that NGOs were perceived as legitimate social actors by the public and thus could deliver the much needed credibility to forest certification systems. It became quickly clear that to have a real impact on consumers, the standards had to be approved by independent organisations that were credible to the majority of consumers. The NGO movement was able to fill this emerging void.[15] Furthermore, NGOs provided expert knowledge on many complex issues related to the technical aspects of certification, as well as to their ecological functions. Retailers for their part could exercise pressure on the forest industry by demanding certified raw materials and products, inducing change in the actual practices of forestry.

Forest managers perceived the chance to increase their profit margins by positioning themselves on the newly emerging market for sustainable timber.

### Summary

In sum, the case of the FSC confirms the importance of a distinct problem structure creating demand for regulation that cannot be met by an international agreement. With NGOs making timber trade a real consumer issue and governments unable to agree on binding regulations, companies sought new allies to save their core business interests. NGOs not only emerged as corporate critics, but also possible solutions to the problem. An integrative idea, based on the norms embodied in the Brundtland Report and Agenda 21, served as the common point of reference within the negotiations. What proved decisive was the fact that a novel idea emerged that was visionary enough to unite different actors to a common cause. In this sense the early FSC was much more an experiment than just a suitable policy tool.

Drawing on the empirical evidence presented in the sections above, the following narrative can be presented. In this view, a distinct problem structure of interconnected interests, different levels of information and knowledge, as well as adversarial relationships among stakeholders create demand that is not met by public regulation. The ability to create private demand for regulation and to find a common solution rests on the organisational resources of distinct actors. These resources are a result of rather large-scale transformations. NGOs and other social actors have emerged as an accepted corrective to public actors, while at the same time corporations acquired both greater environmental impact and public visibility. In this situation, ideas can help to integrate these resources (civil society pressure, public acceptance and environmental impact) into a joint solution. In short, when private regulatory demand, being a result of strategy and macro-systemic transformations, is not met by adequate public supply, a broad inclusive idea can help to integrate resources that can be mutually exchanged to solve the multi-party problem.

## FUNCTIONS AND INFLUENCES OF PRIVATE FOREST GOVERNANCE

This section approaches the question of whether and how the FSC is involved in the construction and maintenance of private governance by carefully assessing its regulatory, cognitive/discursive and integrative functions and the resulting influences on a range of different actors. I start with a brief assessment of the constitutive rules and the resulting roles and responsibilities for actors within the FSC structure to better illustrate how the FSC works as a private governance system. This first section also assesses the degree of formalisation observable within the FSC.

## The Constitutive Rules: Roles and Responsibilities in Private Forest Governance

The FSC is constituted as a membership association. Its highest organ is the General Assembly (GA) of individual members or duly designated delegates of member organisations, representing business, social and environmental interests within three chambers. Each chamber holds an equal voting power of 33.3 per cent; internally they have a 50 per cent quorum from North and South[16] representation, as well as a limitation on individual votes to 10 per cent of the respective chamber. As a consequence, each chamber is subdivided into a Northern and Southern division, in which organisations have 90 per cent of the sub-chamber vote, while individual members hold the remaining 10 per cent (FSC 2002b: §12-13). Table 5.1 shows the current membership pattern accurately as of June 2006.

*Table 5.1 FSC General Assembly membership according to chamber and geographic origin*

| General Assembly | ENV | ECO | SOC | Total |
|---|---|---|---|---|
| North | 114 | 161 | 60 | 335 |
| South | 140 | 113 | 52 | 305 |
| Total | 254 | 274 | 112 | 640 |

While the criteria for membership in the North–South sub-chamber are based on international definitions (cf. footnote 16), eligibility for the economic (ECO), social (SOC) and environmental (ENV) chambers are detailed in the FSC by-laws. For example, commercial vested interests include forest product organisations, certification bodies, industry associations, wholesalers, retailers, traders and consulting companies active in forestry. Prospective members have to demonstrate 'active commitment to implementing the FSC Principles and Criteria in their operations' (FSC 2002b: §29). In addition, it is expected that applicants have already made a considerable commitment to FSC-based certification, accreditation or retailing or that such a commitment is implemented in the next two years. While environmental interests are relatively balanced with regard to North/South representation, economic interests are clearly biased against the South, and social concerns are relatively un-derdeveloped in general. Due to the three chamber voting system and the 50 per cent quorum, this representation structure does not lead to formal under-representation but to a structural advantage of the South. However, larger Northern membership may lead to discursive disadvantages for actors from the South, especially for social organisations that share fewer resources and have less experience.

As specified in the FSC by-laws, the GA delegates operational activities and most decision making to the Board. In addition, the GA will 'normally restrict its decisions to revising the Statutes and Principles and Criteria, ad-mitting and destituting members, electing the Board and being the final au-thority in dispute resolutions' (FSC 2002b: §18). The GA convenes in three forms: as the Ordinary General Assembly, held at regular intervals, not ex-ceeding three years; the Extraordinary GA, requested by the Board or by one-third of the members of each chamber; and finally, as a postal ballot to annu-ally elect Board members or decide on other issues at the discretion of the Board (FSC 2002b: §19-21). General Assembly decisions are adopted by the vote of 66.6 per cent of the total voting power of the association provided for a 50 per cent plus one vote quorum in each chamber in a first ballot. In case such a quorum of voting percentages is not obtained in the first ballot, a second ballot is held, wherein no quorum is required and decisions are adopted by the a total vote of 66.6 per cent of the registered associates (FSC 2002b: §15).

The GA's main function is to elect the Board of Directors that mirrors the tripartite structure of business, social and environmental interests represented in the association. Each chamber elects three members to the Board for a three-year term.[17] Elected representatives should represent the views and concerns of their respective chamber and category (for example Environ-mental/North) in all board deliberations and decisions, rather than reflecting the views of the organisation with which they are affiliated. While in princi-ple every FSC member, in its individual or organisational capacity, is eligible for board membership, 'commercial interests not demonstratively committed to FSC, Certification Bodies, and industry Associations may not be represented on the Board' (FSC 2002b: §50). The representation of Northern and Southern interests alternates between four and five, changing every three years. In June 2006, the North/South ratio is four to five. In addition, in electing the Board, the GA 'shall aim for regional and gender balance' (FSC 2002b: §53).[18] The board decides on all issues of major importance, from ap-proving national representatives and initiatives of the FSC, to allocating the annual budget, to approving new standards.

The Statutes recognise three distinct offices within the Board: first, the Chairman of the Board of Directors, whose duties include presiding over the

GA and board meetings, submitting a financial statement and provisional budget to the GA, as well as representing the Board to the GA and the FSC association to third parties. Second, the Vice-chairman assists the Chairman in the preparation of meetings and during those meetings. Finally, the Treasurer is responsible for the preparation and filing of all necessary financial reports. These offices are designated during the first annual meeting of the Board (FSC 2002d: §19-26). The Board has also established a Dispute Resolution and Accreditation Appeals Committee for dealing with disputes and grievances from members as well as a Technical Committee for reviewing and making recommendations on the international, regional and national forestry standards.

Board meeting decisions are motions approved and decisions taken formally during legally constituted board meetings, with or without a vote, recorded in the minutes. This is most suitable for key decisions, such as: accreditation decisions, especially the approval of accreditation evaluation reports, with pre-conditions or conditions attached; approval of applications from new members, and cancellation of existing membership (subject to confirmation by the General Assembly); approval of annual or periodic workplans, annual accounts, annual audits, as well as approval of major items of policy and documentation. It is further specified that

> [p]olicy decisions, especially decisions which affect the implementation of the statutes, taken during legally constituted board meetings are legally valid and binding. They may be changed or reversed by other decisions with equal legal status, such as valid board decisions taken by ballot or in a later meeting. Such formal board decisions cannot be reversed simply by registering objections or changes of opinion. Board decisions can be invalidated if it is established that the board meeting itself, or the decision taken at the board meeting, was invalid. ... Minor operational decisions taken at a board meeting (such as the dates of subsequent meetings) may be reversed or changed with less formality when appropriate. In case of doubt, the Chair of the Board will determine whether a formal board decision is required, or whether informal consultations among board members will suffice. (FSC 1999)

The day-to-day operations of the FSC are handled by the FSC international secretariat located in Bonn, Germany, and supervised by the Executive Director (ED) who is appointed by and responsible to the Board. The ED is the Chief Executive (FSC 2002b: §60), serves as the Board Secretary (FSC 2002b: §57), the legal representative of the FSC (FSC 2002d: Title 5) and the head of the secretariat, recruited by the Board and responsible to the Board for: (1) effective implementation of FSC policies and programmes; finances, accounting, administration and compliance with legal requirements; (2) staff appointments; (3) presentation of annual reports, annual audited accounts, annual budgets and work-plans; (4) encouraging collaboration with people and organisations who can contribute to the FSC's mission; (5) taking appropriate steps to obtain the necessary legal status in countries in which the FSC has activities.

The secretariat staff is responsible to the ED. The work of the secretariat is an elaboration of the responsibilities of the ED for the implementation of FSC policies and programmes, including: international marketing, promotion and fund-raising; coordination of activities, including collecting and distributing information across the FSC network; accreditation and related dealings with certification bodies; standards decisions and harmonisation; and operational and administrative decisions, based on appropriate studies and consultations within a policy framework determined by the board. On these issues, the decision rests with the senior management team of the secretariat. This will decide the mechanism for decision making, taking account of advice from board members and others as required. In addition, staff members provide support to the board by organising board and committee meetings, distributing regular reports and financial information, company secretarial duties, coordination of policy formulation for board approval. Furthermore, staff members ensure the implementation of guidelines and legal requirements for ballots and elections and provide guidance and information for members when voting. Other roles of the secretariat and its staff are described in staff contracts, job descriptions, terms of reference, the FSC Quality System Manual and local legislation (cf. FSC 1999).

The international secretariat is organised in different operational units among which the Policy and Standards Unit, the Accreditation Business Unit, and the Communication and Marketing Unit are the most important with regard to understanding the process of private governance. Additional organisational units and responsibilities within the international secretariat include the Office Management and Human Resources Unit, the Finance and Fundraising Unit, the regional coordinator, and other usual elements of a bureaucracy such as office support and computer network administration.

Next to the division of the secretariat into specialised units, the FSC as a whole is organised in several operational layers that are connected through the substantive rules of the institution. Next to the FSC international secretariat, there are regional offices and a number of national FSC processes that, after having received accreditation by the FSC board, become national initiatives that independently develop appropriate national FSC standards based on the FSC international standards. According to the by-laws, FSC-related processes in regions and countries fall into the following four categories (FSC 2002b: §71): first, the FSC contact person, who is an individual FSC member or a designated delegate of a member organisation and promotes the FSC mission and consequently facilitates discussions on the theory and practice of forest certification within the country or region concerned.

Second, the FSC Working Group, which facilitates a consultative process involving environmental, social and economic interests of the respective country. Third, once a consultative process has been completed, a national or regional assembly of stakeholders, reflecting the provisions made in the FSC by-laws for the GA, formally elects a national or regional Advisory Board. Finally, the Advisory Board may establish a National Office that performs tasks similar to those of the international secretariat, only limited to the national context. In 2006, a majority of 23 national initiatives out of 36 are located in OECD countries.

To react to specific demands and concerns of national initiatives and to better integrate the valuable knowledge of respective stakeholders, the FSC has set up four regional offices in Europe, Africa, Asia, and Latin America.[19] The regional offices act as focal points for the national initiatives within that particular region and, as a result, create the opportunity for discussions on topics of common concern. Specific regional interests thus can be appropriately developed and formulated. For example, discussions within the regional office for Latin America have raised concerns about the different importance attached to social issues in the region and in the FSC international. Participants felt that in European debates, measurable environmental impacts are of most importance, while concerns about social and cultural matters feature relatively low on the agenda. In contrast to this environmental and economic focus, stakeholders in Latin America stress the importance of addressing cultural and spiritual needs in achieving sustainable forestry.[20]

To adequately monitor and support the decentralisation of the FSC network into National Initiatives and regional offices, the international secretariat has established a unit for regional coordination. Its primary occupation is the organisation of capacity-building sessions and training seminars, as well as the facilitation of discussions via the Internet and telephone. The latter point is of particular importance in regions where NIs are scarce because here in-person meetings are relatively costly and time consuming. The regional coordination unit acts as a clearing house and focal point for national initiatives and the regional offices with regard to a range of technical issues. Its main challenge in this respect is to accommodate the divergent demands of a decentralised and thereby highly dissimilar network of actors without jeopardising its credibility.[21]

In addition to the GA, the Board, and the international secretariat that together form the organisational core of the FSC, and the decentralised network of FSC national initiatives and regional offices, the independent certification bodies (CB) constitute the third institutional element of the FSC as a private governance system. The role and responsibility of CBs with regard to their function in private governance through regulation is discussed in the following section.

Following this brief analysis of the constitutive rules underlying the FSC and the organisational structure resulting from them, I now turn to the actual influence of private forest governance by carefully assessing its effects at different levels of the political system and with regard to different stakeholders. Based on the discussion of the potential functions of private governance in Chapter 3, I distinguish between governance through regulation, governance through discourse and learning, and governance through integration.

### Governance Through Regulation: What is Labelled, that can be Sold

To better understand the different functions the FSC performs, the operational procedures it carries out and the regulatory effects it induces, I disaggregate the operation of a private governance system in forestry into two basic concepts: first, rule making, and second, implementation.

One prime function of the FSC as an example of private governance is to develop and implement detailed rules for sustainable forest management (SFM). As a rule maker, the FSC produces three different types of standards, which constitute the regulative rules of the institution.[22] Global forest management standards represent the first type of standard the FSC developed; they form the basis for national and regional standards development. Forest management standards are certified on the ground. The second type of standard is the chain of custody standard (CoC) that prescribes detailed rules along the production chain, which includes log transport and processing, shipping and further processing. The third standard prescribes rules for the accreditation of independent certifiers and national FSC processes. All standard types are developed and drafted by the Standards and Policies Unit within the international secretariat and later approved by the board of directors.[23]

The 'Principles and Criteria' (P&C), the rules agreed on after the founding meeting in Toronto in October 1993, form the basis of the FSC's work. They define which practices are considered socially beneficial, environmentally appropriate and economically viable. In detail, the P&C (FSC 2000) require compliance with all applicable national laws and international treaties and agreements, including the provisions of CITES, the ITTA and the CBD (principle 1), assurance of long-term tenure and use rights for forest resources (principle 2), the recognition and respect of the rights of indigenous peoples to own, use and manage their lands (principle 3), the maintenance of the long-term social and economic well being of forest workers and local communities (principle 4), efficient use of the forest's multiple products and services (principle 5), the conservation of biological diversity and other non-monetary values (principle 6), an appropriate management plan (principle 7), an adequate monitoring system to assess the condition of the forest, yields of forest products, management activities and their social and environmental impacts (principle 8), the maintenance of high conservation value forests (principle 9), and finally, assurance that forest plantations are in accordance with principles 1 to 9. The ten generic principles are accompanied by 56 criteria that specify the content of the regulations. More detailed standards that take into account regional, national and local differences may be developed by appropriate consultation process that are formally recognised by the FSC.

The second step central to private regulation is implementation. It can best be described in terms of three different, but interrelated processes: certification, accreditation, and labelling. In general terms, certification refers to a 'system by which the conformity of products, services, etc. to an applicable standards is determined and confirmed' (Rundgren 1997: 14). While some certification programmes rely on the internal verification by the applying organisation itself, most programmes prefer the more rigorous approach of 'third party certification',[24] 'wherein a person or organization that is neither part of the FMO [forest management organization, author's note] nor one of its customers or suppliers, is given authority to assess compliance with the program standards' (Meidinger, Elliott and Oesten 2003: 7).

The FSC does not conduct forestry certification itself. Instead, independent organisations, both profit-making and non-profit entities, perform the actual on-the-ground assessment of forest management operations and the supply chain.[25] Hence, accreditation refers to the process of accrediting the certifying organisations according to some general rule.[26] According to the FSC accreditation standard, it is defined as 'the procedure by which an accreditation body gives written assurance that a certification body conforms with the requirements of an accreditation system' (FSC 2002c: Glossary). This definition conforms to the respective ISO guidelines (ISO/IEC Guide 2: 1991 paragraph 13.7). Some programmes prefer their own certifiers, whereas others, such as the FSC, engage independent organisations (Meidinger, Elliott and Oesten 2003: 7).

Becoming an accredited FSC certification body involves a detailed process carried out and supervised by the accreditation business unit. Interested parties will start the accreditation process by ordering an information package or the full application package at a cost of 200 Euro. Once the applicant organisation has officially agreed to seek accreditation, the process starts. The FSC accreditation business unit then checks whether the procedures of the applicant are consistent with those laid down in the FSC accreditation manual and standards (cf. FSC 2002c). The auditing process involves field visits to the applicant organisation. Accreditation is generally granted for five years. The process of accreditation can take up to one year, depending on how well the applicant is organised and how much experience it has with forest certification in general. The accreditation process costs approximately 20,000 Euro, covering only the expenses such as travel costs and costs for personnel. The FSC makes no profit from accreditation. However, turning the accreditation process into a source of revenue has recently been discussed within the context of organisational restructuring. Once the accreditation business unit has filed a final recommendation to be adopted by the board of directors, the CB can begin its certification work.

Compliance with the FSC standards for CB can be monitored through un-announced surveillance audits, but in most cases FSC auditors are acting as 'shadows' in an actual certification process on the ground. The accreditation officers write reports and can file a corrective action request to the accredited certification body in case procedures are not in line with FSC standards or other applicable regulations. CBs can get suspended from accreditation by the accreditation business unit if a corrective action request is not im-plemented. The second monitoring tool at the disposal of the FSC is office visits. In this case, the FSC auditors check the office of the accredited certi-fier and look for shortcomings (for example appropriate files on local experts that are required for the field visits; appropriate documentation of their certification processes). Field or office visits by the FSC accreditation business unit happen at least once a year, depending on the number and kind of accreditation that a specific certification body holds.

Finally, the third process of implementation, next to certification and ac-creditation, is labelling. This refers to the process and practice of attaching a label to products or production chains to inform consumers about existing choices (cf. Eritja 2004).

In sum, it is through the process of rule making and the subsequent im-plementation of these sustainable forestry standards through certification, accreditation and labelling, that private governance is established in the for-estry arena. But what are the measurable effects of this *governance through regulation*? The following sections give a detailed account of the regulatory influence of private forest governance along six sets of indicators: standard-uptake and implementation, geographical scope, trade flows and economic incentives, environmental improvements, norm convergence and changing roles of actors.

### Standard-uptake and implementation

In June 2006, approximately 76 million hectares of forest area worldwide were certified in FSC terms, located in 72 countries.[27] The 15 CBs accredited by the FSC have issued more than 4800 certificates to forestry companies and businesses. Conservative estimates are that 100 million cubic meters of timber from FSC-certified sources reach the market each year, while the total supply of certified timber products is estimated at about 234 million m³ on an annual basis (Atyi and Simula 2002: 17). However, only a small fraction of certified timber is actually traded as a certified forest product (CFP),[28] while the large majority of timber reaches the market without reference to its certification status (Rametsteiner 2002: 160). The FSC's share of total certified area stands at approximately 30 per cent in 2006, competing with two other major certification schemes, the industry-based Sustainable Forestry Initiative, SFI (24 per cent), and the Pan European Forest Certification Council, PEFC (33 per cent). The FSC believes it will be possible to increase its certified area to 140 million hectares by 2010.[29] Figure 5.1 shows the increase of FSC FM certificates, CoC certificates, and the total FSC-certified area.

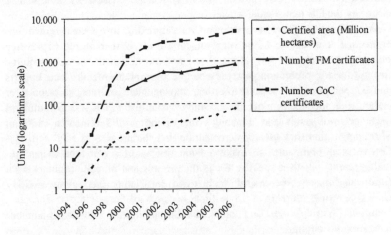

*Sources:* FSC (2001; 2003; 2004b; 2005b), FSC and WWF-Germany (2002).

*Figure 5.1 FSC area and certificate increase from 1994 to 2006*

After the first FM certificates had been issued, the area certified according to the FSC standards quickly rose from less than 500,000 ha in 1994 to 21 million in 2000 and than more than triple over the next five years to reach well over 76 million ha in 2006. Similar to the area increase, the important chain-of-custody certification, which allows products to be recognised in the market, grew from a modest 268 in 1998 to over 2000 in 2001, only to more double again to almost 5,000 by June 2006.

While it is obvious that these developments have occurred as a result of the institutionalisation of the FSC as a mechanism of private governance, it is less clear how high the regulatory impact on the standard-takers really was. Figures from Germany indicate that about one-third of the applicants for FSC forest management certification already conform to the FSC standards before the certification process starts. However, it can be assumed that forest managers in developing countries, lacking the long-standing experience of industrialised nations in sustainable forestry, will have to make more substantial adjustments to their operations. One possibility to approximately determine the level of changes made in reaction to the FSC regulation is analysing the corrective action requests issued by the CBs in the initial auditing process. A corrective action request (CAR) is defined as 'the formal document which details non-conformity with the requirements of the certification scheme and which specifies actions which must be taken to achieve conformity' (FSC 2002c: Glossary). It may be issued by the FSC to a CB or by the CB to a standard-taker.

A 1999 study (Thornber) reviews CARs issued to forest management operations. For example, 42 per cent of companies were required to develop plans for the protection of water and soil resources, 38 per cent were required to improve the protection of representative ecosystems within their borders and 37 per cent had to improve their management of rare, threatened or endangered species. A more recent study by Gullison (2003: 158) confirms these general trends and concludes that '[t]he results reinforce those of Thornber in that they clearly demonstrate that the process of FSC certification requires companies to make a wide variety of significant changes to management'. With a specific focus on the impacts of FSC regulation on European forestry, the World Wide Fund for Nature has reviewed 2817 CARs covering more than 18 million hectares of forest in six European countries (World Wide Fund for Nature Europe 2005). The report summarises its key findings:

> The analysis across six countries shows that FSC certification is delivering a number of benefits for a wide range of stakeholders in the forest industry, and provides hard evidence of tangible improvements that the voluntary mechanism of credible certification delivers for society, the environment and the economy.

In sum, the analysis of corrective action requests issued to forest companies suggests that in general, successful certification involves substantial behavioural changes as a result of FSC regulation, both in developed and developing countries and potentially across all types of forests.

**Geographical scope**
The FSC has been heralded as the first truly global approach towards sustainable forestry. According to the FSC by-laws in their current version, the FSC 'shall promote environmentally appropriate, socially beneficial, and economically viable management of the world's forests' (FSC 2002b: 1). Paragraph 8 specifies: '[t]he FSC Principles and Criteria are intended to apply without discrimination to tropical, temperate and boreal forests world wide, which are managed for production of forest products' (FSC 2006b: 2). However, actual figures look somewhat different. Currently, roughly 79 per cent of the certified area is in Europe and North America, while Africa, Asia, Oceania and Latin America account for only 21 per cent. For forest management and chain-of-custody certificates the relation is 28.5 to 71.5 per cent in favour of North America and Europe.

One reason for this disparity is inadequate infrastructure and economic disequilibria in developing countries. It is not difficult for well-organised forestry companies in temperate regions to meet FSC standards and criteria as the core standards of forestry have primarily been developed in Western Europe. For example, a recent survey on community forests in Germany and their experiences with FSC certification shows that 37 per cent of the forest operations studied did not have to change their management procedures at all to secure certification (FSC Arbeitsgruppe Deutschland 2005). In contrast, tropical countries often lack the infrastructure to facilitate certification. In particular, underdeveloped management routines and lack of expertise raise the cost of certification. A second explanation for the geographical disparity can be found in the well-organised networks of environmental NGOs, retailers and forest owners that have developed in most industrial countries and effectively convinced forest managers to seek certification. In contrast, there is generally less pressure from domestic civil society organisations to shift to sustainable forestry practices in the tropics. Reasons include a lower awareness of environmental problems, limited organisational capacity of NGOs, and, resulting from this point, less influence in decision making processes (Ebeling 2005). A third explanation is the existing structures of the international timber trade. The key markets for tropical timber producers are domestic or regional and show very little demand for certified products in general. Sufficient demand for certified timber exists predominantly in a few European countries, and to a lesser extent in the US and Canada. At present, the average market share of certified forest products is estimated at 5 per cent in Europe, while the share of CFP in Japan, the world's leading tropical hardwood importer, is only 0.02 per cent of total wood consumption (Rametsteiner 2002).

An unintended consequence of the uneven distribution of certified forest area between North and South could well be the institutionalisation of trade barriers between developing and industrialised countries.[30] With only 6–8 per cent of global timber production entering international trade, the majority traded between countries of the same region, and environmentally sensitive markets only existing in Europe and North America, producers from developing countries have significantly less access to premium markets and therefore their incentive to seek costly certification is relatively low (Gullison 2003: 158). Hence, it is an open question whether the FSC can be considered a successful steering mechanism towards sustainability, or rather it could be seen as a strategy tool for companies to drive others out of the valuable 'green' market.

### Economic incentive structures in private forest governance

Another question central in this context is: What are the costs of certification and who pays for them? In other words, how does the FSC as a private governance system affect the economic incentive structures and the distribution of costs and benefits within the forest arena? Costs related to forest certification fall into the two broad categories of indirect and direct costs (Simula 1996: 126-134). Indirect costs include the incremental costs of forest management to meet the certification standards, such as additional silviculture and harvesting costs, additional management and planning costs and costs derived from lower yield per area unit. In addition, indirect costs also contain the information costs of certification, both for forest management and chain-of-custody standards. These costs derive from investment into resource inventories and surveys, forest management planning, reporting and recording of activities, as well as from the necessity to mark and track logs and products along the supply chain. The direct costs are those linked to the actual process of auditing, including application fees and the initial as well as annual inspections.

This theoretical distinction may be convincing and clear-cut, however, comparative empirical data on the costs of certification is largely absent or simply does not keep up with the growth of forest certification, both in area and geographical distribution. Nevertheless, some general conclusions can be drawn. First, the incremental costs of forest management will largely depend on the general management level within a particular forest economy. As the prevailing levels of infrastructure, management know-how, information systems and human resources vary from country to country, and often from region to region, costs will also vary accordingly. With regard to the direct costs that result from forest management certification, there is evidence that FSC certification in the tropics is more costly than in temperate or boreal forest for two reasons: first, non-tropical forests are less complex and thus require less auditing time and preparation; and second, temperate and boreal forests often already have well-established management procedures in place.

Consequently, raising management standards to the required level is less costly. In addition, smaller forests also seem to be disadvantaged. A study of six natural forest areas in Latin America (de Camino and Alfaro 1998) found certification costs for small-scale forestry to be up to four times higher than for larger operations. Similar figures can be derived from an early study of the SmartWood certification programme (Heaton 1994). Here the unit cost per ha is found to be $1.30 for a 5,000 ha operation, while it already significantly drops to only $0.24 for an area of 100,000 ha. As a result, direct costs are higher in total for larger operations, however, with a lower per unit cost.

With regard to the question of who bears the additional costs of certification that derive from raising existing forestry standards to the level of FSC rules and regulations, studies have shown that costs have not been evenly distributed but tended to be concentrated at the lower end of the value chain. Bass et al. (2001: 71) conclude that '[f]or the most part, costs borne at the producer end of the chain have not been passed on to buyers in the retail sector'.

The initial expectation of most forest managers and timber exporters with regard to certification has been a rise in exports and higher profits through premium prices.[31] However, there seems to be no sign of higher prices in general. Early market studies (Winterhalter and Cassens 1993; Baharuddin and Simula 1996) have shown some interest in some market segments for paying a premium price, but the analysis at that time suggested that there is not yet convincing evidence of an existing price premium for sustainably produced, certified timber. This assessment seems still valid today. A recent study from the International Institute for Environment and Development (IIED) finds that premium prices are rare in DIY retailer supply chains. The only situation where premium prices for certified timber have occurred is 'when there has been a mismatch between supply and demand, if buyers are competing for certified wood with few sources' (Bass et al. 2001: 64). However, the same report acknowledges that there have been instances of enduring premium prices for tropical hardwood. For example, producers from Brazil and Papua New Guinea report that they are receiving premiums of up to 20 per cent for well-known commercial species (Bass et al. 2001: 64). In sum, the incentive structures prevalent in most tropical countries do not lend support to the assumption that there will be rapid increases in the area of FSC-certified forests in the near future, although premium markets may exist in some areas for some time. To conclude, few producers have been able to receive a premium from FSC-certification or to shift costs to retailers and consumers.

**Environmental improvement**

Another central question with regard to the influence of private forest governance centres on its environmental effects. The possible negative ecological impacts of FSC certification are reflected in debates about appropriate strategies for achieving sustainable forestry and halting the negative trend of deforestation. Critics of certification fear that this strategy of 'commodification' and its framing as the 'solution' to problems of deforestation and forest degradation may impinge on other strategies such as the forest conservation preferred by some actors. One example is the concerns raised by some NGOs about the FSC strategy of creating buyers networks for virgin tropical forests because economic incentives could lead to the creation of a logging-economy in the Amazon (Councell and Loraas 2002).

Therefore, it is important to assess the actual and potential impacts of forest certification on ecological parameters such as biodiversity conservation. There are three potential ways in which certification may have a positive impact on natural high conservation value forests (HCVF) in the South[32] (Gullison 2003: 156). First, certification may improve the biodiversity value of forest by raising existing management standards to the FSC level. Second, certification may raise the profitability of a forest operation above the level of alternative uses such as grazing land or agricultural cultivation. And third, certification may take away pressure from HCVF because it offers alternative products from well-managed sources. A recent study (Gullison 2003: 162) concludes that

> there is only clear evidence that certification produces biodiversity benefits by im-
> proving management of existing timber production forests during the auditing
> process. In contrast, the incentives offered by certification are insufficient to
> prevent deforestation, and the volume of certified forest products currently on the
> market is too small to significantly reduce logging pressure on HCVF.

In sum, although forest certification potentially contributes to environmentally appropriate forestry, existing empirical evidence is scarce and largely confined to tropical forests with high conservation values. However, on a more abstract level, the FSC has clearly demonstrated its environmental impact. Many observers attribute the FSC to be one of the most influential sources of the current convergence towards more sustainable and ecologically appropriate forestry practices.

**Converging forest practices**

Next to large industrial operations, small-scale community forestry[33] is of particular importance, especially in the South. Community forestry differs from larger corporate-driven enterprises in four ways: first, management practices are often informal and limited; second, harvesting is on a smaller scale, often as a result of limited financial resources; third, commercial activities are sporadic, occurring in times of agricultural inactivity; and fourth, community forestry is often located in remote geographical areas. Case studies from Bolivia, Honduras, Mexico, Zambia and Papua New Guinea (Bass et al. 2001) have found that, as a result of these differences, in some cases private regulation has shifted the perception of 'good forest management' towards western, scientific standards. However, the economic effects of certification have been rather limited to date. The study concludes that 'although there have been some positive experiences, most community enterprises have yet to see a significant increase in their income following certification' (Bass et al. 2001: 31). In most cases, initial certification created higher costs. The funds to implement costly certification standards came predominantly from external sources. In some cases, communities have used certification to attract additional funds from development agencies and NGOs; in other cases, certification has been a condition for future support. In sum, similar to larger forestry operations, the initial expectation of premium prices for certified timber has not been fulfilled. As costs are concentrated at the lower end of the supply chain, certification of community forestry made only modest inroads because donors were willing to fund the extra costs. However, private governance through forestry regulation has shifted professional perceptions and thereby supported convergence within the forestry sector.

**Changing roles and responsibilities**
So far, I have considered the direct impacts of FSC certification, those that affect the standard-takers. However, the regulatory function of private governance systems also induces effects on those actors not formerly under regulation. New roles and responsibilities emerge as a consequence of the indirect involvement of actors with the FSC. For example, a leading German DIY store reports that taking FSC certified products into the product range was cheap, but resulted in many positive externalities. First, many environmental organisations supported the company while abandoning hostile campaigns against retailers in general. Second, comparative advantages to other companies played an important role at the beginning. This created advantages in image, especially because there was widespread attention in the media. This positive experience made the company become a supporter of the FSC, for example by acting through the BHB (Verband der Baumärkte) association to make competitors also join the WWF-wood group – a buyers group in support of the FSC – instead of joining one of the rival schemes.[34] In sum, positive externalities that derive from certification can change the behaviour of actors that are only loosely connected to the rules of the FSC.

To conclude, the influence of private forest governance through its regulatory function can be summarised in five points. First, the analysis of standard-uptake and the subsequent implementation of private rules in global forestry indicate that while the market share for certified timber products remains limited and the percentage of certified forests in relation to the global forest cover is small, the standards de facto change forest management practices on the ground, across regions and across forests types.

Second, the analysis of the FSC's geographic representation has drawn our attention to the fact that private governance in the form of forest certification may systematically benefit some types of actors, while it clearly disadvantages other players in the field. For Northern companies, compliance with relatively tight standards is easy compared to those in developing countries, because the regulatory environment is already tight in industrial nations and key concepts such as sustainability have – to a large extent – originated in the West. As a result, private environmental and social regulation might in fact be considered more of a strategy tool for companies to drive others out of the valuable 'green' market, than a substantial steering mechanism towards sustainability.

Third, and substantiating the former claim, producers, particularly those in the South, have been largely unable to secure premium prices for certified timber. On the contrary, the costs of certification are concentrated at the lower end of the supply chain due to the power of large retailers in the North. Although it has not resulted in higher profits through a premium, certification has helped Southern companies access new markets or at least to guarantee existing ones. As a general observation, private governance through certification has more impact on countries that have strong export markets to Europe and the US, while countries with rather weak ties to green markets are less affected.

Fourth, the FSC has had a relatively low impact on key environmental parameters such as biodiversity. Although it has improved existing management practices to the FSC level, additional impacts such as taking away the pressure from HCVF or avoiding land conversion to non-forestry uses has not been substantiated by exiting case studies. In addition, figures from Germany suggest that a substantial number of forest operations already conform to the FSC standards prior to formally seeking certification. If this observation is a general trend, the FSC has contributed to making existing good forestry from industrialised countries visible, rather than raising standards to a new optimum on a global scale.

Finally, private forest governance has resulted in a shift of perceptions towards sustainable forestry at the local level, in particular in community forestry in developing countries. This shift towards a more 'scientific' understanding of forestry underscores the general trend of convergence in global forestry discourses and practices.

## Governance Through Discourse and Learning: a Network for Change

The second function through which the FSC gains influence on actors in the forestry arena can be labelled *discourse and learning* and contains the following elements: (1) producing and disseminating information, (2) providing the institutional setting for learning processes, (3) allowing for problem solving by providing a forum for discourse and debates, and finally (4) the diffusion of the regulatory model. This cognitive/discursive function is a result of the FSC's distinct network structure and the specific roles and responsibilities that also influence the behaviour of a range of actors outside the narrower reach of rule making and regulation via standards.

### Producing and disseminating information

Through its network structure and the different organisational levels – the international secretariat, the regional offices and the national working groups and initiates – the FSC produces and disseminates information to a wide range of stakeholders. This function is of particular importance for actors from the South because certification of tropical forests, especially in small-scale operations, requires more informational capacity than well-organised commercial forest management. Partially in response to these demands, the FSC has successfully implemented regional offices to help producers and local communities to get the right information.[35]

Connected to the process of knowledge dissemination is the question of awareness raising with regard to the idea of forest certification and the underlying global forest crisis. With regard to the former objective, FSC has been relatively successful in areas where sustainable forestry already existed as an important issue. However, with regard to recognition by the public in general and consumers in particular, interviewees held the opinion that the FSC still has a lot of work ahead of it.[36] Although consumers in OECD countries show general interest in eco-friendly products and have strong sentiments on deforestation and biodiversity loss, in particular with reference to tropical forests (Rametsteiner 1999), consumer awareness of established logos such as the FSC's is low. Partially as a reaction to low recognition by consumers, FSC international agreed to improve its entire communication structure and outside appearance. As a result, in August 2003, FSC international hired a head for the newly structured communications unit. Early results of a more consumer-oriented strategy can be seen in the Netherlands. Here, the FSC teamed up with the WWF to launch a countrywide campaign to increase the recognition of the FSC label. In 2004, after three consecutive years of campaigning, the initial recognition of the FSC logo stood at 33 per cent, while more than 60 per cent recognized the label after some brief explanations. For people under 35 years of age, the initial recognition was even higher, around 42 per cent. The business sector has a role to play in awareness raising, too. For example, as a member of FSC international and the national initiative in Germany, the large DIY retailer OBI prominently markets the FSC label in its stores, as well as in its communication brochures and annual business reports. In the case of the FSC–WWF campaign in the Netherlands, more than 30 companies have participated and supported the effort (FSC 2005a).

With regard to the second objective of raising awareness of the underlying causes of the forest problem, the FSC has been quite passive. Although the issue of forest destruction has become less important in public debates, the FSC is not the prime mover in generating and sustaining awareness of the problems related to forestry, but rather focuses on communicating the idea that by buying certain products, people can become part of the solution.

**Learning networks**

The institutional structure of the FSC as a private system of governance facilitates two types of learning processes. The first could be described as *intra-organisational learning* and includes processes of self-evaluation and the resulting organisational restructuring. This topic has been extensively covered within management science, especially in the literatures on economic history, industrial economics and the theory of the firm (Dodgson 1993: 375). Although the concept of organisational learning is highly contested (Fiol and Lyles 1995) and there is no commonly accepted definition of what the concept refers to in terms of outcome and process, I propose the following minimal definition: organisational learning can be described as the way an organisation builds, supplements and organises knowledge around its activities, resulting in a change in organisational structures and procedures.

One example for organisational learning within the FSC is the self-evaluation process conducted by the so-called 'Change Management Team' (CMT). Established by the former executive director Maharaj Muthoo in 2000, the six-member team conducted a range of interviews with stakeholders and staff members to identify internal and external challenges as well as possible strategic directions for the FSC. The CMT presented a report that the board adopted in 2001. It recommended eight steps to ensure the FSC's future success in its mission of promoting environmentally appropriate, socially responsible and economically viable forest management, such as empowering national and regional initiatives, improving the recognition of the FSC brand and moving the headquarters to an international setting (FSC 2002a). Further priorities to ensure a healthy future for the FSC were suggested, *inter alia*: professionalising the communication activities, separating accreditation and standard setting functions and securing an independent financial basis through enhanced fundraising efforts and additional revenues.

Many of these recommendations are currently in practice. For example, the FSC's communication services have substantially improved since the year 2000, today offering standardized communication templates, comprehensive fact sheets for quick information, as well as a more service-orientated web site. In addition, the strategic relocation of FSC headquarters to an international setting has been completed with moving to Bonn in 2002, as well as the envisaged decentralisation, which was finalised by the establishment of the fourth independent regional centre, located in Africa in 2003. Currently, another major organisational restructuring is taking place, as a result of the CMT's recommendations. The FSC is preparing to establish its accreditation unit as an independent body, thus reacting to the development of international norms and rules in the field of accreditation and certification and within the context of the International Organisation for Standardization.

These observations suggest that organisational learning is taking place within the FSC. Although the described process is quite formalised and was imposed by the FSC leadership, organisational learning drew on the many individual resources of staff members and stakeholders to change the organisation's procedures and practices in key areas. From this perspective, organisational learning in the case of the FSC is not only the result of a management decision, but also an outcome of the specific organisational structure and culture of the FSC, which supports flexible knowledge production and stakeholder involvement as important prerequisites for effective organisational learning (Fiol and Lyles 1995: 804-805). In sum, the existence of intra-organisational learning processes within the FSC supports the assumption that private governance systems, although highly institutionalised, have considerable capacity for adaptation to external demands, especially from key stakeholders.

The second type of learning could be labelled *inter-organisational learning*, involving different types of actors. From this perspective, the FSC constitutes the institutional core of a wider learning network, including members, first- and second-order stakeholders[37] as well as the general public. A learning network can be defined as an inter-organisational network combining the voluntary efforts of autonomous organisations in order to overcome complex challenges through the formal and informal exchange of knowledge. Such inter-organisational networks are characterised by three distinct features: first, inter-organisational networks operate as rather abstract conceptual systems that enable organisations to overcome complex problems; second, networks evolve around shared visions, purposes and goals; and third, inter-organisational networks rest on horizontal organising principles, rather than centralised power (Chisholm 1998: 6). Learning is facilitated by these features of inter-organisational networks for two reasons: first, horizontal structures and the lack of central power are important prerequisites for the exchange of information within a network; second, mutual visions and a shared perception of problems and possible solutions enable communication between diverse organisations.

The FSC constitutes a learning network that includes different organisational actors. This organisational diversity, both in structure and content, seems to facilitate effective learning processes. Consider the example of leading retailers of wood products. It was the specific structure of the FSC as a network of local, regional and global organisations that has led to successful learning. Only the involvement of local and regional experts, forest managers and producers enabled retailers to learn about the many unnecessary intermediate traders participating in the business. The result was not only a cheaper product for the retailers and a higher profit margin for local producers and managers, but also a decline in illegal logging activities in the respective areas.[38]

In addition to new knowledge about their supply chain, leading retailers have also benefited from insights into the environmental community and their strategies. One representative of a leading retailer for home and wood products[39] summarises what the company has gained from participating in the FSC:

> What we have learned in the process of partnership through both FSC International and FSC Germany was what others expected from us as a leading company in home-construction and do-it-yourself products in the field of environmental management and engagement. In addition, we also learned what was possible and what not in terms of strategies and policies with regard to environmental issues.

In return, what the environmental community learned from business was a better understanding of economic thinking and basic concepts of business strategy. This provided the environmental organisations with information that changed their strategic approach to business, too. As one observer to this learning process notes, it was quite difficult at the beginning to reach an understanding because environmental organisations had a lot of brilliant ideas, but little knowledge of the internal processes of business and what is and is not possible from a business perspective. Some seven years later, however, the two sets of organisations are close partners with a good understanding of each other's goals and strategies.[40]

From an NGO perspective, the key lessons have been summarised as a better understanding of how companies function, what their constraints are, what they can know and what they have to take into account from an economic perspective. As a result, NGOs may benefit from this knowledge by formulating better ideas that are specifically tailored with respect to the individual requirement of the company involved. In addition, long-term cooperation with companies may lead to better understanding in future conflicts. A second impact may well be that good results in the forest sector may enable progress in other sectors.[41]

However, network-learning processes within the FSC not only occur because dissimilar organisations learn about possible win–win situations, but also because similar organisations learn from dissimilar procedures. The general assembly and other formal or informal meetings between stakeholders provide opportunities for learning that would not exist in the absence of the network. Social organisations, such as trade unions or indigenous peoples associations, meet with environmental NGOs to exchange strategies and substantive information. As a result, organisations often enrich their strategic toolkit as well as their general organisational culture. For historical reasons, the environmental chamber of the FSC has been the best organised in terms of resource mobilisation, shared visions and resulting policy motions. But business and social interests are catching up as a direct result of learning processes within the FSC network.

In sum, the FSC can be considered a learning institution in two ways: first, the FSC shows distinct features of intra-organisational learning, mobilising the very different experiences of its staff members and stakeholders and turning them into effective organisational restructuring; second, the FSC is an inter-organisational learning network of many diverse actors, which facilitates effective learning processes exactly because of the organisational dissimilarity of its members.

**Deliberative problem solving**
Next to inter- and intra-organisational learning, the cognitive/discursive function of the FSC is also reflected in providing a forum for diverse discussions and deliberations among a wide range of actors. This enables stakeholders to find common solutions to their everyday problems. In addition, there is evidence that the FSC enables actors in the network to take up new roles and enter new environments by strategically using their FSC involvement as an argument in negotiations and debates.

Analysing complaints raised by the FSC's stakeholders, we find business actors and civil society organisations in rather uncommon roles. Surprisingly, companies are relatively reluctant towards general criticism of the FSC. The Confederation of European Paper Industries (CEPI), for example, comparatively examined 24 different forest certification schemes and concluded that among all those analysed, the FSC is the most credible scheme measured against the CEPI criteria (Confederation of European Paper Industries 2001). In contrast, non-governmental organisations play a more ambivalent role. One the one hand, NGO criticism may direct the FSC towards existing shortcomings in certification or actual forest management practices, thereby allowing the FSC to constantly improve the overall performance of its regulatory system. As one board member mentioned in an interview conducted for this study, a substantial number of NGOs put a great deal of energy into monitoring compliance, acting as watchdogs for the FSC. On the other hand, non-governmental organisations also direct their criticism towards the FSC directly, thereby putting pressure not only on the organisation, but also on its non-profit members and supporters. One particular example is the criticism contained in a recent report by the UK-based NGO, Rainforest Foundation (2002). The report highlighted – among other shortcomings – the problematic relationship between certifiers and forest managers, wherein vested economic interests may impinge on the outcome of certification, as well as the FSC's fast growth strategy that tends to put quantity over quality (Rainforest Foundation 2002: 5-7). Interestingly enough, it was Greenpeace that came to the FSC's rescue by publicly stating that much of the report was overstated and that many of the shortcomings were currently being remedied.[42]

Another example is a scandal uncovered by Greenpeace in early 2005. The organisation found that timber from Russian old-growth forests in the region of Archangelsk was being sold in seven German retail stores labelled as coming from German forests and being harvested in a sustainable manner. Greenpeace made this a public scandal and not only criticised the behaviour of the companies trading, processing and selling the wrongly labelled wood to the retailers, but also criticized the retailers, among them the leading German DIY store OBI. This has initially led to tension between Greenpeace and OBI. However, the informal links that had been established between the two organisations as a direct result of their involvement with the FSC provided a forum to fruitfully discuss the controversy. In general, participating in both FSC Germany and International makes it easier for companies to handle crisis situations. One of the obvious functions of a private governance system thus seems to be providing institutional channels through which information can be exchanged to disarm a situation. A forum for discussion makes it easier to cope with crisis situations.

OBI and Greenpeace convened a meeting to discuss the recent scandal and its implications for the future strategy of OBI. This has led to a success for Greenpeace because the responsible managers at OBI began to pay much higher attention to the issue of sustainable forestry vis-à-vis their suppliers, who in the past had been chosen mainly on the basis of a simple cost calculation. As one interviewee familiar with this particular conflict reported, the scandal and the resulting discussion with Greenpeace made it easier for the environmental representative of the company to justify stricter environmental policies to the board and other members of senior management. This observation confirms the assumption that the FSC may play a strategic role in discourses. Similar to states that use their commitment to international policies as a strategic tool to justify domestic decisions, the FSC enables environmentally oriented staff in companies to put pressure on their executives by pointing to present and future NGO campaigns.

In addition to the strategy meeting between OBI and Greenpeace representatives, the two organisations, together with the WWF, the business association BHB and the German retailers Bahr and Hornbach, organised a two day conference and a field trip to Archangelsk to meet with the stakeholders and discuss measures to support trade and environmental integrity at the same time (World Wide Fund for Nature Deutschland 2004). The deliberations led to a common understanding that timber from this region was needed on the market, but at the same time that it should not come from old-growth natural forests, but from managed forest within the area. One direct result was that the forest managers and timber processors from Russia agreed to starting an FSC certification process for the region to maintain the good contacts they have with German traders and retailers. In sum, both Greenpeace and the WWF used their environmental credibility to persuade Russian foresters and producers to seek FSC certification. In this example, the FSC has enabled environmental organisations to both criticise occurring practices, but at the same time offer a credible and practical solution.

Next to learning about the rationales and organisational limitations of business actors, environmental organisations have also benefited from being part of the FSC network in a more strategic sense. For example, the FSC allows Greenpeace a better position in many difficult environments, for example the Amazon, where there are substantial business interests that need to be aligned with the idea of conservation of forests. Thus, having the FSC as a credible example and instrument at hand, Greenpeace gets more flexibility in difficult environments. In addition, and although Greenpeace has cooperated with business on a range of different issues such as eco-efficient cars and ozone-friendly refrigerators, the FSC experience is different because it has developed into a long-lasting institutional relationships.[43] In sum, the FSC has not only facilitated learning processes between NGOs and business actors, but also contributed to a change in perceptions of key players in the forestry arena by being a forum for problem solving and a strategic instrument in difficult environments.

**Diffusion of the regulatory model**
The fourth aspect of the cognitive/discursive function analysed in this section is providing an institutional model within the environmental arena and

beyond. Within the forestry arena, the FSC has forced other actors to react. To protect their specific interests, forest owners and the forest industry developed their own certification schemes (for example SFI, PEFC). In addition, governments have also implemented or supported certification schemes to protect their domestic forest industry. For example, the Finnish government supports the Finnish Forest Certification Scheme (FFSC). As a result, there is only one FSC certified forest operation in Finland, while neighbouring Sweden is the biggest European FSC certificate holder with over 10 million ha. In addition to this example from Finland, the Malaysian government is actively involved in the Malaysian certification schemes, the Malaysian Timber Certification Council (MTCC). Next to the forestry arena, the idea of a stewardship council has been taken up in the fisheries sector (Marine Stewardship Council, MSC), marine conservation (Marine Aquarium Council, MAC) and the tourism industry (Sustainable Tourism Certification Scheme, STCS).

To conclude, the influence of private forest governance through its cognitive/discursive function can be summarised in four points. First, producing and disseminating knowledge and information enables the FSC, in many cases through its supporting organisations, to change the perceptions actors have about sustainable forestry and the underlying causes of the current forest crisis. Second, the FSC constitutes a dual type of learning institution. As a result, the FSC was adaptive to external demands and thereby made several behavioural changes possible. Third, the FSC has functioned as a conflict-resolution mechanism by providing room for debates. Hence, it can be seen as a main driver for changing the perceptions of a range of actors on various issues. And finally, the FSC provides a well-established model for environmental governance beyond the state and public–private partnerships, although imitation has not always been accurate.

**Governance Through Integration: the Legalisation of Functional Spaces**

The third function through which private governance is constructed in the forestry arena is integration. This concept has a twofold connotation: first, integration refers to the transfer of international or transnational norms and standards to the level of private governance. The impact is mainly a 'legalisation' of functional spaces wherein rules become enforceable (through the process of certification and the threat of withdrawing the respective certificate) that were not or only reluctantly enforced beforehand. And second, integration refers to FSC principles, their underlying rational and resulting procedures, being integrated into national political systems or international agreements. In this case, governments may formally or informally endorse FSC standards, former state functions may be outsourced to the FSC or public policies, both at the national and international level, may be influenced by the operation of the FSC. Closely connected to the latter mechanism, formerly marginalized actors may gain access to policy debates and decisions at national or local levels.

## Downward integration

Analysing the first mode of integration, the influence on actors in the South is potentially high because the existing level of regulation is relatively low and compliance measures including sanctions are often only reluctantly enforced in developing countries. The FSC P&C demand that '[i]n signatory countries, the provisions of all binding international agreements such as CITES, ILO Conventions, ITTA and the Convention on Biological Diversity, shall be respected' (FSC 2000: principle 1.3). The recent inclusion of the core ILO conventions[44] into the FSC standards is of particular importance because government compliance with these treaties has been relatively weak in many developing countries. As one FSC board member observes, the FSC is successfully bringing worker rights to the people on the ground. In this view, the process of certification leads to the convergence of rights for local workers. As a result, and often for the first time, social interests are considered through the influence of the FSC.[45] The WWF's study on corrective action requests comes to a similar conclusion for temperate forest regions (2005: 3):

> Those employed in the forests industry have been some of the biggest beneficiaries of FSC certification, through the improvement in the implementation of legislation and guidelines on health and safety. A reliance on properly qualified staff, backed by improved training and a compliance with social taxation requirements have all lead to improved working conditions for those working in FSC certified forests.

As a result of these positive developments, unions, initially cautious of the certification issue, have 'especially over the last two or three years become more involved in certification efforts. They are now actively participating in a number of national initiatives including those in Sweden, Germany and Ghana, where they have been involved in the negotiation of national standards' (Bowling 2000: 134).

A second example for the integration of international or transnational norms into the FSC framework and the resulting impact on actors involved in forest certification can be found in the FSC accreditation standards for CBs that comply with the regulations of the ISO. Case studies from South Africa for example indicate that certification according to FSC standards was achieved more easily when ISO standards were already in place. In effect, the integration of existing standards benefits companies because costly conformance with multiple standards can thus be avoided.

### Upward integration

Turning to the integration of FSC standards into national political systems, three potential mechanisms can be observed. A first possibility is that governments endorse the FSC, for example through their public procurement policies. A recent forest products market review by the UN Economic Commission for Europe (UNECE) and the FAO (Rametsteiner 2002: 163) states that '[p]ublic procurement continued to become a growing source of demand for CFPs'. In addition to a range of policies already existing at the municipal level, in most cases due to the early involvement of city governments in timber boycott activities, several national governments have announced public procurement measures that directly or indirectly favour certified timber. The German government, for example, decided in 2002 that public procurement should solely rely on the FSC for wood products (Trittin 2003). In addition, the red-green coalition government also clearly stated their commitment to forest certification in general and the FSC in particular in their 2002 coalition contract (World Wide Fund for Nature Deutschland 2002). In a similar vein, the British government has enacted the 'Central Government Timber Procurement Policy'. The government of Denmark provides another example: within the context of the fight against illegal logging, a decision in 2001 recognised the FSC label as an example of a credible instrument to provide assurance that timber is not only sustainably, but also legally produced. All together, procurement policies and public endorsement of forest certification exist in Austria, Belgium, France, Germany, the Netherlands, the Nordic States, Switzerland, the UK and some states of the US. However, as a strong environmental consciousness among voters is largely confined to OECD countries and governmental action to accommodate such views is correspondingly limited, endorsement seems to have little impact beyond industrialised countries.

A second form of integrating FSC standards into national systems seem to have been more influential in developing countries. South Africa for example has effectively outsourced its forest surveillance to the FSC as a consequence of its strict monitoring practices. Potentially, this strategy could well spread to other developing countries that control considerable portions of its forests and seek budgetary relief.

A third form of integration is better documented, namely the influence of the FSC on national policies and the corresponding empowerment of actors in national debates. The multi-stakeholder process of the FSC is credited with having had a beneficial influence on policy discussions and stakeholder relations, especially in countries with otherwise weak forestry governance (cf. Bass, Font and Danielson 2001). A study in South Africa (Mayers, Evans and Foy 2001) has revealed that stakeholder consultations on forestry have contributed to bringing actors to national debates that have so far been excluded. With regard to the actual influence of private forest governance on national forest policies, a recent study argues that while certification has in most cases been a complementary instrument to induce compliance with national laws, '[i]n countries like Bolivia, there has been a more interactive process between recent legal forest reforms and certification, where incentives to landowners that engage in certification have been specifically introduced into the forestry law' (Segura 2004: 9). A second example is Mexico that has reacted to the increase of FSC certification occurring after 1996 (the FSC headquarter was situated in Oaxaca until 2002) with a national forestry law closely mirroring the FSC standards on SFM.

Despite considerable impact on national forest politics, the FSC's influence on policy makers has not been driven by a coherent strategy.[46] Rather than proactively influencing the problem perception of key players, the FSC more passively provided an example of a credible solution in sustainable forestry. FSC staff members report that especially on issues relating to indigenous people, the FSC has had some success in influencing policy makers and convincing them that the FSC is a solution to their problem.[47]

In addition to the integration of private governance into domestic environments, private governance may also be integrated into international norms, although this is somewhat more clandestine. Consider for example the World Bank policy towards forest certification. It has changed from rejection to approval as a result of the Bank's involvement with the World Wide Fund for Nature (WWF). The resulting WWF–World Bank alliance was founded in 1998 and has agreed to reach a target of 200 million hectares of certified forests by the end of 2005. As the WWF has been a key player in the establishment of the FSC and has demonstrated its support for the FSC as the only credible global solution to forest certification on several occasions, the new Bank policy can be analysed as one influence that the FSC has on the international political level. The Alliance states that it does not recognise any one specific certification scheme, but instead has developed its own set of nine principles and 11 criteria for certification. However, '[a]t present, the Forest Stewardship Council (FSC) is the only certification scheme that clearly meets the Alliance criteria, although non-FSC certification schemes will be counted toward the Alliance's target in the future' (World Bank/WWF Alliance 2003: 3).

To conclude, the integrative function of private governance is reflected in two major trends. First, binding international agreements and national legislation, as well as transnational norms, are transferred to spaces regulated by private governance systems. As a result, norms and rules that have not been implemented sufficiently become enforceable through the private arrangement operating on the ground. Evidence from tropical and temperate forest regions supports the assumption that the FSC has successfully influenced, for example, the safety and health conditions of forest workers. The second integrative trend can be observed in the influence distinct FSC rules and procedures have on national forest politics. Impacts range from endorsement of the FSC through public procurement policies to devising national forest laws that mirror the FSC's definition of sustainable forestry. Both mechanisms of integration clearly show how closely the public policy arena is connected with the field of private governance. On many occasions, the FSC has utilised international norms complexes, such as sustainable development and the partnership paradigm, to legitimise its distinct standards and procedures. On the other hand, public actors have equally often looked to the private governance realm for support of their policies or simply for solutions for their pressing problems.

## BETWEEN THE FOREST AND THE TREES: LIMITS TO PRIVATE FOREST GOVERNANCE

This section will briefly discuss the potential and shortcomings of the FSC as a private governance system in global sustainability politics. The evaluation of possible shortcomings of any political process or institution will most likely depend on the points of reference identified prior to the analysis. One valuable methodological approach in doing so is triangulation (Schwandt 1997). Different possible perspectives are integrated to arrive at a general representation of the problem under consideration. In the FSC case, the following three reference points are addressed: first, the consistency with its own organisational goals and general objectives (compliance perspective); second, the researchers own view on the organisation based on participatory observation (inner-organisational perspective); and third, a larger systematic perspective on forest politics and private regulation within the context of world politics (structural perspective).

As we have seen above, the FSC's current geographical disparity in terms of hectares certified reflects existing market structures in the international timber trade. Only producers from countries that are connected to the valuable green markets in the OECD have so far economically benefited from FSC certification and hence are willing to bear the higher costs of certification. However, as the tropical timber trade predominantly takes place between countries of the same region, the FSC's impact on the negative implications of forestry is structurally limited. It is an open question whether the FSC and forest certification in general can change the existing structures in the timber trade and work towards an equal share of the emerging benefits. These observations must be seen as a major backdrop against the organisation's own goal of providing a solution to the global forest crisis.[48]

In addition to the shortcomings resulting from the current system of the timber trade, several structural limitations to certification and private governance in the forestry sector have been put forward (Gulbrandsen 2004). First, participation of wood and paper producers in a certification system is contingent on the expected added value for these business actors. In addition, firms may exit a distinct system at any time. This might well lead to a race-to-the-bottom in private forest governance because various systems compete for participants via the price mechanism. Second, in contrast to public systems of rule, compliance in private systems of rule tends to be relatively weak. And third, without the assistance of states, incentives to join a private regulatory system may be too weak (Gulbrandsen 2004: 77-78).

In addition to a disparity in geographical representation, the current growth trend – between December 2000 and June 2006, the certified forest area has increased more than tri-fold from 22 million hectares to 76 million hectares – might not continue uninterrupted. Whereas the forest areas that have been certified first are not controversial, problematic areas, especially in tropical rain forests and in temperate old-growth forests are only slowly coming to the fore. In the meantime, the assessment of plantation forests is also contentious. The FSC drew up rules for their management after long, controversial debates. Plantations currently make up approximately 12 per cent of the total certified area. The credibility of many civil society organisations is on the line, since many environmentalists fundamentally criticise the plantation economy.[49] The FSC, therefore, launched a two-year Plantations Review process in September 2004 to accommodate the criticism raised by non-profit stakeholders.

An additional challenge is the tough competition among various forestry practice regulatory systems. There are now at least 23 different national, regional and global standards competing with the FSC. Consider, for example, the Pan European Forest Certification Council. Forest owners and the timber industry started it in 1999 as an umbrella scheme for national forestry standards. But unlike the FSC, PEFC does not rely on any independent on-the-spot inspections. Nor does it demand annual inspections and only applies random checks. Founded primarily as a reaction to the success and public perception of the FSC (Cashore, Auld and Newsom 2004: 160-185), PEFC has successfully challenged the FSC, currently covering more than 50 million hectares of certified forest in Europe. As a result of the competing forestry standards, the timber industry and forest owners can choose which of various regulatory systems suits them best. However, consumers, without detailed knowledge, are in no position to assess the actual value of the various certificates, a situation that might well undermine the general idea of sustainability certification.

FSC funding is another problem area. Until now the Council has depended on the support of non-profit foundations such as the Ford Foundation, the Rockefeller Brothers Foundation, the MacArthur Foundation or the Wallace Global Fund. The FSC generated over US$14.3 million in the period between 1996 until 2003. But roughly 77 per cent came from donations and only 17 per cent were generated through membership fees and accreditation billings (FSC 2002a, 2004a).[50] Figure 5.2 shows the FSC's annual revenues, including donations, membership fees and accreditation fees.

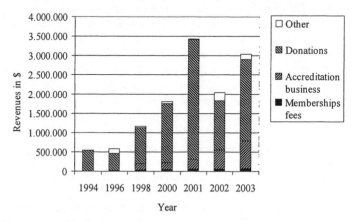

*Figure 5.2 FSC annual revenues from 1994 to 2003*

Greater profit-orientation might become a fundamental strategic necessity, but also runs counter to the fundamental idea of the FSC and thus jeopardizes its credibility. There are several indicators for a growing service provider mentality within the FSC. In the 2002 annual report, Executive Director Heiko Liedeker summarises the ongoing strategy: 'Also, we have undertaken internal restructuring, separating and consolidating the different business areas of FSC to improve service provision worldwide' (FSC 2003: 4). This development included separating the FSC's accreditation services from its standard-setting function. Furthermore, the accreditation unit has been transformed into a legally independent body to secure sufficient income to cover the costs of accreditation. In addition, the FSC set up a marketing and communications unit in early 2002 to enhance brand reputation and trademark use.

Despite the various weaknesses discussed above, the FSC is perceived as a success on the whole. One indication of this is the cooperation of the various environmental and social organisations and the constant endorsement by various public actors. The analysis of the different functional pathways the FSC employs for achieving its governance task has also pointed to the potential of private forest politics. There are three possible scenarios for the future. First, if public attention for sustainability and justice continues or grows, the demand for certified products should increase or at least remain constant. The FSC could then develop into a globally accepted industry standard, given its high level of credibility. However, the further fragmentation of private forest regulation systems depending on diverse consumer demands is also feasible, at least in the medium term. Probably, the FSC would then have to increase its environmental and socio-political profile at the expense of profit considerations to fulfil its own claims and satisfy civil-society supporters. A third scenario is also conceivable. If the long-awaited consensus on an effective forest protection policy should be reached at an international level in the foreseeable future, the FSC would, to a large extent, lose its autonomy and be integrated into international efforts along with the other regulatory systems. However, it is also conceivable that the FSC maintains its key characteristics, such as the tripartite governance structure and the regional differentiation, while at the same time mandatory elements are added under public oversight.

A future strategy towards forest certification as an integral part of global forest politics is only slowly emerging within the FSC. What seems clear, however, is the effort to develop the FSC into a standard business practice, whether on a voluntary basis or with intergovernmental support. Therefore, becoming part of the global sustainable forestry routine, rather than being perceived as a 'political' issue, is the FSC's major strategic goal. Whether this goal is achieved through mutual recognition and convergence between different private schemes or through a reintegration into international processes does not seem to be the central question. As one FSC insider put it: although most people involved in the FSC are committed to solving the global forest crisis, there is no intention 'to keep the animal alive beyond need'.[51]


## CONCLUSION

Why have private rules that transcend boundaries and target business actors rather than citizens or governments emerged in the global forestry sector? What real-world impacts do these private rules have? I have argued that the FSC constitutes a novel institutional model of global governance in the forest arena. As a highly institutionalised private arrangement, the FSC induces a range of effects in its stakeholders and the wider public. The purpose of this chapter has hence been to understand in detail the factors that have led to the institutionalisation of private governance in the forestry sector and the resulting influences of the rule system on its standard-takers, business and civil society supporters as well as on governments and international processes.

To achieve this aim, I first provided a brief overview of the current state of the world's forests, their social, economic and ecological benefits, as well as the major obstacles for reaching an appropriate agreement. Subsequently, I analysed the demand for a credible solution to the global forest crisis as well as the available supply, both in organisational and ideational terms. I argued that it was the novel strategy of leading environmental organisations that turned an abstract and so far uncontroversial issue area – the international timber trade – into a serious risk to major producing, exporting and retailing companies. This new strategy of boycotts acknowledged the increasing role of the private sector in creating or solving environmental problems, as well as the decline in public steering capacity. However, as boycotts quickly led to an explosion of self-labelled sustainability assurances, a credible solution was needed. In this situation, the failure of the international negotiation process in combination with a range of existing ideas, such as the partnership paradigm and certification, bridged existing gaps between actors looking for an appropriate solution to their individual problems.

The resulting institutionalisation of private governance, including precise constitutive and regulative rules, was the focus the third section. Following the analytical framework advanced in Chapter 3, I discussed the FSC's influence as a private governance system along the three functional dimensions of regulation, cognitive and discursive processes and integration.

The regulatory function is achieved through rule making (the development of applicable sustainable forest management standards) and the subsequent implementation of these rules involving the processes of accreditation, certification and labelling. With regard to the observable influence of private regulation, five points have emerged in the analysis. First, although limited in terms of standard-uptake, forest management practices have changed across regions and forest types as a result of FSC policies. Second, under the constraints of existing structures in the timber trade and the prominent role of the market, private governance in the form of forest certification may systematically benefit some types of actors, while it clearly disadvantages other players in the field. Third, while the costs of certification were predominantly transferred to the lower end of the supply chain, envisaged economic benefits deriving from price premiums have not occurred on a broad scale. However, with regard to social and environmental impacts, the FSC has been a main driver of change. Fourth, private rules deriving from the FSC have resulted in a shift of perceptions towards sustainable forestry at the local level, in particular in community forestry in developing countries. This shift towards a more 'scientific' understanding of forestry underscores the general trend of convergence in global forestry discourses and practices.

Finally, new roles and responsibilities have emerged among actors as a consequence of their rather indirect involvement in the FSC.

With regard to the cognitive/discursive function of the FSC, the analysis highlighted the importance of learning processes and the role of the network supporting the FSC therein. The dissemination of knowledge and information, learning processes within the institution and between its stakeholders, as well as strategic positioning have all benefited from the distinct organisational structure of the FSC. In more detail, four types of influence have been highlighted. First, producing and disseminating knowledge and information enables the FSC, in many cases through its supporting organisations, to change the perceptions actors have about sustainable forestry and the underlying causes of the current forest crisis. Second, the FSC constitutes a dual type of learning institution. As a result, the FSC was adaptive to external demands and thereby made several behavioural changes possible. As well as learning occurring between dissimilar organisations, similar organisations also benefited from participation. Third, the FSC provides a formal as a well as informal conflict-resolution mechanism and hence can be seen as a main driver for changing the perceptions of stakeholders on various issues. And finally, the FSC provides a well-established model of private governance, within the forestry arena and well beyond.

The third function through which the FSC realises its influence on different stakeholders has been termed 'integration'. I have argued that the integrative function of private governance is reflected in two major trends. First, the FSC bases its authority on existing international norms and applicable national legislation. As a result, the transnational space the FSC occupies has gradually become more ordered. The second integrative trend can be observed in the influence distinct FSC rules and procedures have on national forest politics and the behaviour of public actors more generally. Evidence for this assumption can be found in the various endorsement strategies of governments, ranging from procurement policies to the outsourcing of forest surveillance and the adoption of FSC-based criteria and indicators for national forestry laws.

After I have substantiated the claim that the FSC constitutes a distinct mechanism of global governance through the institutionalisation of precise and verifiable regulations, the subsequent section paid considerable attention to the potential limits to FSC governance in the forestry realm. Three limitations emerged in this analysis: First, structural factors, deriving from the prominent role of trade and the market systematically limit the scope of private forest governance as well as discriminate against particular actors. Second, existing alternative governance systems limit the influence of the FSC. In addition, competition empowers standard-takers because they can adopt the lowest standards available without losing the positive impacts on brand reputation and access to green markets. Finally, the current structure of funds supporting the FSC is not sustainable. With a majority of funds flowing from foundations, the FSC is easily affected by a strategic reassessment of their cost–benefit calculations. After almost 15 years of operation, funding institutions may look for areas where the invested capital has a higher impact. As a reaction to insecure funding perspectives, the FSC has embarked on a strategy of higher revenue generation through commercial activities. However, such a strategy may run counter to the FSC's efforts to maintain its status as the most credible private solution to the global forest crisis currently available.

## NOTES

1. This rather abstract concept is often referred to as forest certification. It can be defined as a procedure to assess the quality of forest management in relation to the criteria of a forest management standard.
2. According to the Food and Agriculture Organisation of the United Nations (FAO) and the consensus definition provided by the International Forum on Forests (IFF) in 1997, forests are defined as ecosystems dominated by trees with a 10 per cent minimum crown cover.
3. About 95 per cent of the forest cover is in natural forest, the remaining 5 per cent being plantations. The distribution of forest area by ecological zones is as follows: 47 per cent is in the tropics, 33 per cent in the boreal zone, 11 per cent in the temperate areas, and 9 per cent in the subtropics (Food and Agriculture Organisation of the United Nations 2001: xxii).
4. Dimitrov (2004) even argues that the institutions devised at the international level such as the Intergovernmental Panel on Forests (IPF, 1995-1997) or its successor, the Intergovernmental Forum on Forests (IFF, 1997-1999) were consciously designed to preempt effective governance of the global forest problem. However, it should be noted that the permanent discussions facilitated the emergence of trust among its members and thus provided the basis for a slow convergence of perceptions on sustainable forestry.
5. Founding members include the World Wide Fund for Nature, Greenpeace, Friends of the Earth, retailers, trade unions and indigenous interest groups. In 2005, the FSC has over 600 individual and organisational members including large corporations (for example IKEA, Habitat, Home Depot, and B&Q) and well-known environmental organisations (for example Natural Resources Defence Council, Sierra Club, The Nature Conservancy, Rainforest Action Network, and Rainforest Alliance).
6. During the early stages of the NGO responses to the problem of deforestation, strategies were largely reactive and were confined to raising awareness and pressuring key players, predominantly states, and, to a lesser extent, companies (Domask 2003: 159).
7. Personal interview with FSC staff member and participant in the early negotiations, November 2003.
8. Personal interview with environmental NGO representative, July 2004.
9. Personal interview with FSC staff member, November 2003.
10. In addition to UNCED and the ITTO, the ISO, a third important process in global environmental politics, failed to consider forest certification as an appropriate instrument at the time.
11. However, certification as a novel policy instrument was not heralded throughout the whole forest industry. As John P. McMahon, vice president of Weyerhaeuser Company in 1996, notes: 'Given the processes that are in place to promote sustainable forestry in the United

States, most members of our industry question whether the incremental improvements in forest practices that might be gained through certification are worth the added expense, duplication of effort, and management complexity that any certification system would require. Few producers believe that the added expense of certification will be rewarded in the marketplace with a price premium for 'green' products' (cited in Viana et al. 1996: 195).

12. Personal interview with FSC staff member, November 2003.
13. FSC Founding Group Minutes, 16 March 1992, on file with author.
14. Personal interview with FSC staff member, November 2003.
15. Personal interview with FSC staff member, November 2003.
16. The FSC defines Northern organisations and individuals as those based in high income countries and Southern organisations and individuals as based in low, middle and upper-middle income countries (FSC 2002b: §14). According to the World Bank Group definition, low income countries are those with less than $765 gross national income (GNI); middle income those between $766 and $3,035; upper-middle those between $3,036 and $9,385; high income countries are those which generate more than $9,386 GNI per capita.
17. The Statutes clarify that '[d]irectors are allowed to serve two consecutive, three-year terms, subject to re-election by the membership according to the existing statutes' (FSC 2002d: §19).
18. However, theory and practice currently do not match. As of June 2006, only three out of nine board members are female. Cf.
    http://www.fsc.org/fsc/how_fsc_works/governance/board_directors.
19. However, for reasons of the complexity and diversity of forest operations and the size of its markets, Canada, the United States, Russia and China are not coordinated by a regional office, but directly from the international secretariat.
20. Personal interview with FSC regional officer, November 2003.
21. Personal interview with FSC staff member, November 2003.
22. Standard setting, as opposed to the more general process of establishing and maintaining constitutive regulations, is defined as the making of voluntary, expertise-based structural, procedural or substantive regulations (Kerwer 2002: 297-298). Standards can take the form of management schemes, guidelines, product and process labels or general codes of conduct and can further be specified as product and process standards (cf. Nadvi and Wältring 2002).
23. For a detailed elaboration on the process of rule making by the FSC, in particular with reference to its democratic quality, see Dingwerth (2005b).
24. Cf. Chapter 4, section two.
25. For a detailed description of the certification process carried out by one of the FSC accredited CBs, see Maser and Smith (2001).
26. Within the specific context of the FSC, accreditation also refers to the process of approving national FSC initiatives and national or regional forest stewardship standards. These tasks are also conducted by the accreditation business unit and approved by the board of directors.
27. The world's total forest cover – including commercially operated as well as protected areas – is 3.9 billion hectares. The FSC certified forest area makes up 1.9 per cent of the total forest cover.
28. CFPs 'bear labels demonstrating in a verifiable manner by independent bodies that they come from forests that meet standards for sustainable forest management' (Rametsteiner 2002: 158).
29. Personal interview with FSC staff member, November 2003.
30. For a discussion of possible clashes between WTO law and forest certification, see Klabbers (1999).
31. Other expected benefits include increased forest yield as a result of improved forest management procedures, as well as improved efficiency in harvesting, timber processing

and marketing (cf. Simula 1996). Retailers for their part also expected an economic benefit from a 'green' corporate image.

32. In 2005, 4,055,392 ha of natural forests are FSC certified in Indonesia, Malaysia, Bolivia, Brazil, Mexico, Namibia, South Africa and Zimbabwe, while certification of plantations for the same regions stands at 3,481,490 ha.

33. The term community forestry refers to forest management where communities are involved in the planning, management or overall control of a forestry operation.

34. Personal interview with business representative, June 2004.

35. Personal interview with FSC staff member, November 2003.

36. Personal interview with FSC staff member, November 2003.

37. The term first-order stakeholders refers to all those individuals and collective actors that have a direct institutionalised relationship with the FSC, such as certification bodies, national initiatives and national contact persons. Second-order stakeholders include all those actors that have no direct link to the FSC, but are addressed by FSC policies, such as the forest managers and certification holders, retailers and consumers.

38. Personal interview with environmental NGO representative, July 2004.

39. Personal interview with business representative, June 2004.

40. Personal interview with business representative, June 2004.

41. Personal interview with environmental NGO representative, July 2004.

42. For details, see www.greenpeace.org/deutschland/fakten/wald. In addition, over 30 North American environmental organisations signed a 'Joint NGO Statement on Forest Certification' in March 2003 that stated, 'the Forest Stewardship Council is the only certification system that is currently worthy of our support' (document on file with author).

43. Personal interview with environmental NGO representative, June 2004.

44. The FSC standards demand compliance with all ILO labour conventions that are related to forestry, in particular numbers 29, 87, 97, 100, 105, 111, 131, 138, 141, 142, 143, 155, 169, 182 as well as the ILO Code of Practice on Safety and Health in Forestry Work.

45. Personal interview with FSC board member, November 2003.

46. Personal interview with FSC staff member, November 2003.

47. Personal interview with FSC staff member, November 2003.

48. For a discussion of the risk and potential of private forest governance in general, see Pattberg (2005a). For a discussion with reference to private governance in the South, see Dingwerth (Forthcoming) and Pattberg (2006a).

49. See for example the World Rainforest Movement's plantation campaign: http://www.wrm.org.uy/plantations/information.html.

50. The by-laws list five sources of revenue: evaluation fees for certification bodies, licensing fees for logo use, grants and donations, membership dues and returns from investment and services (FSC 2002b: 2).

51. Personal interview with FSC board member, December 2003.

# 6. The Coalition for Environmentally Responsible Economies

This chapter analyses the institutionalisation of private governance in the area of corporate environmental performance, reporting and management practices.[1] The case study will take a detailed look at an early example of business co-regulation that has been credited as one of the key drivers of corporate 'greening' in the 1990s. The Coalition for Environmentally Responsible Economies developed out of intense negotiations and dialogue between environmental groups and institutional investors in the late 1980s. The US-based coalition agreed upon a set of ten principles for environmentally responsible business practices in 1989. These were named the Valdez Principles, referring to the then recent oil slick catastrophe in Prince William Sound, Alaska, involving the Exxon Valdez tanker. The principles were renamed in 1992 to become the CERES Principles, and still function as the basis for CERES' work. As a key innovation, the principles include a commitment to constant improvement of environmental performance and public disclosure of this improvement via a corporate environmental report.

CERES has been primarily analysed as a US-based coalition that aims at greening standard business practices by demanding corporate environmental reporting and thereby creating incentives for the endorsement of broader environmental principles. In the preceding sections, however, I argue that CERES can be analysed as a private governance arrangement in global sustainability politics that institutionalises the behaviour and interaction of profit and non-profit actors at the transnational level through a range of distinct functions and along a set of specific rules and principles.

To assess the conditions for the emergence of CERES in the late 1980s and its influence in global sustainability politics, the case study is structured in the following way. First, I provide a brief background to the debate about corporate reporting, socially responsible investment and the role of shareholders in corporate environmental reporting. Second, I address the formation of CERES, including a detailed account of how the demand for corporate environmental reporting has developed, as well as the 'supply' that an appropriate private instrument could draw from. Third, I analyse the different functional pathways through which CERES influences stakeholders and the wider political arena in global sustainability politics. Similar to the case study on the FSC, this section is based on a detailed assessment of both the constitutive and the regulative rules of the private governance arrangement. Fourth, I critically discuss the prospects for and limitations of private voluntary environmental reporting and management, while the concluding section summarises the key findings with regard to the emergence and influence of CERES as an example of private governance in global sustainability politics.


## CORPORATE ENVIRONMENTAL REPORTING, PERFORMANCE AND SHAREHOLDER VALUE: THE REGULATORY BACKGROUND

Today, corporate environmental reporting and management are ubiquitous. Firms increasingly subject their environmental performance to external auditing and public disclosure (Eisner 2004: 149). This has occurred for a variety of reasons, including: to comply with existing regulation and to reduce the cost of future compliance; to comply with codes of conduct and more general contextual norms; to decrease operating costs, to improve the environmental visibility of a company and use this as a competitive advantage against other firms; to advance the firm's legitimacy and to improve stakeholder and community relations (Morhardt, Baird and Freeman 2002: 215-216).[2] The latest surveys on corporate reporting conducted by KPMG (Kolk et al. 1999, 2005; Kolk and van der Veen 2002) show that the percentage of the 100 largest corporations in different countries publishing an environmental/sustainability report has risen from 12 per cent in 1993, to 17 per cent in 1996, to 24 per cent in 1999, to 28 per cent in 2002, reaching 33 per cent in 2005. Similar figures have been estimated for the world's 250 largest TNCs, the so-called Global 250. While in 1999, 35 per cent produced an environmental/sustainability report, 45 per cent did so in 2002 and 52 per cent in 2005. Although reporting performance varies considerably across industry sectors,[3] it is undisputable that '[s]ince the publication of the first separate environmental reports in 1989, the number of companies that has started to publish information on its environmental, social or sustainability policies and/or impacts has increased substantially' (Kolk 2004: 51).

Corporate reporting and disclosure, however, has a longer history (cf. Hoogervorst 2005). It first appeared in the 1930s in the form of financial reporting as a tool for informing shareholders about corporate financial performance. This basic instrument of communication has been complemented, by social accounting in the 1970s, environmental reporting in the late 1980s and early 1990s and, most recently, by sustainability reporting as embodied in the reporting guidelines of the Global Reporting Initiative, GRI (cf. Global Reporting Initiative 2002). Communications to external audiences have developed from being primarily directed towards the shareholders to addressing a wide range of stakeholders such as customers, neighbours and communities, investors, governments, non-governmental organisations and the general public. In addition, corporate environmental and sustainability reporting has been endorsed by the international community, mainly through UNEP's involvement in the formation of the GRI and the Johannesburg Plan of Implementation, which makes specific reference to the role of business in meeting the challenges of sustainable development.[4] This significant success of the general idea of corporate environmental reporting and the parallel development of appropriate environmental management systems can be linked, at least to a large extent, to the successful institutionalisation of private governance within CERES. In sum, 'while causation is clearly difficult to establish, the CERES Principles have played an important role in improving corporate environmental reporting over the past 15 years' (Goel 2005: 13).

The emergence of corporate environmental reporting and the integration of environmental considerations into standard business practices must be analysed in relation to growing societal concerns about corporate behaviour and the resulting environmental impacts that have occurred since the 1980s. Different to environmental regulation of policy fields such as forestry, fisheries or the apparel industry, corporate environmental performance constitutes a crosscutting issue and an integrated problem. In the following paragraphs, I will briefly sketch the regulatory environment of corporate performance and reporting, the corresponding corporate responsibility debate and the role of shareholders and socially responsible investors in corporate environmental reporting.

The perception of corporations in wider society has profoundly changed during the last 150 years. With the landmark *Santa Clara County vs. Southern Pacific Railroad* case (1886), which granted legal personhood to the modern corporation, business began to emancipate itself from its former principal, the state. Whereas older organisational forms of the corporation, such as the British East India Company, evolved in close relation to the state and in fact carried characteristics of state-like organisation themselves, the modern corporation increasingly focused on profit making as its sole raison d'être. This one-dimensional strategy, however, quickly began to distance the corporation from the communities it operated in and the people it thereby profoundly affected. One answer to this early legitimacy crisis can be observed in the philanthropic activities of many corporate leaders in the early 20th century. Andrew Carnegie, for example, funded the construction and filling of libraries all over the United States. But it was not until the 1960s that business interest began to pay considerable attention to corporate reputation management and the resulting necessity to communicate with a growing range of stakeholders (Rowe 2005: 134-135).

The increasing environmental impacts of standard business operations and the powerful image of environmental catastrophes started to create demand for corporate regulation, accountability and responsibility from the 1960s onwards. Rachel Carson's book *Silent Spring* (2002 [1962]) is an early embodiment of the growing mistrust against the by-products of modern industrialised capitalism. In the post World War II economic order, the acceptance of corporate behaviour in industrialised countries was based on the notion 'that corporate activity was subject to state control and that profit maximizing was a societal good' (Weiss 2002: 87). However, as a result of major economic reconfigurations after the 1973 oil crisis and the demise of the Bretton Woods system, corporate power has escalated in the context of increasing internationalisation of production and the relatively unrestricted mobility of capital and this has led to a considerable decline in acceptance of corporate behaviour. In sum, as a result of the accelerating process of globalisation, a governance gap has emerged between internationalising business activities and the capabilities of governments to secure acceptable levels of societal benefits.

Responses to the growing demand for business regulation in general and environmental regulation in particular can be observed within both the domestic and the international regulatory environments. International attempts to regulate corporations emerged in the 1970s. In particular, the newly independent governments from developing nations attempted to curtail business influence within a New International Economic Order negotiated at the United Nations (cf. Chapter 4). Although this political move was quickly and successfully countered by the industrialised nations through proposing the voluntary Guidelines for Multinational Enterprises in 1976, business interests began to reorganise on a more international level. During the 1970s, a range of corporate agencies, think tanks and global business planning forums emerged to better coordinate internationalising business interests.[5] In addition, as Rowe (2005) argues, the fractions of money and productive capital were bridged and jointly engaged in the development of the neo-liberal counter ideology that opposed the prevalent embedded liberalism compromise that favoured a strong regulatory state over business-friendly laissez-faire. The result of this trend was a new and stronger role for business in articulating the benefits of free markets and industrial production vis-à-vis the state.

Domestic attempts to cope with the environmental problems caused by business activities mainly relied on command-and-control regulation until the 1980s. Command-and-control refers to a public policy approach 'that relies on centralized regulatory commands to implement environmental goals. Governments issue detailed requirements and follow up with inspections, enforcement, and punishment' (Nash and Ehrenfeld 1997: 488). The early environmental problems addressed within this framework, such as river pollution and urban area smog, were analysed as singular and isolated occurrences with no, or very little, systemic components. Hence, early domestic regulatory approaches focused on environmental performance standards or technology-based controls. Although command-and-control legislation has successfully mitigated a range of environmental problems affiliated with industrial processes, it could not prevent the emergence of a range of new environmental issues of a more complex and systemic nature (cf. Biermann and Pattberg 2004). As a result, many observers view command-and-control approaches as a rather crude first-generation strategy (Nash and Ehrenfeld 1997: 489) and criticize them for being economically inefficient and ineffective in addressing the complex nature of many contemporary environmental problems (Weiss 2002: 90).

Several factors are put forward to explain why legislative approaches of command-and-control are limited in their ability to deliver an acceptable compromise between societal and economic demands. First, command-and-control legislation sets minimum standards, but does not create incentives for constant improvement in corporate environmental performance. As a result, environmental innovations often only occur after the costs of resistance against a specific regulation are deemed too great (Nash and Ehrenfeld 1997: 490). Second, as laws are relatively inflexible and time-intensive to enact, appropriate regulations are often devised only after severe disruptions of environmental equilibria have occurred. And third, as legislation is an important instrument of symbolic politics, regulations may be implemented to react to acute demands from society without the necessary knowledge about causes, effects and outcomes, often creating vague and inconsistent answers to pressing environmental problems (Weiss 2002: 90).

In the context of the decline of the domestic regulatory paradigm, growing societal dissatisfaction with corporate performance and a realignment of the fractions of money and productive capital, the corporate social responsibility debate emerged as an overarching idea and strategic tool of business. As discussed in some detail in Chapter 4, corporate social responsibility refers to 'a concept whereby companies integrate social and environmental concerns in their business operations and in their interactions with their stakeholders on a voluntary basis' (Commission of the European Communities 2001: 6). The attempt to hold economic actors accountable for their actions has a considerable history. As early as 1787, concerned British citizens formed a society that demanded the end of British involvement in the slave trade (cf. Oliviero and Simmons 2002). Today, 'two in three citizens want companies to go beyond their historical role of making profit, paying taxes, employing people, and obeying all laws; they want companies to contribute to broader societal gaols as well' (Environics International Ltd 1999: 2). As I will argue in the following sections, CERES can be credited for being one influential source in this recent development of corporate responsibility mainstreaming. However, voluntary codes of environmental conduct, reporting and management emerging from private sources have been complemented by government voluntary programmes, such as the US Emergency Planning and Right-to-know Act of 1986, the US Pollution Prevention Act of 1990, the US Environmental Protection Agency's (EPA) Industrial Toxics Project and its Common Sense Initiative as well as the European Union's Eco-Management and Audit Scheme of 1993. All these examples can be primarily considered as information-based approaches towards business regulation, as opposed to more market-based approaches such as those employing the tool of certification (for example FSC, MSC, MAC, FLA).

In addition, not only has the international and domestic regulatory environment shifted in favour of voluntary codes of conduct, but economic theory has also started to support environmental improvements as a strategic move to increase shareholder value. In standard finance theory, maximisation of shareholder wealth is seen as the pre-eminent goal of the financial manager. Accordingly, socially or environmentally desirable investment that does not benefit the corporations' shareholders should be avoided (Friedman 1970). However, a range of arguments have been put forward that see clear advantages in environmentally responsible behaviour in firms. In particular, shareholders will benefit from opportunities from the sale of 'green' products and services, reduced waste treatment and disposal costs, decreased litigation and future liability for environmental damages, improved public credibility, more productive employees and benefits deriving from less antagonistic relationships with regulators and public interest groups (cf. White 1996).

The emergence of private voluntary information-based governance approaches must be analysed in close relation to the specific institutional context of corporate America. In more detail, the idea of public disclosure and the resulting power of shareholders in holding their corporations accountable have developed in close relation to the specific corporate governance model prevalent in the US. As Detomasi (2002: 429) summarises it,

> [c]orporate governance in the United States emphasizes protecting shareholder rights and maximizing shareholder return, and in meeting the metrics imposed by an active, liquid, and deep capital market. These concerns were a product of specific historical experience characterized by a widespread diffusion of public stock ownership and a deep cultural mistrust of the possible centralization of financial power in large domestic banks.

Shareholder activism in relation to environmental and social concerns can be interpreted as a new civil society strategy to counter the neo-liberal corporate resurgence with its own methods. Shareholder resolutions as an instrument of business regulation first emerged during the South Africa divestment campaign and the Vietnam War, where shareholders called upon companies to withdraw from South Africa or to stop manufacturing controversial wartime products such as napalm.[6] Next to the technique of using shareholder resolutions, a second aspect has played a considerable role in bringing about corporate environmental reporting and performance management as a novel institutional form of business regulation: the practice of socially responsible investing. Investor action first gained prominence when student activists in the United States began to demand that universities sell stocks in corporations involved in the South African Apartheid regime in the 1980s. In addition, religious groups have maintained investment portfolios excluding specific products and corporations for some time (Oliviero and Simmons 2002). Socially responsible investment has become a major source of financial capital, representing over $2.2 trillion in 2000 from a modest beginning of $40 billion in 1985 (Balmaceda and Larson 2000: 35).[7]

In sum, the decline of the regulatory paradigm at the domestic level, in particular in the US, and a reconfiguration of economic forces at the international level following Southern attempts to regulate international business activity helped to create an environment of corporate social responsibility, wherein both corporations and non-profit organisations could develop novel strategies. In particular, the distinct structure of corporate governance in the US and the growing socially responsible investment camp provided opportunities to use innovative instruments to regulate corporate (mis)behaviour. In addition, economic theories that acknowledged the benefits of environmental stewardship for the shareholder value also contributed to a more open atmosphere with regard to voluntary, information-based instruments of business regulation. How these contextual factors have created the demand for private rules in corporate environmental reporting, and how supply could be effectively organised, is the focus of the following section.

## THE EMERGENCE OF CORPORATE ENVIRONMENTAL REPORTING AND ENVIRONMENTAL MANAGEMENT: FROM THE EXXON VALDEZ TO CERES

What are the enabling factors for the institutionalisation of private regulation involving companies and civil society organisations in the area of corporate environmental reporting and performance management? I assess the conditions for institutionalisation along the four recurrent themes identified in the analytical framework – macro-systemic transformations, the problem structure, organisational resources and the discursive environment of ideas and models – starting with the demand side (that is: What is the distinct problem structure and how has it evolved?) and followed by the supply side (that is: What regulation exists at the international level? What are the decisive resources organisations hold to solve the problem?). Similar to the analysis of the emergence of private rules in the global forestry arena, the underlying assumption is that the ability of civil society actors to construct a business risk for corporations and their specific responses can be understood as the result of rather large-scale transformations reconfiguring the strategies and abilities of both corporate and civil society actors in an era of globalisation.

## Making Corporate Environmental Performance a Business Case

The Coalition for Environmentally Responsible Economies started operating in 1989 after publishing the so called Valdez Principles, utilising the huge public outrage around the Exxon Valdez oil spill, which occurred on 24 March the same year. A group of socially responsible investors, mainly organised into the Social Investment Forum (SIF),[8] and 15 large environmental groups started discussing the possibility of using the power of investors (shareholder resolutions) against the power of the boardroom. The idea behind CERES is to engage companies in dialogue and work towards the subsequent endorsement of environmental principles[9] that establish long-term corporate commitment to continual progress in environmental performance. The ten-point code of corporate environmental conduct establishes 'an environmental ethic with criteria by which investors and others can assess the environmental performance of companies' (CERES 2002c: 31). Principle ten requires an annual self-evaluation by the endorsing company, based on the CERES reporting form, by which the required continual progress towards environmental responsibility can be measured. As a result, environmental improvements, lowered investment risks and positive corporate performance were expected to go hand in hand. In the words of Nash and Ehrenfeld (1997: 512), '[t]he vision of CERES' organizers was for firms to release to the public "consistent and comparable" environmental data similar to what is used by investors for analysis of corporate financial performance'.

The original idea for CERES emerged at a board meeting of the Social Investment Forum in 1988. The catalyst was the fact that most of their clients considered environmental performance a key issue for investment decisions. However, serving those clients proved difficult because there was no publicly available information on the overall environmental performance of companies, or it was simply very hard to obtain. In the words of one SIF board member:[10]

Big companies had little coherent information on the issue [of environmental performance]; advocacy group information was not always applicable and accurate. Some of us had the idea of approaching environmental groups to do work on the environment to try to find out how to get information more consistently that would benefit the environment and serve investor interests.

Consequently, the SFI convened a committee to explore ways for its members and environmental advocates to work together (CERES 2004: 10). This team was formed after the board meeting and headed straight to Washington to find out about the opinions and strategies of the leading environmental organisations such as the Sierra Club; but most organisations rejected cooperation with social investment. It took over a year to convince 15 major environmental organisations to work with the investment community.[11] During its first joint meeting in April 1989, the new coalition agreed to focus on two priority issues: first, the development of an environmental mission statement for companies, which was envisaged as being more than a management tool, but rather a kind of environmental ethic for corporations; and second, the development of adequate instruments for gathering and disclosing important corporate environmental information.

The original demand for a new institutional arrangement of corporate environmental reporting and performance had grown mainly out of the concerns of institutional investors and their clients about the adequacy of corporate environmental information. Although reluctant in the beginning, environmental organisations soon began to support this new approach because strategic perceptions were already changing profoundly. Environmental NGOs increasingly realised that with a regulatory environment favouring voluntary approaches and systemic de-regulation, both at national and international levels, companies were of paramount importance with regard to realising measurable environmental improvements. According to Doane (2005: 23-24), NGOs realised that 'more momentum could be achieved by partnering with the enemy'. The processes of economic integration and the increasing velocity of globalisation dynamics have given TNCs a stronger voice in influencing policy outcomes; however, these processes also expose companies to public scrutiny and thereby led to the imposition of external rules on these actors (Clapp 2005: 284). With reference to the first and most well-known codes of environmental management practice, among them Responsible Care, the ICC charter, the ISO 14000 series and CERES, Nash and Ehrenfeld (1996: 18) contend: 'These codes have grown out of public concern about corporate environmental performance and corporate fears about a new round of regulation'. The decisive event that convinced companies of the usefulness of corporate codes of conduct coupled with a reporting obligation was the use of shareholder petitions by institutional investors.

In sum, social investors came together with environmental NGOs with a view to building bridges with business, understanding that the success of many programmes to protect the environment would depend on designing an economy that is sustainable over the long run, requiring corporate involvement and commitments. Among investors and environmental activists, there was growing agreement that companies are one of the central causes for many current environmental problems because it is they who emit pollutants, extract the raw materials and use high quantities of energy. As one observer of the early negotiations comments: 'We came together with a view that we could influence corporations in a positive way by entering into a dialogue'.[12]

To conclude, it seems that the emerging demand for distinct private regulation in the field of corporate environmental performance and reporting has largely been driven by the macro-systemic transformations in the nature of global capital formation and the resulting strategy changes, both within firms and NGOs (cf. Bartley 2003). In sum, '[i]n 1989, CERES was founded on the belief that a thriving economy need not, and indeed cannot, drain the world relentlessly of its resources without replenishment' (CERES 2002c: 2).

After this analysis of the demand side of private governance in the area of corporate environmental reporting and management, I now turn to arguments about the actual supply of solutions, both at systemic and organisational levels.

### Towards a Private Framework for Corporate Environmental Reporting and Management

When institutional investors and the representatives of major environmental organisations convened at Chapel Hill, North Carolina, in April 1989 to discuss ways to improve the environmental and social impacts of investments, a whole range of controversial issues was waiting to be solved. For social investors and their clients, the lack of information about the environmental performance of companies was a real risk for their business. Either information came from the companies themselves, displaying advanced public relations skills rather than substantial information, or from advocacy groups addressing their specific constituencies. Neither served the need of a growing social investment community. Little help came from governmental regulation at that time, because measures focused on specific substances, such as the case of the Toxic Release Inventory (TRI) established in 1987,[13] rather than on environmental performance in its entirety. NGOs, for their part, began to realize that conventional lobbying strategies aimed at governments were becoming less effective, while at the same time business actors emerged as the real threats to the environment. In particular, the catastrophe of Bhopal in 1984 and the Exxon Valdez oil spill of 1989 brought corporate misbehaviour to the forefront of public concern. As a result, companies, although reluctant at the beginning, started to look for credible ways to secure brand reputation and profits in the midst of a hostile public environment. In sum, the problem structure was characterised by interdependent stakeholders having vested interests in the problem, disproportional levels of expertise and information, as well as different perspectives resulting in an adversarial relationship.

After a couple more meetings among the original coalition members, the negotiations led to the formulation and public announcement of the Valdez Principles on 7 September 1989, resulting in considerable media coverage and attention. Already this early phase of negotiations showed a remarkable feature. Debates were not based on positional negotiation and confrontational strategies, but on a common framework of reference from where future visions could develop.[14] Two ideas, one practical, the other more visionary, served as influential institutional models. First, there is the system of standardized financial accounting that emerged in collaboration between public and private actors in the United States and is controlled and monitored by the Financial Accounting Standards Board (FASB). As Nash and Ehrenfeld comment (1997: 512), 'Ceres ambitiously aspired to play a role like that of the Financial Accounting Standards Board and to eventually formulate generally accepted principles for environmental reporting'.

The second idea that had a considerable impact on the coalition members in finding mutual grounds for common action was the approach of using shareholder petitions to change corporate behaviour, as in the case of the Sullivan Principles applied to US companies operating in South Africa under the Apartheid regime. The Sullivan Principles originated in 1977 when Reverend Leon Sullivan, a Baptist minister, issued his code of conduct in an attempt to end discrimination against black workers in South Africa oppressed by the nation's policy of apartheid. This initiative helped to focus attention on the issue of racial injustice in South Africa within international business by promoting criteria for socially responsible investment practices. The Sullivan Principles are even credited with contributing to the end of apartheid. These strategies used by activists and concerned consumers to pressure corporate behaviour in South Africa served as 'the basic blueprint for CERES' (Nash and Ehrenfeld 1997: 513). Similar to the provisions made in the Sullivan Principles, CERES' organisers sought to establish an independent monitoring body to report compliance with their Principles. In sum, both the idea of financial accounting and the Sullivan Principles were of considerable importance in the process of institutionalisation, because they created a common framework of reference under which adversarial standpoints could be integrated into a shared practical vision.

Shortly after the public announcement of the Valdez Principles, coalition members engaged in an intense dialogue with corporations to test their willingness to adopt the principles and commit themselves to periodic reporting. However, although the Aveda Corporation became the first signatory to the Valdez Principles on 22 November 1989 (CERES 1999d), it took another three years to institutionalise cooperation with a wider range of corporate actors. In its own words (CERES 1998: 4),

> [i]n the early years (1989-92), the CERES Principles were mainly adopted by companies that already had strong 'green' reputations, as exemplified by such firms as The Body Shop, Ben & Jerry's, Seventh Generation and Aveda. But the momentum behind the CERES concept continued to build.

This happened as a result of strategic changes within the coalition. After the campaign to win corporate supporters to the CERES principles had not produced the envisaged results,[15] the various investment groups represented in CERES began to place resolutions before the stockholders of influential companies.[16] In many cases, shareholder resolutions are the first step towards intense dialogue with corporations, often at the highest executive level, that leads to formal endorsement of the Principles. In the words of SIF (Social Investment Forum 1999), a coalition member,

> [f]rom the beginning, a distinctive strategy of the CERES coalition was the utilization of the shareholder resolution to raise the question of a firm's environmental responsibility with its board. The right of shareholders as the owners of a corporation to insist on formal responses to such questions was firmly established by Congress and has been upheld for decades by the courts. Many of CERES' institutional investor members ... have since filed numerous proxy resolutions asking companies to endorse the CERES Principles. Such requests made by investors directly to senior management are often the catalyst for an on-going dialogue between the CERES Coalition and a company that may lead to endorsement.

After several rounds of talks with companies, the principles were amended and renamed in 1992. Corporate actors had repeatedly voiced concern about the name of the principles, associating good environmental performance with a major environmental catastrophe. As a result, the principles were renamed the CERES Principles, but also included substantial revisions (Nash and Ehrenfeld 1997: 514). First, different from the original Valdez Principles that demanded a third-party reporting and auditing system, the new principles replaced this provision with the requirement to an annual report on company environmental performance using a 'CERES Report form' (for example CERES 1995). Second, the Valdez Principles required a board-level environmental committee within each company, while the new principles only called upon firms to consider environmental commitment as one factor when choosing a director. And finally, while the original document asked companies to sign the principles, the new one added a disclaimer stating that:

These principles are not intended to create new legal liabilities, expand existing rights or obligations, waive legal defenses, or otherwise affect the legal position of any endorsing company, and are not intended to be used against an endorser in any legal proceeding for any purpose. (CERES 1993)

Sunoco became the first Fortune 500 Company to endorse the CERES Principles in February 1993, General Motors followed in 1994.[17] Several contextual factors can be identified that affected the early process of institutionalisation between investors, advocacy groups and corporations. First, environmental catastrophes, especially the Exxon Valdez incident, triggered widespread public concern about the environmental integrity of major companies. Second, the beginning of the information revolution and increasing business activity at the global level radically changed both the importance and availability of information. As Joan Bavaria, a founding member of CERES and a current board member, recalls (CERES 1998: 2),

this need [for principles and reporting] arose just as an information revolution was starting to race around the world. We sensed that this was a real revolution, with implications for our economy, environment, and culture as sweeping as those that accompanied the agricultural revolution or the industrial revolution.

As a third contextual factor, the rhetorical as well as practical support that the Clinton administration gave to cooperative approaches, voluntary initiatives and partnership concepts seems to have played a role too.[18]

When CERES began to get more institutionalised neither the investment community and the environmental organisations, nor the endorsing companies knew what the outcome would be in terms of joint gains and mutual benefits. A good example is the engagement with GM, the world's largest automobile corporation. The CERES *Performance Review* of GM (2002a: 5), conducted in 2001 and covering the first five years of institutional cooperation, notes:

The world's largest corporation was joining hands with a relatively unfamiliar, yet potentially very influential, coalition of environmental groups and socially responsible investors. The outcomes were uncertain, and there were many skeptics on both sides. ... Together GM and CERES hoped to harvest potential benefits in admittedly unknown and probably rough terrain.

What has proved more important than a clear understanding of future gains were four distinct organisational resources involved in the process of institutionalisation: the ability to frame the problem in a way that is meaningful to other stakeholders, the information necessary to solve it, the impact to make an actual difference in the given issue area and the credibility to construct a joint solution acceptable to all the participants. Social investors were able to address the problem of corporate environmental performance because they not only represented social visions, but substantial capital interests as well. Through filing shareholder petitions, they made companies aware of the growing demand for environmental disclosure. But investors needed the support of non-partisan environmental organisations to offer corporations the reputational benefit and added value necessary to engage them in cooperation. The companies, for their part, provided the information requested by investors and the commitment envisaged by the NGOs to make a real difference on the ground.

In addition to organisational resources, individual capacities and commitment played a role too. In the late 1980s, Joan Bavaria was getting an increasing number of requests from customers who demanded accurate information about the environmental performance of those companies being considered for investment. As one account of this early phase of institutionalisation states, Bavaria found that the answers to this question would differ considerably when posed to companies on the one hand and environmental NGOs and local community groups on the other. What resulted out of this experience was the idea of a coalition between investment professionals and environmental activists (Northeast Utilities Systems 2005). Confirming this story, Nash and Ehrenfeld (1996: 19) summarise:

> The driving force behind the Coalition for Environmentally Responsible Economies is Joan Bavaria, president of Franklin Research and Development Corporation, a firm dedicated to socially responsible investment. Bavaria and Dennis Hayes, an environmental advocate, began to organize CERES in the late 1980s. Bavaria's primary goal was to institutionalize the capability to generate data on corporate environmental management that investors could use in decision-making.

## Summary

In sum, the CERES case study confirms the importance of private demand for a certain regulatory framework in the absence of appropriate governmental or international responses. A distinct problem structure creates demand from different sides of the stakeholder spectrum. What seems important is that one actor holds the power to make the problem a business issue, in this case the social investors through the intense use or threat of shareholder petitions and the resulting risk for corporate reputation. Furthermore, ideas seem to matter in allowing dissimilar actors to agree on a mutual frame of reference as the basis for future action. Although the environmental community did reject the approach at the very beginning, the idea of environmental principles coupled with standardised reporting provided a common point of reference that was used as a strong long-term vision to bridge existing differences. The macro-level of conditions played a twofold role in the case. First, contextual factors, such as the Exxon Valdez catastrophe, provided an additional impulse for successful private regulation; second, macro-shifts in the economic realm drove corporate actors to the forefront of public attention.

What could not be confirmed was a simple power or interest-based explanation. What rather seems to have been influential are available organisational resources that are exchangeable to create a zone of joint gains. Although companies did achieve gains, such as positive brand reputation, the initial cooperation process was marked by uncertainty with regard to the possible outcome. What seems to have been of further importance is the existence of an institutional entrepreneur, a committed individual generating momentum for the idea, similar to the concept of an norm entrepreneur discussed by Finnemore and Sikkink (1998). These findings indicate that an integrated model, combining micro- and macro-structures, is better equipped to understand the emergence of private business co-regulation in the field of environmental management and reporting than a single-factor account.

## FUNCTIONS AND INFLUENCES OF CORPORATE ENVIRONMENTAL REPORTING AND MANAGEMENT

This section approaches the question of whether and how CERES is involved in the construction and maintenance of private governance by carefully assessing its regulatory, cognitive/discursive and integrative functions and the resulting influences on a range of different actors within global sustainability politics. I start with a brief assessment of the constitutive rules and the resulting roles and responsibilities for actors within the CERES structure to better illustrate how the coalition works as a private governance system. This first section also assesses the degree of formalisation observable within CERES.

### The Constitutive Rules: Roles and Responsibilities in Corporate Environmental Reporting and Management

Before I engage in a detailed analysis of CERES' constitutive rules, an important difference to the FSC case study needs to be addressed. While the FSC's organisational structure has remained relatively constant over time, it is important to understand that CERES is a more flexible institution in terms of its actual programmes and work areas. The following discussion reflects the volatile nature of the object of study, however it is most interested in the stable features of the institution, with the exception of internal learning processes and the resulting organisational restructuring. In fact, the website and the general corporate appearance of CERES have changed over the course of this analysis. I will therefore try to refer to current documents, however in some cases reference is made to older documents that cannot be accessed via the World Wide Web, but are on file with the author.

As of 2006, more than 60 companies had endorsed the CERES Principles, including the annual reporting commitment. Among the CERES endorsers are large multinational corporations such as American Airlines, Bank of America Corporation, Baxter International Inc., Coca-Cola North America, Ford Motor Company, General Motors, McDonald's Corporation, Nike and Sunoco, as well as small and medium-sized firms, including environmental front-runners such as The Body Shop International or Aveda Corporation. The second pillar CERES rests on is the CERES coalition, a network of over 100 organisations, including environmental advocacy groups, public interest and community groups and labour unions, as well as an array of investors, analysts and financial advisors representing more than $400 billion in invested capital.[19]

Different from the FSC, CERES is not a membership, but a board-driven organisation. The board has 22 distinguished members and is self-electing, based on the recommendations of the board's Nominating Committee. A list of nominees for election as directors shall be prepared by the committee that is appointed by the Chair of the Board. The nominees shall consist of individuals qualified to represent the class and category of the director they would succeed (CERES 1999a). Elected board members serve for a three-year term and can be re-elected twice.[20] The by-laws specify three interest groups to be represented on the board: investors, environmental organisations and other organisations at large. Representatives of endorsing companies are excluded from board membership, however, the by-laws do not exclude business representation per se. In 2006, six board members were environmental directors, seven served as investor directors, and nine were at-large directors. Next to the Nominating Committee, the board has set up a range of other committees, such as an Executive Committee, an Accountability Committee, an Endorsement Committee and an Investor Programs Committee. The board takes decisions on the following issues, among others: the executive director and other board officers, the annual budget and general financial oversight, endorsing companies and coalition members and strategic issues, for example CERES' recent engagement in the area of climate change and business risk.

The day-to-day operations are supervised by an executive director[21] and carried out by a staff of 22 people located in Boston, MA. As of 2005, CERES is organised around four thematic areas, reflecting its initial set-up as a coalition of environmental organisations and investors on the one hand and

corporate endorsers on the other. The first programme area (company programmes) contains the CERES coalition's engagement with companies on
environmental and social issues, in particular endorsement of the CERES
Principles. Endorsing the principles is a two-way process; it includes the
commitment by a company and the approval of the CERES board of directors. Although companies may approach CERES to enter into collaboration,
they cannot unilaterally decide to endorse the principles, but depend on the
board for approval. The process of mutual endorsement typically consists of
three steps: first, the opening stage, in which both parties agree to enter into
discussions; second, the stage of engagement, in which substantive issues are
discussed and conflicts solved; and finally, the stage of agreement, in which
companies formalise their relationship to CERES, as well as their own roles
in the institution.[22] The endorsement of the CERES Principles by companies
involves three basic responsibilities, although not in legal terms:[23] first,
companies should agree on public disclosure of their environmental
performance through the CERES standard report form (for example CERES
1999c) or other adequate metrics such as CERES' guidelines for small enterprises and non-profit organisations (CERES 2002b) or the GRI guidelines
(Global Reporting Initiative 2002). Second, firms are expected to integrate
the values and goals embodied in the CERES Principles into their everyday
operations and strategic planning; and third, companies should maintain an
open-door relationship with CERES. More specific expectations are defined
in endorsement agreements between CERES and individual companies. For
example, companies may agree to make staff assignments to specific projects
such as stakeholder contacts, or commit to continued dialogue with coalition
members on contested issues.[24]

Companies, for their part, are invited to actively influence the general
course of CERES by participating in various committees or working groups.
One important avenue of influence for endorsing companies has been the
possibility to comment on the CERES report form they were using each year
and to propose changes or amendments that may be incorporated into the
annual revision of the document.[25] In addition, corporate representatives that
are active in committee work can attend the CERES board meetings. A
further avenue of influence for corporations is the annual CERES conference,
drawing together almost all coalition members and endorsers to discuss the
issue of corporate environmental commitment in a long-term perspective. As
William Clay Ford, Chairman of the board of Ford Motor Company, notes
(cited in CERES 2001: 9), '[t]he CERES annual conference is helping to
establish not only the agenda of the next century, but also the relationships
we will need to solve some very daunting issues'.

The second programme area that is directly related to endorsing companies
and their roles and responsibilities in CERES is the sustainability reporting

programme. It is through this programme that companies are expected to report annually on their environmental performance, engage with the coalition to seek advice on sustainability reporting and hence achieve continual improvement of their environmental performance (CERES 2005e). Until 2004, CERES convened Report Working Groups of 15–20 representatives of coalition organisations and endorsing companies to conduct a review of corporate environmental reports prior to their publication.[26] This approach allowed for a resolution of conflicts before they reached the public and thereby increased the willingness of corporations to participate in environmental disclosure. However, participation in these working groups was highly volatile and lacked long-term commitment. Therefore, starting in 2004, CERES reorganised the report review process. It is now the responsibility of Stakeholder Teams to engage with companies. Every large endorsing company and several smaller companies, based on the respective sector, are overviewed by one Stakeholder Team. This new approach is a clear sign of increasing institutionalisation of roles and responsibilities within CERES. In its own words (CERES 2005e),

> [m]any companies have used CERES staff and particular stakeholders in this way [providing expertise and information on reporting issues and future areas of conflict] over the years, but now all CERES companies and a majority of our coalition organizations have a more intentional commitment to this enhanced level of engagement.

Industry programmes are the third area CERES is working in. The focus is predominantly on dialogue between coalition members and companies from different sectors, the main thematic issue being climate change as a business risk. Recent initiatives include an attempt to convince the insurance sector to pay more attention to the issue of climate change. Following the lead of one of the world's largest re-insurance companies, Swiss Re, dialogues with ten leading US and international oil and gas companies as well as an intense dialogue with the electric power sector have begun.

CERES' relation to investors and its investor programme, the fourth area of engagement, is the most flexible and least regulated area of operation. CERES works closely with its coalition members in the investment sector, for example by preparing and coordinating shareholder resolutions, a practice that had been downscaled in CERES' work for some time (to demonstrate good standing with companies that CERES wanted as endorsers), but now seems to have returned to a more prominent level. Shareholder resolutions were filed with a range of companies in 2005, predominantly addressing the issue of business risk and financial adjustments to climate change, including GM Corp., Ford Motor Co., ChevronTexaco Corp., Dow Chemicals and J.P. Morgan Chase&Co (CERES 2005d).

These campaigns are embedded in a larger strategy that aims at engaging and educating investors on climate risk and connecting the issue of corporate governance with that of the challenge of climate change. One strategy of CERES has been to publish a range of reports making the connection between climate change and financial risks, both for companies and investors (CERES 2003c; Cogan 2003; Mansley 2003). A second strategy was the launch and coordination of the Investor Network on Climate Risk (INCR) in cooperation with the United Nations Foundation. As of 2005, this CERES-led network comprises over 40 US and European institutional investors with assets of over $2.7 trillion.

Similar to endorsing companies that are approved by the CERES board, coalition members also have to undergo a thorough review process before they formally join the coalition. This process involves a formal application, an interview, a staff report and a recommendation to the board, a decision by the board committee responsible for the coalition members and finally a definite decision by the whole board. Both coalition members and endorsing companies pay an annual fee that ranges from a few hundred dollars for small coalition members to $30,000 for large corporations.

In sum, the analysis of CERES' constitutive rules has shown that they tend to be more flexible than those of the FSC. However, certain identifiable roles and responsibilities can be attributed to the main actors within the private governance arrangement of CERES. First, the board of directors takes the major decisions including the approval of endorsing companies and coalition members, as well as the general strategic direction of CERES. Second, the secretariat and its staff manage the day-to-day operations and engage with endorsing companies and coalition members on various issue of mutual interest. Third, endorsing companies agree to accept the CERES Principles as normative guidelines for their environmental behaviour, including a commitment to continual improvement and annual reporting. Finally, the coalition members offer their organisational resources on various issues and engage in promoting the CERES mission in their respective networks. Following this brief analysis of the constitutive rules underlying CERES' work and the organisational structure resulting from them, I now turn to the actual influence of private governance in the environmental reporting and management domain by carefully assessing its effects at different levels of the political system and with regard to different stakeholders. Based on the discussion of potential functions of private governance in Chapter 3, and mirroring the analysis of the FSC in Chapter 5, I distinguish between govern-ance through regulation, governance through learning and discourse and governance through integration.

**Governance Through Regulation: What can be Measured, that can be Managed**

The regulatory dimension of CERES as a private governance system contains two related aspects: first, the principles, establishing a normative framework for companies to operate in; and second, a standardized format for corporate environmental reporting, describing the form and content of public disclosure (CERES 1999c). According to CERES,

> Over the past thirteen years, CERES has emerged as the worldwide leader in standardized corporate environmental reporting and the promotion of transformed environmental management within firms.[27]

To understand the nature of regulation in the case of corporate environmental reporting and management, I will discuss the principles of corporate conduct and the standardized reporting scheme in some detail. The ten-point code of environmental conduct, the CERES Principles, forms the basis of CERES' work. They define the normative framework of corporate behaviour. In detail, the CERES Principles (CERES 1999d) demand the protection of the biosphere based on continual progress toward eliminating the release of substances that may damage water, air or the earth and its inhabitants (principle 1); the sustainable use of natural resources including a commitment to make sustainable use of renewable natural resources (principle 2); the reduction of waste through source reduction and recycling (principle 3); the conservation of energy by improving the energy efficiency of internal operations (principle 4); the reduction of risk including environmental, health and safety risks to employees and communities (principle 5); the reduction and, where possible, elimination of products that cause environmental damage or health and safety hazards (principle 6); the prompt correction of conditions that endanger health, safety or the environment (principle 7); regular communication with affected people and communities on all relevant issues (principle 8); a commitment toward environmental representation on the board of directors, as well as toward general integration of environmental practices into the everyday operations of companies (principle 9) and finally the commitment to an annual self-evaluation of progress towards these principles and the resulting public report. Different from the FSC P&C, the CERES Principles are not accompanied by further indicators or comments. As a result, the precise content of the principles is contested and open to debate among CERES' members.

The second regulatory dimension of CERES is the commitment to public disclosure of environmental performance and improvement through an annual report. In the formative phase in the late 1980s and early 1990s, the CERES founders envisaged an independent audit procedure conducted by accountants or specialised certification organisations. However, this proposal met fierce resistance from business actors and disappeared when the principles were renamed in 1992. Today, the reporting requirement takes the form of a second-party reporting scheme where rule making and compliance reporting are separated, but not independently controlled, as for example in the FSC case.

The first version of the CERES report form was published in 1991. As endorsement of the CERES Principles grew over the years, the report form was constantly revised to match the increasing demand for informative, but easy-to-use disclosure. Despite these constant changes, some key elements of the CERES report form can be identified. The document asks for information on a range of issues that derive from the overall normative orientation and concrete demands of the CERES Principles. In this sense, the report form takes over the function that more detailed criteria and indicators have in the FSC case. For example, under the heading 'Use and Conservation of Natural Resources' (section 7) the 1998 CERES report form asks for information on how the company incorporates environmental guidelines into its selection of goods and services; whether the company has a formal written policy regarding material/resource conservation including water conservation, energy conservation, habitat conservation, risk reduction and recycling of solid waste, among others; and information on specific targets for material/resource conservation with reference to a baseline year (CERES 1999c: 20-21). The report form also asks for detailed information on the company-owned or leased-fleet vehicle fuel use (CERES 1999c: 24) as well as on greenhouse gas emissions and other key air pollutants such as carbon monoxide, lead, VOCs; NOx, and SOx (CERES 1999c: 26-27). In addition, section 9 asks for data on compliance with national and international regulations including information on the number and value of penalties (CERES 1999c: 34-35). In total, the report form has 36 pages and covers nine sections.

In addition to constantly updating the report form, CERES also created a range of more specific forms that are tailored to the needs of smaller companies or the requirements of specific industries. In 1998, for example, CERES published a financial services as well as an electrical and gas industries report form. Since the inauguration of the GRI, CERES has asked its endorsing companies to use the appropriate GRI standard for reporting. However, companies can still use the CERES form for guidance. In most cases, a company will edit its report according to public relations necessities, taking into account different formats and reporting requirements. According to CERES, companies fulfil their reporting requirement when using the environmental section of the GRI guidelines; however, they are strongly encouraged to go beyond environmental disclosure and provide information on social performance as well.[28]

Similar to the FSC case, compliance with the regulatory rules is mainly ensured through the threat of public withdrawal of endorsement. CERES has a review procedure in place that allows the referral of serious questions or concerns about a participating company's activities or intentions to the Engagement and Review Committee.[29] Referring to this committee and its procedures, Nash and Ehrenfeld (1997: 515) report:

> CERES has developed a protocol by which it can revoke the endorser status of companies that violate the letter or spirit of its principles. CERES recently dropped the names of more than 20 companies from its list of endorsers because these firms had failed to submit CERES reports or pay membership dues. While CERES considers the remaining firms active and committed, it is prepared to take action against any endorsing company that betrays its trust.

Such actions might be caused by the company's failure to report on its constant improvements or pay the annual fee, known and deliberate falsification of the reported data and misrepresentation of the firm's relation with CERES or clear environmental mismanagement. It is important to note that the review procedures have been developed 'with the full awareness, support and participation of endorsers'.[30]

On a fairly abstract level, both aspects of CERES' regulatory dimension, the corporate code of conduct and the reporting scheme, can be considered a success. Many companies have published an environmental mission statement drawing on the original Valdez Principles.[31] To date, more than 2,000 companies worldwide regularly publish environmental or sustainability reports. The CERES report form has gained so much credibility that it provides the basis for the global sustainability reporting guidelines operated by the GRI. In CERES' own words (CERES 2002c: 2),

> [i]n 1990, when we presented our 10 principles of corporate environmental responsibility, some ridiculed the idea. Today, the concept of continual environmental improvement has become embedded in international standards and corporate goals. When we embarked on dialogues with companies, such dialogues were rare. Today, hundreds or even thousands of companies are engaged in discussions and are building voluntary partnerships to achieve economic growth, social responsibility, and environmental protection.

In sum, CERES' attempts to regulate corporate behaviour through its code of environmental conduct and the accompanying reporting requirement, which is the key instrument of rule-implementation in the corporate environmental reporting and management domain. But what are the measurable effects of this *governance through regulation*? To answer this question, I will address the development in corporate endorsement and reporting over time, performance reviews conducted by CERES, the influence of reporting on shareholder value and core business performance, as well as emerging norms and values.

**Standard-uptake and implementation**
CERES influence on companies measured by the standard-uptake is quite modest at first glance. After three years of intense debates and shareholder resolutions filed with major companies, only 14 companies had endorsed the CERES Principles in 1992, out of over 3,000 corporations originally envisaged by the founding organisations. However, CERES has been able to increase the endorsement rate over the years. In 2006, more than 70 companies are active CERES endorsers and a number are expected to join in the near future.[32] In addition to business endorsing the idea behind CERES, an increasing number of civil society organisations have joined CERES and thereby increased its general acceptance. In 2006, more than 110 civil society organizations are listed as coalition members. Figure 6.1 shows the increase in endorsing companies and CERES coalition members from 1989 to 2006.

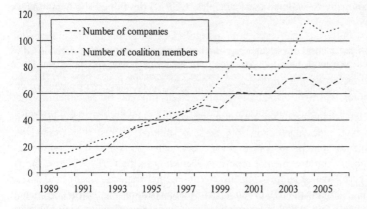

*Figure 6.1 The increase in CERES' endorsing companies and coalition members, 1989 to 2006*

What seems more important than the plain number of endorsing companies is both the impact of corporations and the quality of the actual report. With regard to the first point, CERES has been rather successful at integrating large corporations that really could make a difference. Next to Sunoco and GM, who are early endorsers, CERES has been able to secure the support of companies such as American Airlines, Coca-Cola, and

McDonalds. Endorsing companies today cover most economic sectors, from finance, to oil and gas, to automobiles, to chemical companies. With regard to the second point, available studies indicate that CERES reports perform above average compared to other standards when it comes to completeness and quality of information (Davis-Walling and Batterman 1997). In sum, CERES has a modest influence on companies through its regulatory function when measuring the standard-uptake only. However, when taking into account the companies and sectors they represent as well as the actual quality of corporate environmental reporting, the judgement may be slightly more positive. In addition, when compared to standard-uptake in the FSC case (ha of forests certified compared to global forest cover), which is roughly 1.8 per cent, the CERES figure of 2.1 per cent (number of companies endorsing CERES compared to 3000 originally envisaged) is slightly better.

**Performance reviews**
Another way of assessing the influence of the CERES Principles on a company is looking at the detailed performance reviews CERES has conducted for its interaction with General Motors (CERES 2002a), the world's largest corporation, and Sunoco (CERES 1999b), the first Fortune 500 company to endorse the Principles. CERES developed the performance review

> as a mechanism for examining whether companies that endorsed the CERES Principles more than five years ago are achieving continuous improvement in corporate reporting, facility and product performance, and how the CERES Principles are influencing their culture, programs and policies. (CERES 2002a: 6)

At the beginning of the formal collaboration between CERES and GM in 1994, both sides agreed on four areas of mutual interest that formed the baseline for the performance review conducted in 1999/2000: public accountability (environmental reporting according to the CERES report form), plant performance (improving the environmental impacts, health and safety conditions at GM plants), product performance (improving the fuel efficiency of its fleet) and stakeholder relationships (building a lasting dialogue with CERES coalition members and other stakeholders). All of these priority areas are based on the CERES Principles. The results of this major performance review, however, are mixed (CERES 2002a: 8-22). Addressing the issue of public accountability, GM has published eight annual environmental reports, expanding their scope from US-only to global metrics. Issues addressed cover direct company impacts as well as supply chain issues. In addition, GM is described as a leader in promoting the use of the GRI guidelines. With regard to plant performance, the report shows that GM was able to achieve improved environmental performance at the plant level over the seven years covered by the review. Significant achievement was also made in stakeholder relationships. However, and most important, GM did not show improvement in product performance with its fleet fuel performance stagnating due to higher demand for fuel-intensive automobiles such as SUVs. This latter observation is of particular importance when assessing the actual influence of private governance in corporate environmental reporting and management.

Although the results of the GM performance review are not representative and very much reflect the specific situation of the company and the sector, it seems plausible to assume that performance improvements will occur in sectors that are least prone to market developments and hard financial performance. While environmental reporting and improving stakeholder relations are of secondary importance to the core operations of an automobile company, and plant site improvements are relatively easy to achieve in the context of constant technological improvements, GM was unable to increase its fuel efficiency because of the demand situation and global competition.

The Sunoco performance review is slightly more positive, concluding that Sunoco 'has made improvements over the last five years in these important areas [health, environment, and safety performance (HES); public accountability; relationship to external stakeholders; business process and culture; public policy]' (CERES 1999b: 2). What is most important, the review states that through the endorsement of the CERES Principles and the resulting close interaction with coalition members and CERES staff, Sunoco 'has achieved important results in driving culture change by strengthening and changing its HES business process', and '[o]ver the six-year span, Sunoco's CERES commitment has affected the corporate culture in many ways' (CERES 1999b: 14-15).

In sum, existing performance reviews of CERES endorsers highlight that changes in business practices and corporate culture occur. However, changes seem to be distributed unevenly across issue areas. Whereas corporate environmental reporting and improvements in health, environmental and safety performance have become standard practices and institutional goals, few changes have occurred in products and services. Comparative studies of corporate codes of practices come to similar conclusions (Nash and Ehrenfeld 1997: 519, 524). In general, 'codes have helped to institutionalize some significant new practices in participating firms'. With regard to CERES, interviewees 'believe they are seeing signs of changing consciousness in several participating firms. They describe the changes as soft or attitudinal. They have not yet observed changes in products or processes that reflect this new consciousness'.

**Economic incentive structures of corporate environmental reporting and management**

A third possible indicator for CERES' regulatory influences are the economic effects it generates, in particular with regard to the shareholder value and general economic performance of endorsing companies. The essential question is: can firms do well while doing good? Recently, this belief has been reinvigorated by Wall Street through the creation of the Dow Jones Sustainability Index and FTSE4Good. This 'myth of CSR', however, it is also heavily contested (Doane 2005). Why should companies voluntarily go beyond compliance? A straightforward answer is that by implementing environmental management systems and reporting on the progress achieved, companies can reduce costs that occur from waste treatment, pollution prevention, bad press and lawsuits, among other factors. More important, firms may use environmental performance as an asset in differentiation-based strategies that aim at signalling to investors and consumers that there is something unique about the company, setting it aside from competitors (Eisner 2004: 150). In addition, as companies are embedded in larger networks, pressure from competitors or a large market-leader may force firms to adopt existing best practices in order to survive.[33] After having argued that there is an instrumental value to corporate environmental reporting and management, the problem of causality remains. In simple terms, it is difficult to determine whether increased levels of corporate environmental responsibility cause higher returns on investment and profits in general, or whether more profitable companies are simply able to invest more of their resources in environmentally friendly behaviour.

Acknowledging this difficulty, research over the past 30 years has nevertheless established clear links between good financial and environmental performance.[34] According to Eisner (2004: 149), 'there is a growing body of evidence that firms with superior environmental performance (SEP) are reaping financial rewards, although there are ongoing questions about causality'. With regard to six companies endorsing the CERES Principles, White (1996) found that it pays to be 'green'. Over a period of 48 months, the six CERES companies performed above the average of companies not using any environmental reporting scheme. In addition, qualitative data suggests that companies were able to benefit from involvement in CERES. For example, 'Sunoco believes that there is a direct correlation between HES performance and the company's profitability' (CERES 1999b: 15). According to this account, the challenge for CERES and Sunoco has been to demonstrate to Wall Street 'the specific dollars saved over the course of the relationship' (CERES 1999b: 15). For example, several lawsuits were avoided through the collaboration with CERES. In sum, given the generally positive correlation between corporate environmental and economic performance and the findings on CERES companies, we can conclude that one clear influence of private governance in the environmental reporting and management domain is the improved financial performance of participating firms, although data on the full sample of CERES companies is missing.

**Converging norms in corporate governance**
A fourth instance of regulatory influence is the establishment of norms. One example is the increasing recognition that environmental interests should be represented at the highest levels of corporate governance. As some scholars have emphasised, based on research with experts on voluntary business regulation and standards, to be effective approaches must have a top management commitment (Krehbiel and Erekson 2001: 110). CERES acted as a norm-entrepreneur in this issue-area. As early as 1990, Exxon Mobil created the new position of Vice President for Environment and Safety as a reaction to the Valdez Principles and the negative press following the Exxon Valdez catastrophe. As a general trend, the number of environmentally committed people on boards has grown since the early 1990s. In addition, companies who did not place an environmental representative on their boards have created alternative ways of introducing environmental concerns to their upper-level management (Weiss 2002). With regard to CERES' precise role in this development through its rules on environmental board representation (principle 9) Weiss (2002: 101) notes:

> However, CERES was a motivating force in exerting pressure and defining social expectations for a strong upper management commitment to environmental initiatives and for increased environmental–corporate collaboration. To some extent, when CERES defined the commitment of management a requisite for environmental responsibility, and companies appointed environmental representatives to their board, a norm of environmentally responsible behavior emerged.

In addition to environmental board representation, companies have accepted the concept of environmental mission statements in general. As one interviewee reports, language indicates that many companies have developed their own environmental codes based on the CERES Principles without publicly acknowledging this fact.[35] In sum, 'CERES had a catalysing effect on the idea of mission statements. For a lot of businesses, environmental reporting and mission statements have become a norm'.[36]

A similar observation can be made with regard to the practice of environmental reporting. In the first half of the 1990s, the idea of environmental reporting was still contested:

> Whether public environmental reporting becomes a requirement for Corporate America is an open question. ISO is likely to consider including public reporting of

performance measures. The CERES Principles support reporting of environmental performance, and participation in EMAS in Europe also results in a level of public disclosure ... companies have initiated environmental reporting to proactively satisfy information demands and receive due credit for their significant investments in environmental stewardship. (PricewaterhouseCoopers 1995: 6)

However, in 2005, corporate reporting on sustainable issues, including a wide range of environmental performance indicators, has become a global standard business practice.

To conclude, the influence of corporate environmental reporting and management through its regulatory function can be summarised in four points. First, standard-uptake by business actors has been modest. However, CERES was able to steadily increase the number of endorsing companies and integrate influential global players such as GM, Ford Motor Company and McDonalds. Second, company performance reviews conducted by CERES indicate that business practices have changed as a result of endorsing the CERES Principles. However, while changes in public accountability, stakeholder relations and the environmental performance of individual plants could be observed in both reviews, no significant changes occurred in core business areas such as the fuel efficiency of GM's product range. Third, acknowledging the fundamental problem of attributing causality to the relation between environmental and economic performance, the literature converges in its assessment that firms can do well while doing good. Therefore, adopting the CERES Principles and annually reporting on environmental performance potentially influences a company's core business, although specific data on the total sample of CERES endorsers is lacking. And finally, the analysis suggests that CERES has been an influential driver in establishing sustained environmental commitment in the highest ranks of corporate governance, as well as the general idea of corporate environmental mission statements and reporting.

### Governance Through Discourse and Learning: Changing the 'Conversation'

Next to influencing actors through its regulatory function, CERES affects actors in the corporate environmental reporting and management domain through shaping discourses and initiating learning processes. In more detail, I discuss the following four aspects of this cognitive/discursive governance: (1) producing and disseminating information, (2) providing the institutional setting for learning processes, (3) allowing for problem solving by providing a forum for discourse and debates, and finally (4) the diffusion of the regulatory model within and beyond disuse areas. Similar to the FSC case, this cognitive/discursive function is a result of CERES' distinct network structure and the specific roles and responsibilities of actors therein.

**Producing and disseminating information**
CERES uses its wide network of coalition members to produce and disseminate information on issues of key importance. One example of producing information is the recent attempt made by CERES to (re)define industry's stance towards climate change. Within this project, CERES has produced and commissioned a range of studies that raise the issue of climate change as a risk for business and investors. For example, in a 2002 report (Innovest Strategic Value Advisors: 2) CERES states: '[t]he bottom line ... is straightforward: climate change represents a potential multi-billion dollar risk to a wide variety of US businesses and industries. It should, therefore, command the same level of attention and urgency as any other business risk of this magnitude.'

CERES' attempt to alter the existing discourse on climate change within the business community is also reflected in recent developments in its communications strategy. The media strategy that has been developed from 2001 on reflects the situation that CERES is often perceived as an environmental advocate, while its audience is really the companies and the financial markets. As one staff member recalls, 'the shift that CERES tries to make is really about getting our issues into the financial press; not on the environmental page, but in the business section.'[37] This attempt has been remarkably successful with more than ten articles on the issue of climate change and business risk in major US and international newspapers, including *The Wall Street Journal*, *Financial Times*, and *The New York Times*, in 2003 (for example Ball 2003a, 2003b; Burr 2003; Feder 2003a, 2003b; Murray 2004). Although the articles do not necessarily mention CERES, they make a strong case for the issue of climate change. The *Wall Street Journal* for example comments (Ball 2003a): 'Here's what companies' directors have to worry about these days: accounting scandals ... earnings problems ... oh, and global warming'. And the *Financial Times* recalls (Murray 2003):

> There was a time when the most prominent voices in the debate on climate change were environmental lobby groups, activists and non-governmental organisations. These days, however, new speakers are entering the fray: banks, insurers, investors and other organisations in the financial services sector.

These examples show that CERES acted as a knowledge producer and knowledge broker through its communications strategy. In the words of a CERES staff member, 'CERES has really driven this issue and made it into the press'.[38] This view is remarkable because, according to the same interviewee, two years ago (in 2001) there would not have been an article on climate change and risk in the business press. The triggering events have been shareholder resolutions on climate change and the corresponding risk for investors. CERES has also been active in influencing a new class of actors, public pension funds, utilising its existing coalition network. The 2003 Annual CERES Report (2004: 9) states:

> Much of Ceres' work in 2003 culminated in the historic Institutional Investors Summit on Climate Change held at the United Nations headquarters in New York City on November 21, 2003. There, Ceres, the State of Connecticut Treasurer's Office, and the United Nations Foundation brought together institutional investors representing more than $1 trillion in invested capital together to examine the financial risk of global climate change.

In particular, the changed voting behaviour of large pension funds, which have started to vote in favour of resolutions calling for adequate policies concerning climate change, has attracted much media coverage over the past few years.[39] In the view of one observer, CERES has been a prime mover and organiser of these critical resolutions, particularly in highlighting the business case and approaching mainstream advisors, convincing them that climate change is a business issue and not just an environmental concern.[40]

A clear indicator for the success of CERES' attempt to challenge the existing discourse on business and climate change can be found in the 2005 record high voting support for shareholder resolutions seeking greater analysis and disclosure from companies about the financial impacts of climate change. For example, at the 2005 corporate annual meeting of Exxon Mobil, 28.3 per cent of the shareholders supported

> a resolution requesting that the company's board of directors undertake a comprehensive review on how it will meet the greenhouse gas reductions targets in countries participating in the Kyoto Protocol. The 28.3 per cent support represent 1.5 billion shares with a market value of about $83.8 billion. (CERES 2005c)

Figure 6.2 shows the number of shareholder resolutions on climate change filed with US companies from 1994 to 2005. In sum, CERES' function as a knowledge and information broker has clearly been changing the conversation. In its own words (CERES 2004): 'An important Ceres communication goal is to "change the conversation" from the assumption that climate change solutions will hurt the economy to recognition that inaction is the greater business risk'.[41]

Next to brokering knowledge through its media campaign and communication strategy, CERES also engages in close interaction with its coalition members, for example, when training them in 'environmental responsibility through dialogue and disclosure' in an annual Corporate Accountability Workshop.[42] In addition to media campaigns and capacity-building programmes, CERES has also established, jointly with the Association of Chartered Certified Accountants (ACCA), an award scheme for communicating best practices in sustainability reporting in North America (Association of Chartered Certified Accountants 2005).

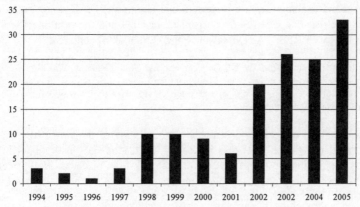

*Figure 6.2 US shareholder resolutions on climate change, 1994 to 2005*

**Learning networks**

CERES' institutional structure as a coalition of diverse actors clearly facilitates inter-organisational learning processes. Three aspects warrant closer attention. First, CERES organises an annual conference to bring together its coalition members and endorsing companies. It was just an annual gathering where people within the CERES network could meet and discuss issues of common concern until 2003, but the conference has recently taken up a more high profile role. The new conference format places more emphasis on engaging endorsing companies and coalition members in strategic projects. This organisational change is based on the recognition that CERES does not make adequate use of its wide resources. As one interviewee reports, many people in member organisations lack a clear understanding of CERES' work and the possible contribution of their own organisation to this work.[43] The conference is an attempt to increase the involvement of coalition members and endorsing companies beyond participating in CERES board meetings and committee work. In addition, greater emphasis is laid on utilising the distinct organisational knowledge of participants in workshops and discussion groups, covering topics from 'How Investors Worldwide are Addressing Sustainability Risks and Opportunities', to 'Oil: Closing the Sustainability Gap', to 'Electric Power and Climate Change: Best Practices in Disclosure and Management', to 'What's Driving

Competition and Change in the Auto Sector?', to 'The Risk to Companies of US Policy Uncertainty on Climate Change', to 'Chemicals, Consumer Products and Environmental Health: Greening Supply Chains to Boost Corporate Reputations and the Bottom Line' (CERES 2005b).

A second example of inter-organisational learning is the investor summit on climate risk that CERES first organised in 2003 and the resulting INCR that is led by CERES.[44] As Dossal and Fanzo (2004: 334) comment,

> [w]hen participants from the US Government, the United Nations, Wall Street and corporate board executives, were brought at the Investors Summit … this allowed participants to explore the linkages between previously separate ways of thinking. This is where innovation lies.

One result of integrating previously separate ways of thinking is the ten-point 'Call for Action' that was issued by ten leading US institutional investors demanding new steps towards climate risk from business, Wall Street and the US Security and Exchange Commission. A report commissioned by CERES in 2005 (David Gardiner & Associates: 6), reviewing the progress that has been made since this first call for action, finds: 'A further indicator of investors concern about climate risk is the degree to which investors are actively engaged in learning about the issue and how to address it'. Since 2003, members of INCR have organised and sponsored four major conferences on the issue of climate change and business risk in the United States and Europe. In sum, both the conferences and the investors' network can be considered major examples of inter-organisational learning involving over 600 different organisations, from large labour pension funds to the United Nations.

The third example of CERES inducing inter-organisational learning is the process of mutual endorsement that leads to the formalisation of relations between companies and CERES. After companies have communicated their willingness to endorse the CERES Principles, a detailed negotiation process commences that includes CERES staff members, CERES board members and the applicant company. According to Robert Massie, CERES' executive director from 1996 to 2003 (cited in Nash and Ehrenfeld 1997: 515),

> this period of negotiation is a mutual learning process in which CERES Board members and firm executives explore what CERES might expect from the company and how the firm's performance might change in the future. This process helps a firm develop a stronger sense of the environmental issues it faces and can be one of the most important benefits a firm derives from its CERES involvement.

With regard to learning processes within CERES, evidence is less obvious. CERES has changed during the course of its 16-year history, from an idea advocated by only a handful of concerned investment professionals and environmental advocates to an influential player in corporate environmental reporting and management, representing over 160 different organisations, millions of members and billions of dollars. However, change within the institution has been driven more by ad-hoc decisions than long-term strategic planning. Nevertheless, intra-organisational change can be observed on at least two occasions. First, CERES has started to put more emphasis on its unique network of experts, from investment to labour unions and churches, by changing the format of the annual CERES conference from one of general meetings and discussions to one of strategic planning and learning. In addition, CERES has reorganised the Report Working Groups into Stakeholder Teams to utilise the strength of its network. And second, CERES has increased its efforts to influence important players on key issues of sustainability such as climate change while it has downplayed its role as the provider of standardised reporting due to the successful inauguration of the GRI.

**Deliberative problem solving**
Turning to the third form of cognitive/discursive governance, I will briefly focus on CERES as a forum for problem solving. As one commentator observers (Anonymous 2000): 'Since its founding in 1989, the Coalition for Environmentally Responsible Economies (CERES) has played an important role in the dialogue between businesses and environmental interests.'

However, CERES has not only acted as a facilitator of dialogue, but also of problem solving. The distinct structure of CERES – with its board meetings, working groups, the annual CERES conference and other major events – provides plenty of opportunity for actors to meet in person and discuss issues of mutual concern. What seems important to companies is the fact that these debates take place behind closed doors, rather than in front of the media. Hence, conflicts can be solved before they get public, an approach rather untypical for business–NGO relations.[45] In addition, the close cooperation with coalition members has also been credited as an early-warning system for corporations, signalling to them what the next big issue could be.[46]

**Diffusion of the regulatory model**
Similar to the FSC in forest certification, CERES has a considerable influence on the policy domain of corporate environmental reporting as a whole. In response to CERES, a range of industrial groups undertook initiatives to define corporate environmental reporting. One example is the Public Environmental Reporting Initiative (PERI) that was jointly developed by ten major US companies between 1992 and 1994, among them industry leaders such as AMOCO, Dow and DuPont, which CERES had initially hoped to win for its own principles.

In addition to passively inducing environmental reporting, like in the case of PERI, CERES was also actively involved in mainstreaming, broadening and essentially globalising the model of corporate environmental reporting with the successful establishment of the Global Reporting Initiative. As detailed accounts of the formative phase of the GRI are given elsewhere (Dingwerth 2005b; Waddell 2002), I will only provide a brief summary, focusing on CERES' distinct role in the process. The GRI was set up in 1997 to harmonise and integrate existing environmental/sustainable reporting schemes. Several companies had approached CERES and raised concerns about the fragmented scope of reporting and its limited geographical reach. At the same time, the Tellus Institute,[47] a major North American think tank in the field of sustainability, published its report *Green Metrics*, a study that compared existing reporting schemes and their requirements in a single matrix and identified overlaps between various schemes (White and Zinkl 1998). Based on this input, initial discussions on establishing a broader and harmonised reporting framework began, leading to the successful establishment of a Steering Committee in December 1997. Shortly after, UNEP could be won as a partner institution, a step that proved decisive, both in terms of enhanced legitimacy through public participation, as well as scientific input.[48] Until the GRI became an independent organisation in 2002, CERES served as its secretariat and provided most of the financial resources.[49] Although being a key driver of the GRI process, CERES managed to involve a range of other players in the deliberations that led to the draft GRI principles. In this context, it was of major importance that CERES had agreed on transforming the GRI into an independent organisation with its own board of directors early in the process (Waddell 2002: 5-6). In 2005, CERES participates in various GRI working groups and is represented on its board by Joan Bavaria.

To conclude, the influence of CERES through its discursive and cognitive functions can be summarised in four points: first, CERES has considerable influence through producing and disseminating information. Its media strategy, with its focus on getting information about CERES and the risk of climate change into the business press, has been successful and can be credited with having influenced the recent increase in shareholder resolutions on climate change filed with US corporations. Second, CERES shows clear signs of being an inter-organisational learning network, mainly through its annual conference and the establishment of INCR. Third, CERES has provided a forum for problem solving and early warning, mainly because it kept conflicts within the institution, rather than making them public before they were solved. And finally, CERES has forced other actors in the field to react to the general idea of corporate environmental reporting, as well as successfully implemented its own global sustainable reporting scheme, the GRI.

### Governance Through Integration: the Mainstreaming of Corporate Sustainability Reporting

The third function through which private governance is constructed in the environmental reporting and management domain is integration. This concept has a twofold connotation: first, existing international norms and regulations may be integrated into the private governance system and thereby enforce existing regulatory structures. Integrating international standards may also increase the authority of private governance arrangements. And second, private rules for corporate environmental reporting may be transferred upwards to the international level through formal acknowledgement or endorsement, as well as horizontally to national or sub-national political arenas.

### Downward integration

With regard to the first mode of integration, evidence is scarce and reference to existing international norms and regulatory frameworks is rather implicit. In a wide sense, a number of the CERES Principles, such as protection of the biosphere, sustainable use of natural resources and energy conservation can be interpreted as relating to the general idea of sustainable development as embodied in the 1987 Brundtland Report. However, and differently from the FSC case, the CERES Principles do not formally relate to international accords.

### Upward integration

With regard to the second mode of integration, three basic patterns can be observed. First, the CERES Principles have been introduced as state legislation in sub-national polities in the US, for example in the state of New Jersey. In addition, several states have passed legislation on voluntary audits, and the EPA has strengthened its guidelines on auditing and public disclosure (Weiss 2002: 104). Second, a range of public actors and agencies endorse the CERES Principles. For example, the Department of Environmental Protection Pennsylvania (2005) states:

> While industry associations like the Chemical Manufacturer's Association and the American Forest&Paper Association deserve recognition for their environmental initiatives, as do the Programs of the Global Environmental Management Initiative and the International Chamber of Commerce, these initiatives do not match the CERES Principles nor the CERES reporting process in several important respects.

CERES has also been supported by public actors such as state comptrollers:[50]

New York City Comptroller Alan G. Havesi, joined by more than 19 key
institutional investment groups, will announce a year-long drive to call on the
nation's leading companies to endorse the CERES principles on environmental
reporting and encourage other institutional investors to join in their demand for
environmental reporting from the world's largest corporations. (Socialfunds.com
1999)

The third pattern of integration relates to the upward transformation of
private rules. Three examples illustrate this development. First, the United
Nations used the Valdez Principles in the design of its sustainable development guidelines for multinational corporations (Weiss 2002: 104). Second,
CERES has been a key driver in launching the GRI, which today provides an
encompassing reporting framework on social, economic and environmental
issues for large corporations, along with small and medium-sized enterprises,
NGOs and public agencies. The GRI has been endorsed by UNEP who
became an early member in the formation process in 1998. The GRI is an
official collaborating centre of the United Nations Environment Programme
and works in cooperation with UN Secretary-General Kofi Annan's Global
Compact. Hence, the idea of standardised reporting advanced by CERES and
mainstreamed into the GRI can be considered to be generally endorsed and
supported at the highest levels of international politics. Substantiating this
claim, the idea of corporate sustainability reporting and management also received public acknowledgement at the 2002 Johannesburg Summit on
Sustainable Development.

In sum, the integrative influence of private governance systems is less
obvious in the CERES, than the FSC case. Very little reference is made to
existing international norms; however, private rules have been endorsed by
public actors at the national, international and transnational levels, including
US public agencies, governments and UN programmes. The most profound
impact that CERES can claim is mainstreaming the corporate environmental
reporting agenda to a global sustainability reporting agenda and securing
support for this development from the United Nations and the international
community.

## PROSPECTS OF AND LIMITS TO CORPORATE
## ENVIRONMENTAL REPORTING AND MANAGEMENT

This section will briefly discuss the potentials and shortcomings of CERES
as a private governance system in global sustainability politics. As in the FSC
case study, I will address three points of reference: first, the consistency with
its own organisational goals and general objectives; second, an inner-

organisational perspective; and third, a larger systemic perspective on corporate reporting and private regulation.

CERES' mission is 'to move businesses, capital and markets to advance lasting prosperity by valuing the health of the planet and its people' (CERES 2005a). This fairly broad mission statement is founded on three core beliefs that are shared among the CERES members: first, environmental stewardship and company value are strongly linked; second, the bedrock of sound corporate governance is measurement and disclosure; and third, responsible companies must provide their investors and stakeholders with complete and transparent information about their environmental performance. With regard to these assumptions and aspirations, the analysis suggests some major shortcomings, but also potential.

With regard to moving businesses, capital and markets in the direction of sustainability, the limited standard-uptake constitutes a major drawback to CERES' mission. Although the number of endorsing and reporting companies – in particular large TNCs – has steadily increased since the announcement of the original Valdez Principles, and is expected to continue to grow by two to four large corporations per year, most companies targeted by CERES have refused to cooperate or joined alternative schemes.

Similar to the case of private forest governance, a number of competing schemes have occurred as a reaction to the CERES Principles. Schemes like PERI or the Global Environmental Management Initiative (GEMI) have also engaged in integrating environmental values into standard business practices and measuring the progress towards this goal via corporate reporting. Early on, CERES understood that competition among different reporting standards and environmental mission statements could severely hinder progress towards a more sustainable economy as envisaged by CERES. Beneficiaries of this situation were the companies that could choose what suited them best from a range of different 'offers'. On the other side of the stakeholder spectrum, social investors suffered from this situation because multiple signals increased the cost of decisions. To overcome this potentially harmful situation, CERES successfully implemented an overarching reporting framework that went beyond environmental disclosure. Different from the forest arena, where an integrative framework is still missing despite ongoing debates about mutual recognition, the GRI provides an accepted reference point for sustainability reporting worldwide.

CERES is regularly supported by foundations, companies and non-profit organisations such as the United Nations Foundation, Pew Charitable Trust, Rockefeller Brothers Fund, Wallace Global Fund, Ford, Nike and the Civil Society Institute. CERES also has considerable sources of income through its endorser and coalition fees, as well as fees for the annual CERES conference. For example, in 2003 and 2004, CERES was able to cover around 19 per cent of its total expenses from its coalition and endorsers' fees. In addition, revenues from coalition and endorser fees, as well as grant revenues have been stable over the last three years, allowing CERES to plan its future strategy with some confidence. However, becoming less reliant on donors through securing higher revenues from services might yet become a strategic necessity for CERES, as it is for the FSC. Figure 6.3 shows the annual endorsers' and coalition fees, conference fees and grant revenues from 1998 to 2004.

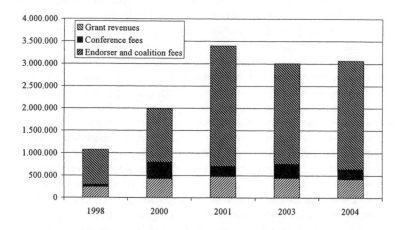

*Figure 6.3 CERES annual revenues from 1998 to 2004*

Another important aspect in determining the potential shortcomings and prospects of private governance in the environmental reporting and management domain is analysing its structural limitations. I will address four themes that are of particular relevance. First, a fundamental prerequisite for successful implementation and institutionalisation of corporate environmental and sustainability reporting is that the demand for public disclosure is also institutionalised among a range of key actors. For example, public relations benefits for companies through reporting will only be realised if the public keeps up demand for environmental and social disclosure. Likewise, benefits for investors will largely depend on the demand for social investment (and the necessary information to make such an investment decision) from customers.

A second important issue is enforcement. As a private, information-based governance system, enforcement in corporate environmental reporting is limited to naming-and-shaming practices and the constant public interest in annual corporate disclosure. With regard to using such practices, CERES seems to be in an ambivalent position. Rules for the exclusion of endorsing companies from the CERES network exist; however, they have been applied only once.[51] The failure to use the instrument of public naming-and-shaming by excluding a company from CERES results from its specific role as an honest broker between coalition members and companies. As most issues that could potentially lead to an exclusion are debated within the CERES network among coalition members, CERES staff and companies prior to any serious action, business actors will rather leave than get expelled. The threat of exclusion thereby loses much of its potential as an enforcement instrument.

A third matter of concern is the fact that participation in corporate environmental reporting schemes is voluntary. This involves at least two problems. First, potential free riders can attach themselves to the general idea of environmental disclosure by creating some kind of environmental report without endorsing the underlying principles of constant improvement and environmental stewardship as embodied in the CERES Principles. In addition, free riders may also benefit from reporting simply because they operate in the same sector as well-known companies that do report. The second problem deriving from the voluntary nature of environmental reporting is competition. In a competitive market environment companies will avoid reporting if it is perceived as a cost and therefore a comparative disadvantage. A partial solution to these two problems is winning large corporations into a particular reporting scheme, thereby utilising their power vis-à-vis smaller competitors and firms along their own supply-chain. CERES has been rather successful in attracting larger TNCs with substantial operations and long supply-chains such as the automobile and food industry.

In addition to the free rider problem, reporting systems may also attract either good performers that have already made substantial investments in their operations or environmental laggards that hope to increase their reputation a lot by doing little. CERES has attracted both kinds of endorsers. Many of CERES' early endorsers were environmentally oriented companies such as The Body Shop or Seventh Generation, while some of the larger endorsers, such as GM, have been linked to anti-environmental lobbying and unsustainable product policies.

Finally, companies only go beyond compliance if it is in their interests. Therefore, to attract business supporters, private governance systems in corporate environmental reporting must prove their added value. In this respect, CERES seems to be in a rather good position. The wide coalition of environmental organisations and investment professionals, together with social interest groups such as churches and labour unions, provides a valuable resource for corporations. Next to using the CERES network as a learning environment, companies are also able to monitor the business-critical scene for potential disturbances. The benefits of this resource network far outweigh the $30,000 some larger corporations pay as their annual CERES fees.


## CONCLUSION

This case study has assessed the institutionalisation of private governance in the corporate environmental reporting and management domain in its dual understanding of emergence and influence. Hence, I have asked: Why do private rules emerge in the corporate environmental reporting domain that transcend boundaries and target business actors rather than citizens or governments? What real-world influence do these rules display? I have argued that CERES constitutes a novel institutional model of global governance in the reporting domain. As an institutionalised governance system, CERES induces a range of effects in its stakeholders and the wider public. The purpose of this chapter has hence been to understand in detail the factors that have led to the institutionalisation of private governance in the reporting domain and the resulting effects of the governance system on its standard-takers, business and civil society supporters, as well as on governments and international processes.

To achieve this aim, I have first provided a brief overview of the current state of corporate environmental reporting and performance, its historical context and its main drivers. Subsequently, I have analysed the demand for a credible solution to the corporate crisis as well as the available supply, both in organisational and ideational terms. I have argued that it was mainly the novel strategy of social investors that turned an abstract and so far uncontroversial issue area into a real threat to business. Shareholder resolutions calling for more public disclosure of environmental performance, as well as demand by customers for adequate information for their investment decisions, created demand on both sides of the stakeholder spectrum. However, investors could not rely on either company or activist information, while corporations lacked a credible system to communicate their environmental commitment to their stakeholders and the wider public. In this situation, ideas matter in allowing dissimilar actors to agree on a mutual frame of reference as the basis for future action. Although the environmental community rejected the initial approaches, the idea of environmental principles coupled with standardized reporting provided a common point of reference that was used as a strong long-term vision to bridge existing differences.

The resulting institutionalisation of private governance, including precise constitutive and regulative rules, was the focus of the third section. Following the analytical framework advanced in Chapter 3, I have discussed CERES' influence as a private governance system along the three functional dimensions of regulation, learning and discourse and integration.

The regulatory function has been achieved by a ten-point code of environmental conduct as the ethical basis of corporate behaviour and a reporting requirement detailed in a number of generic and specific CERES report forms, and, from 2002, in the GRI guidelines on sustainability reporting. With regard to the influence of private regulation, four points have been highlighted in the analysis. First, although standard-uptake has been modest, CERES has been able to attract large and influential companies. In addition, CERES has ensured that the number of endorsing companies constantly increases. Second, existing performance reviews of CERES companies indicate that the integration of environmental behaviour in standard business operations has been achieved in the areas of stakeholder relations, plant-site performance and disclosure, but not in product development and strategic management. Third, the analysis suggests that private governance in corporate environmental reporting affects corporate performance and shareholder value. However, data is inconclusive on the exact causality of this correlation. And finally, CERES appears to have had a strong influence on changing norms in the business arena, in particular on environmental board representation, corporate mission statements and environmental disclosure in general.

With regard to the cognitive/discursive function of CERES, the analysis has highlighted the importance of producing and disseminating information and thereby influencing the 'conversation' in crucial issue areas. In particular, four observations have been made. First, through its media and communication strategy, CERES has influenced the existing discourse on climate risk within the business community. A number of reports and research findings have found their way into the business press and the financial sections of major US and international newspapers. One observable result is the increase in the number of shareholder resolutions filed with US companies on addressing business preparedness for climate change. A second finding underscores the centrality of the supporting network for influential private governance. Similar to the FSC case, CERES has acted as a learning network for a wide range of different actors. However, different from private forest governance, evidence for intra-organisational learning has been scarce. Third, CERES has successfully provided a forum for problem solving among its coalition members and endorsing companies, for example through its annual conference or committee work involving CERES endorsers and firms. The fourth observation with regard to CERES' cognitive/discursive governance function is the diffusion of the regulatory model of corporate environmental reporting. Next to forcing a range of business actors to react to the CERES Principles by establishing their own schemes, CERES has also deliberately engaged in a mainstreaming strategy of corporate environmental reporting that has led to the successful implementation of the independent GRI with its focus on globally applicable sustainability reporting indicators.

The third function through which CERES realises its influence on different stakeholders has been termed 'integration'. While some evidence of integration could be found with regard to public endorsement of CERES, at the national as well as international and transnational levels (upward integration), international norms have not been incorporated into the CERES rules (downward integration). However, in a broader understanding, the CERES code of environmental conduct reflects core themes of the 1987 Brundtland Report that popularised the term sustainable development.

After I have substantiated the claim that CERES constitutes a distinct mechanism of global governance through the institutionalisation of roles and responsibilities in the corporate environmental reporting and management domain, the subsequent section raised some questions with regard to CERES' potential limitations and prospects. Next to problems arising from the relatively low standard-uptake and a high financial reliance on grant revenues, the systemic limits of information-based governance approaches were highlighted. In particular, problems for corporate environmental reporting as a credible and influential governance arrangement result from four major issues: first, in order for corporate reporting to be sustainable, demand also needs to be institutionalised. Second, enforcement is limited to naming-and-shaming practices. However, CERES' close cooperation with companies renders this enforcement mechanism ineffective. Third, the voluntary nature of reporting and performance improvement creates incentives for free riders and might only attract good performers and laggards. Finally, as companies only go beyond compliance if it is in their interests, private governance systems in corporate environmental reporting are increasingly forced to prove their added value to companies.

## NOTES

1.   Corporate environmental reporting can be defined as 'a tool to communicate a company's environmental performance. It is used to demonstrate company-wide integrated environmental management systems, corporate responsibility and the implementation of voluntary initiatives and codes of conduct' (United Nations Environment Programme 2005). Environmental management can be understood as a process to manage the environmental aspects of a company, plant, building etc. This includes both rather informal and ad-hoc procedures, as well as integrated and institutionalised environmental management systems (EMS) that are independently certified according to the ISO 14001 standard or the European Eco-management and Audit scheme (EMAS). Although corporate environmental reporting and management are voluntary, some schemes may emerge as 'de facto industry standards that provide the desired legitimacy, consistency and comparability required by business and its stakeholders' (Ligteringen and Zadek 2004: 1).

2. With reference to the question of why some companies have accepted the conduct of environmental performance reporting as a standard business practice, while others have not, scholars have pointed to individual environmental initiatives of managers, directors and owners, the perception of environmental issues as opportunities for business, the general proactivity of the firm, the cost of obtaining the information to report on and the size and general performance of a company. For detailed literature on these issues, see Morhardt, Baird and Freeman (2002: 216).

3. Environmental and sustainability reporting is found to be higher in industries that are historically connected to visible pollution and environmental restructuring such as chemicals or extracting industries, while banking and finance pay considerably less attention to the issue of reporting (Kolk 2004: 53). Roughly 80 per cent of corporate reporting within the Global 250 group came from the electronics, utilities, automotive as well as oil and gas sector in 2005 (Kolk et al. 2005).

4. For example, see paragraph 17 (a): 'Encourage industry to improve social and environmental performance through voluntary initiatives, including environmental management systems, codes of conduct, certification and public reporting on environmental and social issues, taking into account such initiatives as the International Organization for Standardization (ISO) standards and Global Reporting Initiatives (GRI) guidelines on sustainability reporting, bearing in mind principle 11 of the Rio Declaration on Environment and Development' (United Nations 2002).

5. Consider for example the establishment of the World Economic Forum by Klaus Schwab in 1971 and the establishment of the Trilateral Commission by David Rockefeller in 1973.

6. Shareholder activism in general is regulated by a mix of state and federal law. The US Securities and Exchange Commission takes a dominant role in regulating the process of submitting shareholder resolutions. In simple terms, shareholders are allowed to present proposals if they hold more than $2,000 or 1 per cent of the shares of a corporation. Proposals that fail to win a majority vote can be reintroduced the subsequent years, a minimum support of 3 per cent provided.

7. This trend mirrors the general increase in assets controlled by institutional investors that has risen from $13.8 trillion in 1990 to over $46 trillion in 2003, equalling roughly 157 per cent of OECD countries' GDP in the same year.

8. The SIF is a network of actors focusing on Socially Responsible Investing (SRI), understood as the integration of personal values and societal concerns with investment decisions. See, http://www.socialinvest.org.

9. The former Valdez Principles have been renamed CERES Principles in 1993.

10. Personal interview with CERES staff member, January 2004. A similar view is cited in Nash and Ehrenfeld (1996: 19-20): 'In 1988, when CERES was put together, there was not enough information to make intelligent investment decisions. What we were hearing from environmental advocates like Greenpeace and what we were hearing from companies was often diametrically opposed. There was no way to know about environmental performance without investigating these companies ourselves'.

11. Personal interview with CERES board member and participant in the early formation phase, March 2004.

12. Personal interview with CERES board member, January 2004.

13. The TRI forms part of the Superfund Amendments and Reauthorization Act of 1986, which requires companies to annually report on their releases to air, water and land (cf. White 1999).

14. Personal interview with CERES board member and participant in the early formation phase, March 2004.

15. Only a handful of companies signed the Valdez Principles after their public announcement in 1989.

16. Although the resolutions forwarded by CERES investors received only 9 per cent support on average (Nash and Ehrenfeld 1997: 513), the media coverage of the issue was quite substantial and started to threaten corporate reputations.

17. As Andy Smith, in 1993 a CERES board member and Director of Economic Justice, National Ministries of the American Baptist Churches, recalls the situation: 'When we announced the Valdez Principles in September 1989, little did we realize that it would take three-and-one-half years for the first large company to make the commitment. The endorsement of Sunoco is one of the watersheds in the history of CERES. The relationship that followed is like none I have ever experienced before. The most remarkable result has been the culture change that has occurred on both sides' (cited in: CERES 1999d).
18. See, for example, the administration's involvement in the apparel industry coalition that later led to the establishment of the Fair Labor Association.
19. Among the over 100 coalition members are large organisations such as the American Federation of Labor and Congress of Industrial Organizations (AFL-CIO), a voluntary federation of 53 national and international labour unions (representing more than 9 million members, the Sierra Club (representing more than 750,000 members), and the World Wildlife Fund (WWF US, representing more than 1.2 million members).
20. This limitation was only introduced in 1999 and does not take into account previous board memberships.
21. This position was renamed 'President' in 2005, but contains the same roles and responsibilities vis-à-vis the board of directors.
22. See website document (CERES 2003a), on file with author.
23. To avoid any legal conflicts or liabilities, the disclaimer to the CERES Principles clearly states: 'These principles are not intended to create new legal liabilities, expand existing rights or obligations, waive legal defenses, or otherwise affect the legal position of any endorsing company, and are not intended to be used against an endorser in any legal proceeding for any purpose'.
24. Personal interview with CERES staff member, November 2005.
25. Personal interview with CERES staff member, January 2004.
26. Personal interview with CERES staff member, January 2004.
27. Website document (CERES 2003b), on file with author.
28. Personal interview with CERES staff member, November 2005.
29. Personal interview with CERES staff member, January 2004.
30. Website document (CERES 2003a), on file with author.
31. Personal interview with CERES board member and participant in the early formation phase, March 2004.
32. A staff member estimates that there are around 10 ongoing dialogues with potential companies in 2005. Every year, two to four large corporations are expected to join CERES.
33. In the auto industry, for example, Daimler Chrysler, GM, Toyota and Honda quickly followed Ford in embracing the ISO 14001 standards.
34. For an excellent overview, see Raar (2001).
35. Personal interview with CERES board member, January 2004.
36. Personal interview with CERES board member, March 2004.
37. Personal interview with CERES staff member, January 2004.
38. Personal interview with CERES staff member, January 2004.
39. One of these new actors is CalPERS (California Public Employees Retirement Fund) that started to set aside $200 million in a private equity fund for environmental investing in 2004.
40. Personal interview with CERES staff member, January 2004.
41. CERES has successfully continued this strategy in 2004 and 2005. See, for example, Murray (2004); Harvey (2005).
42. Website document (CERES 2003d), on file with author.
43. Personal Interview with CERES staff member, January 2004.
44. The 2005 progress report on INCR (David Gardiner & Associates 2005: 5) states: 'INCR is a project of CERES, and CERES President Mindy Lubber is the director of INCR'.
45. Personal interview with CERES staff member, January 2004.
46. Personal interview with CERES board member, March 2004.

47. Tellus Institute and CERES not only shared the professional vision of corporate sustainability, but also office space in Boston between 1997 and 2003.
48. Integrating UNEP's Division of Technology, Industry and Economics (DTIE) in Paris was a logical step given their longstanding work on corporate best practices and reporting guidelines.
49. Grants by the Spencer T. and Ann W. Olin Foundation, as well as the United Nations Foundation, secured funding in the formation period.
50. In general, a comptroller is an officer who audits accounts and supervises the financial affairs of a corporation or a governmental body.
51. Personal interview with CERES staff member, November 2005.

# 7. Conclusions

Scholars theorising about global governance and the current shifts in world politics must grapple with a multitude of sources and spheres of authority, issue-specific sites of problem solving and a range of systems of rules spelling out roles and responsibilities for actors from both the profit and non-profit segment of civil society. It is a generally held view that state-centred approaches to problem solving are increasingly complemented by novel approaches, such as public policy networks and private forms of co-regulation between NGOs and companies. These new forms of global policy-making emerge at the intersection of two broadly discussed trends in world politics. First, there is the privatisation of regulation (Clapp 1998; Hummel 2001; Lipschutz 2002), a transfer of regulatory tasks from public actors, such as states and intergovernmental organisations, to a wide range of non-state actors, such as bond-rating agencies or the ISO. The second conceivable trend refers to the ubiquitous talk about partnership and cooperation as an emerging mode of interaction between divergent actors in world politics (McQuaid 2000; Dossal and Fanzo 2004). Empirically, these trends signify the transformation of global sustainability regulation from public international to private multi-stakeholder approaches (cf. Chapter 4).

Within the wider context of changing state–society relations, blurring boundaries between public and private responsibilities and a growing societal demand for effective and legitimate problem solving, this study examined in detail the phenomenon of private business co-regulation in the field of global sustainability politics. The empirical phenomenon of private business co-regulation appears to be new for several reasons: first, novel governance arrangements involve NGOs and business actors, agents who are believed to follow different logics of action in traditional accounts of international politics; second, they involve both the ordering elements of markets and norms, combining claims to moral superiority with the incentive of higher profits, enhanced brand reputation and access to new markets; third, they transcend state-centred, territorially-based forms of politics, thereby establishing new spaces of transnational organisation; and fourth, they are highly institutionalised, in the form of rules, standards and regulations, and thus go beyond the cooperation, alliances and partnerships discussed in most previous debates. My work on business regulation in global sustainability politics highlights the institutionalisation of private governance – in its dual understanding of emerging transnational rules and the influences that these rules have on actors – as one source of transnational organisation.

In this wider context, this study has answered four specific questions:

- What is the nature of private governance beyond the state within the general analytical framework of global governance?
- What explains the emergence of private governance systems in the forest certification and environmental reporting domain?
- What are the influences of private governance systems in global sustainability politics and how are they realised?
- Why do some governance systems have more influence than others?

With regard to these questions, I have argued that an analytical global governance perspective is most adequate in analysing the emergence and impact of private arrangements in world politics. In particular, I have introduced an institutional view towards business co-regulation that centres on constitutive and regulative rules and their systemic interaction as the prime unit of analysis. Within this context, I present four answers to the questions outlined above.

First, private governance beyond the state can be understood as a source of transnational organisation. From this perspective, the empirical phenomenon of private business co-regulation is analysed as a distinct arrangement of private governance that institutionalises the behaviour of profit and non-profit actors around a set of consciously devised and relatively specific rules. As a result, the regulative and constitutive rules give rise to a system of governance wherein actors take up specific roles and agree to have defined responsibilities. In contrast to views that find the transnational arena to be anomic and shapeless, the analysis of private governance suggests that not only is interaction at the international level increasingly rule-based, but at the transnational too.

Second, this study suggests that the explanatory factors for the emergence of private governance systems in sustainability politics are best thought of as a set of four integrated conditions, two at a macro- and two at a micro-level of political structures. In this view, macro-systemic transformations, resulting in the perceived or actual decline of public regulatory power, the emergence of civil society as a legitimate and credible actor and the increased environmental and social impact of corporate players, as well as powerful ideas that serve as common points of reference constitute the macro-level of necessary conditions. At the micro-level, the problem structure of interrelated interests and the available organisational resources of the actors involved, in particular public credibility and actual environmental impact, constitute the necessary conditions for private governance systems to emerge. In this sense, a macro/micro account overcomes some of the weaknesses of single-factor explanations and consequently bridges the divide between structure- and agency-based accounts of institutional formation.

Third, the impacts of private governance systems in global sustainability politics fall broadly within three categories: first, direct influence that is the result of the regulatory function of FSC and CERES; second, cognitive and discursive influences that result from inter-organisational learning processes and the general function of knowledge-brokering and dialogue-facilitation; and third, structural influences that are mainly the result of the integrative function of private governance systems. The empirical analysis of private forest governance and corporate environmental reporting suggests that in addition to their regulatory function through rules and standards, private institutions exert a number of cognitive and discursive influences whose magnitude goes beyond standard accounts of non-state politics.

And finally, with reference to explanations of the differences in the actual influence of private governance systems, this study engaged in a preliminary discussion of plausible explanatory factors of the influence of private governance. The analysis suggests that some variables hold promising explanatory power, while others could not be confirmed on the grounds of the empirical studies. First, the degree of formalisation of a private governance system (degree of obligation, precision of rules and delegation) is correlated with its actual influence through its regulatory function. The comparison suggests that a higher degree of institutionalisation leads to a higher level of influence. However, the data is inconclusive about the potential to generalise this finding, because the CERES case lends some credibility to an alternative explanation. In this view, CERES' rather modest influence through its actual regulatory framework was only possible because the rules were rather informal and lacked the precision of other private schemes. Therefore, flexible rules and a lower degree of formalisation may also be regarded as prerequisites for specific approaches to private governance. Second, the organisational structure and the quality of the network surrounding a private governance system explains the influence through its cognitive and discursive function. Here the comparison shows that in both cases a diverse network of actors and frequent interactions between them have induced substantial learning processes and discursive changes. Third, the comparison suggests that the higher the fit with existing transnational norms, the more influence a private governance system has through its function of downward integration. The reverse trend of upward integration seems to be best explained by existing political interests and contextual factors at the domestic level. Hypotheses based on problem and cost structures could not be verified. Here the analysis shows that a benign problem structure is conducive to cooperation in general. Whether this enhances the influence of private governance is unclear. In addition, cost structures play a different role in the regulatory effects of private governance than conventionally expected. Although corporate environmental reporting is less costly than forest certification, it has demonstrated less influence through its actual rules.

In more detail, this concluding chapter first critically discusses the institutionalisation of private governance in the light of the previous theoretical discussions and empirical findings. Subsequently, this chapter reviews the case studies from a comparative perspective to find a common narrative on the necessary conditions underlying the emergence of private governance systems and the functional patterns through which private governance is exercised. The subsequent section reviews the explanatory propositions suggested in Chapter 3 against the empirical evidence to develop some preliminary hypotheses of private institutional effectiveness. Subsequently, I address the question whether private governance constitutes an adequate answer to the challenges of sustainability within the context of accelerating globalisation. The concluding section discusses the findings from the wider perspective of global governance research and the initial question of adequate ways to understand the current nature of world politics in general. I close with some remarks about possible future directions of private governance research.

# THE NATURE OF PRIVATE GOVERNANCE: TOWARDS TRANSNATIONAL ORGANISATION

In this book, I have analysed the institutionalisation of private governance in global sustainability politics as a dual process. First, the institutionalisation of private governance refers to the emergence of private rules and the subsequent formalisation of the roles and responsibilities of actors within an institutional arrangement or 'system of governance'. Second, the term institutionalisation refers to the process of influencing distinct actors through this institutional arrangement and the functional pathways of influence. The key point is that the institutionalisation of private governance has led to new forms of transnational organisation as an emerging form of post-sovereign order in world politics, complementing international and predominantly state-based forms of organisation. Transnational organisation can be understood as the functional outcome of a multitude of governing processes, actor constellations and transnational policies that in sum give rise to structured behaviour in different types of actors across borders and functional domains. This observation goes beyond well-known forms of coordination and cooperation between private actors. Similar to claims that the international system shows signs of gradually becoming more rule-based and legalised, I contend that this holds true for the transnational level of world politics too. In particular, relations between actors excluding states and international organisations have become more institutionalised. I suggest in my analysis of two distinct forms of business co-regulation – corporate environmental reporting and forest certification – that private governance systems are one such source of transnational organisation that has largely been overlooked in many previous accounts of world politics and the shift from public to shared forms of political steering. As Djelic and Quack (2003b: 27) argue,

> the mainstream of the International Relations (IR) tradition pictures the transnational space as essentially anomic – a shapeless and structureless arena. Agents are essentially free and rational, maximizing their own interests with little burden being put on them by the space in which their action takes place.

My analysis of private governance as a source of transnational organisation is based on an institutional perspective towards business regulation. Such a perspective stresses the importance of rules for understanding both the formation and the effects of problem solving arrangements that involve the profit, as well as non-profit sides of civil society. In particular, I have argued that we can disaggregate a private governance system into two basic analytical components as the core units of analysis: first, the *constitutive* rules of an institution that describe the roles and responsibilities of actors within the system. These rules can be formal, as in the case of General Assembly voting procedures, eligibility for board membership and management structures, or informal such as in the case of internal conflict resolution. Changing these rules means changing the institution as a whole, altering its nature and appearance. The second type of rules I refer to as *regulative* rules, because they direct the behaviour of actors, in my empirical cases that of forest managers, forest producers, forest traders and small, medium and large corporations across a range of industrial and service sectors. Regulative rules take the form of standards or guidelines that give relatively concrete commands for behaviour such as:

> Sites of special cultural, ecological, economic or religious significance to indigenous peoples shall be clearly identified in cooperation with such peoples, and recognized and protected by forest managers. (cf. FSC 2000: §3.3)

or

> We will conduct an annual self-evaluation of our progress in implementing these Principles. We will support the timely creation of generally accepted environmental audit procedures. We will annually complete the CERES Report, which will be made available to the public. (cf. CERES 1993: §10)

Hence, an institutional perspective on the phenomenon of business co-regulation helps to understand how systems of governance operate through their constitutive (internal) and regulative (external) rules. The empirical evidence I have presented highlights the dual process of institutionalisation, the emergence of private rules in forestry and corporate environmental reporting on the one hand, and the influence of these rules on stakeholders and a wide range of political actors on the other. In both the forestry and the corporate reporting domain sets of rules have emerged that define the relations among participating organisations and create institutional constraints towards the standard-takers. As a result, distinct roles and responsibilities arise that indicate a transformation from predominantly strategic interactions to the institutionalisation of private governance. Novel roles, for example, include environmental organisations protecting firms from hostile media campaigns or corporations advocating the adoption of private rules among their own business associations. Responsibilities refer to a range of demands that result from both the regulative as well as the constitutive rules, and are directed at business actors and civil society organisations. For example, in addition to companies agreeing on the annual self-reporting of their environmental performance, environmental organisations and social investors agree to act in ways consistent with the overall mission of CERES. In the FSC case, responsibilities expand to independent certification bodies that are accredited according to FSC rules. In sum, the analysis of business co-regulation in the corporate environmental reporting domain and the forestry arena suggests that private governance systems that include both profit and non-profit actors are one important source of transnational organisation in world politics next to private inter-firm regimes and public–private partnerships.

The research presented in this book is embedded within the larger academic debate about the current nature of world politics, the direction of large scale transformations and the significance of these developments for political theory, both normative and analytical. Within the last decade, 'Global Governance' has emerged as a widely acknowledged debate about these issues. However, stemming from its history as a social science concept predominantly applied to the domestic level and debates about the changing role of government, a range of conceptual misunderstandings have plagued the academic debate about global governance, rendering attempts to build more general theory difficult. To locate this book within the global governance debate without losing its potential as a scientific concept to study the transformation of world politics, I have engaged in a reconstruction of global governance as a useful scientific concept (cf. Chapter 2). Arguing that we can identify three distinct conceptual understandings and academic debates connected to those understandings, I have situated my research within the analytical approach to global governance. This highlights distinct qualities of the governing process, such as non-hierarchical steering modes and the inclusion of private actors within that process. Based on this understanding, I have further proposed analysing global governance with a view to three distinct characteristics: its procedural, structural and output dimension.

Drawing on this distinction, three key lessons can be drawn from the analysis of private governance arrangements in global sustainability politics. First, with regard to the procedural dimension, the analysis has directed our attention to two different policy options: on the one hand, the market-based mechanisms of forest certification, and on the other the information-based approach of corporate environmental reporting. A key lesson is that private policies in global governance combine rational incentive structures with claims of moral superiority (doing well, while being good). In addition, and against conventional wisdom, both instruments rely more on the power of capital (large retailers and institutional investors) than on consumers. Second, with regard to the structural dimension of global governance, the analysis has highlighted new actor constellations, as well as a range of novel actors. Instead of thinking about private governance in terms of business and civil society as opposed categories, the case studies indicate that a more nuanced distinction may be helpful. For example, not all business actors have benefited equally from forest certification; and it was the commercial interests of social investors that created the initial demand for corporate environmental reporting. Finally, with regard to the functional dimension of global governance, this study indicates that norms and shared perceptions are emerging among a range of profit and non-profit actors at the transnational level. For example, the norm of environmental board representation is now a broadly accepted feature of good corporate governance. In sum, the research on private governance informs us about three substantial characteristics of global governance: first, problem solving is no longer confined to the international realm, but also manifests itself in private policies pursued by profit and non-profit actors at the transnational level; second, the architecture of global governance is maintained by a wide variety of actors, who should be perceived in wider terms than states, business and civil society; and third, next to the established area of international organisation, global governance also incorporates the emerging space of transnational organisation, visible in the increasing amount of norms, rules, standards, roles and responsibilities directed towards transnational actors.

To conclude, this book contributes to the broader debate about global governance and post-sovereign structures in world politics. It confirms the fundamental assumption that the Westphalian system is undergoing a profound transformation. Hence, it challenges the still widely held belief that '[t]he texture of international politics remains highly constant, patterns recur, events repeat themselves endlessly' (Waltz 1979: 66). As a result, the study also underscores the need for a new vocabulary, a new map to master this emerging post-sovereign territory (for example Ruggie 1993). However, the author remains cautious about the scope of the current transformation. Far from describing an even process, this study draws our attention to the fact that emerging transnational orders are highly uneven and the underlying rules and standards may have very different influences across geographical areas, actors and functional domains. Rather than uniform in its appearance, transnational organisation is still scattered, with pockets of private authority existing next to shapeless arenas. In addition, actors do not so much change their primary motivations as complement their strategic toolkit. Nevertheless, this study suggests that we are witnessing the gradual emergence of private governance and the development of a transnational arena of interactions that is increasingly rule-based, both in the sense of economic incentives and normative guidance.

## MARKETS, MORALS AND IDEAS: THE EMERGENCE OF PRIVATE GOVERNANCE SYSTEMS

Any attempt to understand the institutionalisation of private governance needs to account for the emergence of private rules in the first place. Hence, this section briefly reviews the theoretical propositions developed in Chapter 3 against the empirical evidence presented in Chapters 5 and 6. Most accounts of institution building at the transnational level have focused on functional explanations. In this view, private rules to regulate business have emerged as a reaction to increased capital flows across borders and the assumed decline in the regulatory capacity of states (Evans 1997; Haufler 2003). However, this functional causality has been questioned, because the need for new institutions becomes their sole explanation. Other theoretical approaches highlight single factors, such as transaction costs and changing market dynamics (North 1990) or the fundamentally political nature of institution building in the global economy (Fligstein 1996). In most cases these explanations fail to account for the interaction of larger systemic transformations and decisive conditions at the organisational level.

Taking this state of affairs into account, I have reviewed three literatures with a view to finding common assumptions about institutional formation in the transnational and private realms. Four key factors have emerged throughout the discussion: first, macro-systemic transformations of political and economic structures (globalisation) and emblematic events (catastrophes); second, discourses, ideas and models that provide actors with a frame of reference; third, the problem structure and distribution of interests; and finally, organisational resources that enable actors to reduce transaction costs or improve their strategic position. I have argued that these aspects can be grouped into two broad categories, one containing the micro-level conditions, the other those observable at the macro-level. Micro-level conditions include the problem structure and organisational resources, because these are dependent on the specific issue area and actors involved. Macro-level conditions, in contrast, relate to large-scale transformations in the structure of the international system, as well as to broad discourses and the resulting, more specific ideas and practices.

To avoid the shortcomings of most single-factor accounts, I have argued in favour of viewing the four conditions as forming an interconnected and integrated model that describes the emergence of private governance as a systematic interaction of distinct variables. This approach has proved helpful because it draws attention to a variety of inter-linkages between the different conditions. First, the relation between shifts at the macro-level and new resources for organisational actors, leading to new strategic choices; second, the relation between resources and the problem structure, addressing the ability of actors to construct a problem in the first place; and third, the relation between ideas that emerge and diffuse at the macro-level and the subsequent integration of competing perspectives in the actual negotiations.

Based on this analytical model, the case studies have discussed the emergence of private rules in the forestry and environmental reporting arena with regard to the demand side and the supply side. Drawing on the empirical evidence, a common narrative can be presented that highlights the key conditions for institutional formation. In this view, initial demand for private regulation was created by non-state actors that turned rather uncontroversial practices (timber trade and corporate reporting) into a business case. As the international or domestic supply of solutions was either missing or inadequate, the initial response of business actors was to seek solutions on their own. Examples include the wide array of self-labelling that occurred in response to civil society campaigns against large timber retailers and corporate environmental mission statements in the wake of the Exxon Valdez oil spill. However, these industry responses were heavily contested, because a neutral frame of reference was missing. Evaluating the rightness of these claims made by business actors was impossible. In this situation, supply for a solution came from the distinct mixture of organisational resources available. NGOs and other civil society actors traded their credibility and knowledge for the possibility of companies making concrete environmental improvements. As a fourth factor, widely accepted ideas, which had already met the test of practicability, helped to bridge existing differences and unite actors around a shared vision for future action. In the case of forestry, this idea has been the practice of certification, well known to representatives of environmental organisations and acceptable to business actors, because the application of a label resembles standard marketing strategies. In the corporate environmental reporting domain, actors used the framework of shareholder petitions developed in the US Anti-Apartheid movement. In addition, the idea of environmental reporting was not too far from conventional business experience, because it implies the same logic as financial reporting.

In sum, accounting for the emergence of private governance in the forestry and corporate environmental reporting domains centres around four explanatory factors. First, transformations at the macro-level have led to a reconfiguration of actors in world politics that have given rise to new strategies. With business actors becoming more visible on the transnational stage and states pursuing a policy of de-regulation, some NGOs shifted their attention to corporations directly. Second, adequate supply for a solution is available neither at the international nor the domestic level. Hence, private actors started to address their concerns bilaterally. Third, specific organisational resources created the grounds for cooperation, that is, finally, sustained and institutionalised through a broadly accepted idea. These ideas are embedded within broader discourses and reflect the wider institutional context of private governance formation. To conclude with Hall and Taylor, private business co-regulation as a consciously devised institution emerges in 'a world already replete with institutions' (1996: 953).

## RULES, ROLES AND RESPONSIBILITIES: THE INFLUENCE OF PRIVATE GOVERNANCE SYSTEMS

Next to analysing the conditions under which private governance systems have emerged in the forestry and corporate reporting domains, understanding the institutionalisation of private governance involves two central tasks: first, measuring the actual influences of distinct private governance systems on actors and structures, linking observed effects with the operation of governance systems through careful process tracing; and second, establishing plausible functional pathways of influence. To achieve this aim, I have provided a detailed discussion of approaches towards assessing the influence of private governance in section three of Chapter 3. Based on a thorough assessment of the literature on regime effectiveness and recent attempts to analyse the effectiveness of international organisations, I have argued for focusing on outcomes as the behavioural change of actors that are, in one way or another, affected by a private governance system. However, departing from most approaches in the environmental regime literature, I have proposed also including the unintended consequences of private governance in the analysis. Hence, Chapter 3 has introduced two complementary ways of assessing the influences of private governance: first, distinguishing between first- and second-order effects, the former referring to those influences directed towards standard-takers and organisations bound by the constitutive rules of an institution, the latter referring to influences occurring outside of the narrow institutional context, including effects on public actors or the wider economic arena. And second, distinguishing between the different characteristics of effects. First, private rules can be expected to have normative effects resulting from the concrete rules and standards if they become socially binding to a certain extent. Second, private rules can have discursive effects. In this case, private rules and procedures become a point of reference in transnational debates that can only be omitted by accepting high reputation costs and other strategic disadvantages. And finally, private rules are expected to have structural effects, such as shifts in markets or power relations between actors.

In addition to discussing different points of measurement, I have proposed assessing the influence of private governance along three hypothetical functions: *regulation, discourse and learning* and *integration*. The following paragraphs summarise the key findings.

(1)    The empirical evidence supporting the assumption that private governance arrangements influence actors through a regulatory function can be grouped into three categories: first, standard-uptake and the resulting changes in behaviour of standard-takers; second, structural changes, including shifts in markets, trade flows and profits; and finally, changes in perceptions and more deeply rooted norms. With regard to standard-uptake, the analysis shows that both schemes had only a modest influence in terms of their standards compared to the possible optimum of either the worldwide total forest cover or the total number of large transnational corporations. However, both cases show considerable and steady growth over time. In addition, a more qualitative stance towards standard-uptake suggests that both examples have been relatively successful in addressing influential players in their respective fields. While the FSC has mustered support from most of the large timber retailers, a key condition for enhanced influence in the forest certification domain, CERES has integrated large and well-known corporations, such as GM, Ford and McDonald's into its operations. With regard to establishing a clear causal link between the governance arrangement and behavioural changes resulting from standard-uptake, both cases suggest that this link exists. The analysis of corrective action requests in the FSC case has clearly shown that successful certification involves substantial behavioural changes as a result of FSC regulation, both in developed and developing countries and potentially across all types of forests. In a similar vein, the analysis of company performance reviews in the CERES case suggests that genuine behavioural changes have occurred at the individual company level.

However, the analysis has also shown that changes are less sustained in the core business areas of companies as they are in other, less business relevant, fields.

Turning to structural changes, both cases suggest the clear influence of private governance through its regulatory function. The FSC study suggests that private governance in the form of forest certification may systematically benefit some types of actors, while it clearly disadvantages other players in the field. For Northern companies, compliance with relatively tight standards is easy compared to those in developing countries because the regulatory environment is already tight in industrial nations and the key concept of sustainability has originated in Western societies. As a result, private environmental and social regulation could be considered more of a strategy tool for companies to drive others out of valuable 'green' markets, than a genuine steering mechanism towards sustainability. In addition, most producers, particularly those in the South, have been largely unable to secure premium prices for certified timber. On the contrary, the costs of certification are concentrated at the lower end of the supply chain due to the power of large retailers in the North. Rather than resulting in higher profits through a premium, certification has merely helped Southern companies to access new markets or at least to guarantee existing ones. As a general observation, private governance through certification has more impact on countries that have strong export markets to Europe and the US, while countries with weaker ties to green markets are less affected. In comparison, the CERES case also suggests that structural changes have occurred as a result of the regulatory function of private governance. In particular, the analysis underscores the often held assumption that companies can do well, while they are doing good.

The third category of evidence is normative changes. Both cases show clear normative influences, however, this is somewhat more obvious in the CERES case. In addition to defining the norm of 'sustainable forestry' within the industry, the FSC has also influenced perceptions of forestry in smaller community forests in the South. The analysis of CERES suggests that it has been an influential driver in establishing sustained environmental commitment on the highest ranks of corporate governance, as well as the general idea of corporate environmental mission statements and reporting. In sum, the empirical evidence collected throughout the case studies supports the assumption that one functional pathway of private governance is regulation.

(2) Comparing evidence on the cognitive/discursive function of private governance, four key observations have been made. First, private governance systems engage in the production and dissemination of information and knowledge. Both the FSC and CERES produce information and disseminate this information to their stakeholders and the wider public. Both cases indi-

cate that due to the information and knowledge produced within the governance systems, actors have changed their perceptions and behaviour. An illustrative example is CERES' media strategy of raising corporate concern about the impacts of climate change on their key business performance that can be credited with having influenced the recent increase in shareholder resolutions on climate change filed with US corporations.

As a second observation, the two cases support the assumption that private governance systems induce both internal and external learning processes. For example, the FSC can be considered a learning institution in two ways: first, the FSC shows distinct features of intra-organisational learning, mobilising the different experiences of its staff members and stakeholders and turning them into effective organisational restructuring; second, the FSC is an inter-organisational learning network of many diverse actors that facilitates effective learning processes exactly because of the organisational dissimilarity of its members.

Next to influencing actors through the production and dissemination of information and knowledge and their operation as large learning networks, both examples also provide an arena for solving problems of mutual concern. Although concrete changes are difficult to assess, actors have changed their strategic positions within a conflict situation, as a result of their involvement in the private governance arrangements.

Finally, private governance systems force other actors to react by establishing their own governance systems; they also engage in the dissemination of the regulatory model themselves. Within the forestry arena, the FSC has clearly forced other actors to react. To protect their specific interests, forest owners and the forest industry developed their own certification schemes (for example SFI, PEFC). In addition, governments have also implemented or supported certification schemes to protect their domestic forest industry (for example FFCS, MTCC). Next to the forestry arena, the idea of a stewardship council has been taken up in the fisheries sector (MSC), marine conservation (MAC) and the tourism industry (STCS). Similar to the FSC in forest certification, CERES has considerable influence on the policy domain of corporate environmental reporting as a whole. In response to CERES, a range of industrial groups undertook initiatives to define corporate environmental reporting; CERES also deliberately mainstreamed the corporate environmental reporting agenda and practice by establishing the GRI jointly with the Tellus Institute and UNEP. In sum, both case studies present strong support for the initial assumption that private governance systems realise some of their effects, in particular discursive effects, through a cognitive/discursive function. In addition, empirical evidence also suggests that structural changes occur as a result of the diffusion or deliberate implementation of the regulatory model to other contexts.

(3) With regard to the integrative function of private governance systems, two major conclusions can be drawn from the case studies. First, with regard to the downward integration of international and transnational norms and rules into private governance systems, the FSC and CERES are remarkably different. While the FSC integrates a range of international and transnational rules within its regulatory scope, CERES is largely unaffected by downward integration. Second, with reference to the reverse trend of private governance affecting public rule systems, both cases suggest that public actors at domestic and international levels have reacted to private governance systems. Reactions included the integration of private rules into domestic forestry law, the endorsement of FSC standards through public procurement policies in major Western European states and the impact of the reporting idea on international debates and international organisations. Table 7.1 summarises the findings with regard to the functional pathway of influence and the empirical evidence supporting it.

In sum, the analysis of two examples of private business co-regulation has shown that actors adopt new behaviour, take up new roles and responsibilities and thereby alter existing political and economic structures. The disaggregation of pathways of influence in three analytical components – regulatory, cognitive/discursive and integrative governance – highlights the specific processes through which actors' perceptions are changed, incentive structures altered and new practices institutionalised.

Although comparative data on private institutions is scarce, a number of scope conditions for the influence of transnational governance systems in the environmental domain can be identified. First, the regulatory influence of a given private institution may depend on – the real or perceived – legitimacy with regard to its principal stakeholders. In particular, in a competitive environment of numerous institutions existing in the same issue area, the support of a credible civil society may be a key asset. In addition to soft factors like legitimacy, the influence of private institutions may also depend on the willingness of states to support such governance forms (Raustiala 1997). However, the 'shadow-of-hierarchy' argument seems to be of minor importance, since most private arrangements in the environmental field have emerged in issue areas where public regulation was absent or at least fragmented and weak. Second, the cognitive and discursive influence of private institutions may largely depend on their internal setup as a learning organization (Pattberg 2005b; Siebenhüner 2005) and their ability to link themselves to larger influential discourses. For example, the FSC's strong influence on the global discourse on sustainable forestry and labelling can be interpreted as a result of its successful attempt to emphasize its link with the broader concept of sustainable development and the embodiment of a tripartite architecture therein (Bass 2002).

Table 7.1 Functions and influences of private governance systems in global sustainability politics

| Function | Evidence | Result | Order of influence |
|---|---|---|---|
| Regulatory governance | Standard-uptake; structural changes; normative changes | Growth in certified area and reporting companies; new markets and economic incentive structures; norm of 'sustainable forestry' and 'corporate environmental board representation' | First order (forest managers, forest traders, reporting companies) |
| Cognitive/discursive governance | Knowledge-brokering; learning; deliberative arenas; model diffusion | Discourse on climate risk, new roles and perceptions; competing regulatory schemes | First and Second order (NGOs, industry, pension funds) |
| Integrative governance | Upward integration; downward integration | International norms in private spaces; private norms in public spaces | Second order (governments, international organisations, local people) |

Finally, material and structural influences, for example the shifts in costs and incentive structures among producers, depend on larger systemic features of the international system. In particular, the integration of countries into world markets and particular into green markets in the North is a central condition for direct influence. This assumption is plausible in particular with regard to institutions that predominantly rely on market instruments (for example certification).[1] However, direct material and structural influences may well be induced by arrangements that have a less market-driven approach.

To conclude, with regard to the second element of institutionalisation, the measurable influence of private rules, this analysis suggests that private governance systems induce a number of concrete normative, discursive and structural changes within their issue area and beyond. However, far from constituting a uniform and evenly structured space, the transnational arena remains one of regulatory disparities, where in fact some actor relations and practices become more institutionalised, while others essentially remain ad-hoc and unrestrained from transnational norms and rules. In fact, the case studies indicate that – differing from other accounts that focus on standard-uptake and compliance – normative, cognitive and discursive influences are profound and hence should figure more prominently in future academic research.

## WHY ARE SOME PRIVATE GOVERNANCE SYSTEMS MORE INFLUENTIAL THAN OTHERS? SOME PRELIMINARY HYPOTHESES

After summarising the different functional pathways of private governance and the distinct influences attributable to private certification and corporate environmental reporting systems in global sustainability politics, this section proposes some preliminary explanatory variables with regard to varying degrees of influence across the two cases. The aim here is not so much to test existing hypotheses, but rather to devise plausible assumptions for future research on the influence and effectiveness of private governance arrangements in general and empirical forms of business co-regulation in particular. Hence, I briefly reassess the five hypotheses presented in the analytical framework in relation to the empirical material presented in Chapters 5 and 6 and discuss their explanatory potential and weaknesses. Similar to the analysis of influence, I discuss each functional pathway separately.

A first hypothesis with regard to the regulatory function of private governance systems is that the degree of formalisation determines regulatory effects. I assume that *the higher the degree of institutionalisation existing within a private governance system, the more influence the arrangement will have through its regulatory function* (predominantly normative effects).

Comparing the FSC and CERES with regard to their regulatory influence, a clear judgement is hard to make. On the one hand, both arrangements have only a modest impact on the stakeholders they address; on the other hand, both have been able to secure the support of influential players in their respective fields. However, if we concentrate on the rate of standard-uptake, the number of economic actors affected and the resulting geographical representation, as well as actual compliance, the FSC scheme seems to be more influential. Looking at the independent variable, the degree of formalisation, the FSC is clearly more formalised than CERES in at least three regards. First, while both schemes have a formal procedure for dealing with non-compliance (withdrawal of certification and endorsement), the FSC's corrective action request system is far more detailed and also more frequently applied. Second, the precision of the FSC rules is higher because they are more detailed (ten principles and 56 criteria in the FSC case compared to only ten broad principles in the CERES case) and adapted to regional and national circumstances through individual rule-making processes by the national initiatives. Finally, with regard to delegation, the FSC has outsourced monitoring and compliance management to independent certification bodies, while CERES relies on self-reporting. In addition, only the FSC has implemented detailed complaint procedures for certificate holders and other interested parties.

In sum, the FSC scores higher than CERES in all three dimensions of formalisation, thus supporting the initial assumption that a higher degree of formality within a private governance system will lead to a greater influence through its regulatory function. However, a closer look at the evidence presented in the case studies also lends support to an alternative explanation. In this view, CERES' more modest influence on business actors is the result of its informality compared to the FSC, because companies prefer informal arrangements to more formal ones out of fear of liability. For example, companies only joined the CERES coalition in greater numbers once a disclaimer had been added to the CERES Principles clarifying that these guidelines do not establish any legal claims against endorsing companies. In this case, a higher degree of formality might have led to even lower regulatory impact. To conclude, although the FSC displays a slightly higher impact through its regulatory function than CERES, and also scores higher on all three dimensions of formality, data on a causal relation is inconclusive because one can argue that it was in fact the lower formality that secured at least some business support for CERES in its early years.

A second hypothesis with regard to the regulatory function of private governance systems is that the costs of implementing private rules determine their regulatory effects. I assume that *the higher the costs of implementing the specific standards, the less influence they will produce on the behaviour of targeted stakeholders.*[2] Hence, governance systems that rely on more costly instruments such as certification (that might involve fundamental changes to existing production processes) are expected to be less influential through their regulatory function than those that rely on less costly approaches such as environmental reporting (wherein fundamental changes to production and management processes are only long-term goals).

With regard to this hypothesis, both case studies disconfirm the relationship between lower costs and higher regulatory influences. The CERES case shows that the lower costs of implementing private rules do not necessarily lead to higher impacts. In addition, companies that endorse the CERES Principles seem to take into account the benefits, such as close contact to environmental organisations and their knowledge, rather than the costs of corporate environmental reporting per se. The FSC case in contrast shows that although certification induces costs for producers that can neither be transferred to consumers nor retailers, business actors are willing to seek certification and implement the necessary changes to their forest operations.

A third hypothesis with regard to the regulatory function of private governance systems is that the problem structure determines the influence. However, taking a closer look at the existing literature on problem structure and institutional effectiveness, it becomes evident that rather than stipulating a causal relation between the benignity/malignity of a problem and the scale and scope of the regulatory effects, there seems to be a relation between the problem structure and the degree of cooperation. Hence, *I assume that a benign problem structure will result in more cooperative and institutionalised relations between actors than a malign problem will eventually produce.* In both cases analysed in this study, the problem structure was characterised by interdependent interests. In neither the FSC nor CERES cases could actors realise their goals independently given that public solutions to the problem were either missing or inadequate. In sum, although not conforming a strict causal relation, the two case studies support the initial hypothesis that a benign problem structure determines the likelihood of cooperation rather than its regulatory influence.

Turning to the cognitive/discursive function of private governance systems and the resulting outcomes, organisational design features warrant closer attention. One hypothesis is that the quality and scope of the supporting network determines influence through learning and other cognitive processes. The production and dissemination of knowledge, the facilitation of problem solving and learning processes, as well as the diffusion of regulatory models is contingent on the qualities of actors involved in a private governance system and adequate organisational procedures and structures defining their interactions. Hence, two relations may occur. First, *the more diversified in terms of expertise and experience a network is, the greater the cognitive/discursive influence of private governance that can be expected*; and second, *the more frequent the interactions between actors participating in the network are, the greater the cognitive influence of private governance that can be expected.*

Re-examining the first relation, both case studies support the hypothesis that diverse actors enhance the quality of discursive and learning processes and thereby lead to cognitive effects. In the FSC example, it was the dissimilarity of large environmental organisations, smaller indigenous groups and transnational corporations that facilitated learning among these actors about the structure of the timber trade and the potential to improve both profits and local livelihoods. I have made similar observations in the CERES case, where profit and non-profit actors used the informational resources of their adversaries to change their own strategies. With regard to the second relation, both case studies support the initial assumption that higher cognitive influences are facilitated by frequent meetings between actors who normally do not meet. Both the FSC and CERES show decisive organisational features in this respect; while the FSC brings together actors through its regional centres, national initiatives and its GA meeting, CERES has institutionalised frequent meetings through its company report review procedure and its annual conference.

With regard to the third functional pathway, the influence through integration, I hypothesise that fit and congruence with international, transnational and domestic norms explains the variance in observed outcomes. As private regulatory systems are voluntary in nature, they use a variety of strategies to gain authority vis-à-vis their stakeholders (cf. Cashore, Auld and Newsom 2004). One obvious strategy is relating their own standards to widely accepted norms that exist at the international or transnational level. Hence, *the more a private governance system refers to existing norms and rules for external authorisation, the higher the influence through its integrative function will be.* This relation has proved plausible in the FSC case, where the downward integration can be linked to widely accepted international norms or transnational schemes like the ISO. However, no such process could be observed in the CERES case. In addition to failing to account for the lack of downward integration in the CERES case, fit and congruence with international norms do not explain the second empirical observation, upward integration of private governance through public endorsement, procurement or integration into public regulatory schemes. Therefore, an alternative explanation that focuses on the political benefits of integrating private rules into public frameworks seems more plausible. For example, we could understand the fact that national procurement policies are calling for FSC certified timber products as a reaction to demand by green constituencies that are largely limited to some few OECD countries. To better assess this claim, future analysis should focus on domestic factors that facilitate public support for private policy making as opposed to those that hinder it. This would also direct our attention to the important question of the role of the state in facilitating or preventing private governance.

## LIMITS AND POTENTIAL OF PRIVATE GOVERNANCE

After having argued that private rules, once they have emerged among business and non-profit actors, construct a space of transnational organisation, although rudimentary and fragmented, what are the implications of these observations for our understanding of the current nature of world politics in general and the prospects of private problem solving in particular?

Both case studies have highlighted a range of shortcomings that need to be overcome in order for private governance systems to reach their full potential as alternatives to international problem solving. First, the FSC's current geographical disparity in terms of hectares certified reflects existing market structures in the international timber trade. Only producers from countries that are connected to the valuable green markets in the OECD have so far economically benefited from FSC certification and hence are willing to bear the higher costs of certification. However, as the tropical timber trade predominantly takes place between countries of the same region, the FSC's impact on the negative implications of forestry is structurally limited and constitutes a major backdrop against its own goal of solving the global forest crisis. In a similar vein, the limited standard-uptake in the CERES case constitutes a major drawback to its mission. Although the number of endorsing and reporting companies – in particular large TNCs – has steadily increased since the announcement of the original Valdez Principles, many companies originally targeted by CERES have refused to cooperate or joined alternative schemes.

A second limitation to private governance in global sustainability politics is the emergence of alternative schemes that compete over supporters, consumers and resources. While CERES has been successful in mainstreaming the idea of corporate sustainability reporting into the GRI, thereby offering a standard towards which other approaches can converge, the FSC has not been able to either prevent alternative schemes, nor implement an acceptable framework for mutual acceptance and, eventually, convergence.[3]

A third potential limitation derives from the current financial situation of private governance systems and potential remedies to this situation. Both the Council and the Coalition largely depend on the support of non-profit foundations such as the Ford, Rockefeller Brothers and MacArthur Foundations or the Wallace Global Fund. The FSC generated over $US14.3 million in the period from 1996 until 2003; but roughly 77 per cent came from donations and only 17 per cent were generated through membership fees and accreditation billings. The figure for CERES is roughly the same, standing at 19 per cent for the years 2003 and 2004. The problem that derives from the current financial situation can be described as the necessity for strategic reorientation towards more service-oriented behaviour. In both cases, first attempts to increase the budget by generating income through services such as consulting are evident, potentially threatening credibility and neutrality vis-à-vis key stakeholders.

And finally, four structural limitations to both market-based and information-based instruments in private governance have occurred throughout the discussion. First, a fundamental prerequisite for successful implementation and institutionalisation of corporate environmental reporting and forest certification is that the demand for public disclosure and sustainable timber is also institutionalised among a range of key actors. A second important issue is enforcement. Both in information-based as well as in market-based governance systems, enforcement is limited to naming-and-shaming practices and the constant public interest in annual corporate disclosure and acceptable forestry practices. A third matter of concern is the fact that participation in private governance schemes is voluntary. As a result, business actors have exit options that may strategically be used to lower the regulatory demand of private systems. Finally, companies only go beyond compliance if it is in their interests. Therefore, in order to attract business supporters, private governance systems in corporate environmental reporting and sustainable forestry must prove their added value to their economic stakeholders. A key observation with regard to the shortcomings of private governance systems is that, while some of them can be overcome within the confines of private governance, others can only be remedied by rethinking the private governance framework as a whole. However, does the trend towards private governance in general signify a regulation *of business* or rather a regulation *for business*?

Whereas some scholars are positive about the problem-solving capacity of private approaches in global sustainability politics, in particular the integration of corporations in decision making and implementation (Reinicke and Deng 2000; Ruggie 2002), others take a more critical stance and question the adequacy of private governance as such. For Newell (2005: 198), '[t]he marketization of environmental policy provides an illustrative case of a broader trend whereby the causes of environmental degradation emanating from global economic processes are increasingly protected from policy interference'.

In this view, private governance is embedded within a larger trend towards the marketization of problem solving, understood as an ensemble of strategies of market-based steering. The increasing application of these strategies is based on the belief that markets can provide public goods in the most efficient way. As I have discussed at some length in Chapter 4, the broad process of 'marketization' is a result of political decisions taken by governments, discursive strategies on the part of corporations and international organisations, as well as the result of the increasing salience of the 'ecological modernization' paradigm. Marketization is not only criticised for being unable to solve the basic problems of environmental degradation, but also for blurring the boundaries between politics and private decisions. As Lipschutz argues (2005a: 229), '[m]arkets are particularly weak arenas in which to seek political goals', because politics is about the visible aggregation of power, while markets disaggregate power into a number of rational, individual decisions.

What then is the significance of private governance and its increasing institutionalisation in global sustainability politics? The institutionalisation described in this book, the emergence of transnational rules and their subsequent influence on actors and structures in world politics, is not a conflict-free and cooperative process. Rather it signifies a profound reconfiguration of actor constellations and strategies within the global system. With governments losing the ability to solve problems unilaterally in a range of issue areas and corporations becoming increasingly visible through economic globalisation, civil society organisations have to redirect their strategies towards business directly. Governments on their part support this strategic reconfiguration because it effectively reduces their costs, while keeping them involved in the process at the same time. For business, civil society organisations emerge as potential partners for two reasons. First, their perceived credibility offers an effective legitimisation of corporate conduct; and second, cooperation has become more appealing as many large NGOs have become more business-like themselves. However, this current state of affairs is not necessarily stable. Actors always have alternative strategies: NGOs may use boycotts, corporations may return to unilateral behaviour and governments may ultimately decide to re-regulate specific issue areas. A key question therefore is: What forces stabilize or destabilize the current configuration of actors within the global sustainability arena and beyond?

In sum, the institutionalisation of private governance signifies a profound shift in the configuration of actors in world politics, a shift that is fundamentally political in nature. As a result, the limits of private governance are the structure of the contemporary economic system and the discourses that support this system. Whereas private governance can overcome its internal limitations, its external limit is simply the adequacy of applying the very same logic that brought much of the current problems about. However, judging this adequacy is a meta-question and cannot adequately be solved here.

## SUMMARY AND OUTLOOK

Increasingly, private policies at the transnational level complement, and in some cases even replace, public interventions. Although this empirical observation is frequently used to illustrate a shift in the dominant mode of governance in world politics, few scholars have actually tried to take a deeper look at the phenomenon and account for both the emergence and the influence of private forms of governance. In an attempt to contribute to the growing literature on global governance and the privatisation of politics, this book has analysed the institutionalisation of private governance in the global sustainability arena in some detail. Focusing on empirical cases of private business co-regulation, I have approached the question of why and how private forms of policy making emerge at the transnational level and how their influences can be analysed. In a first step, I have reconstructed the analytical approach towards global governance as a useful social science concept. Based on this understanding of global governance, Chapter 3 introduced the necessary analytical framework to make sense of private forms of business regulation and the conditions for its emergence and influence. In particular, I have argued for approaching the phenomenon of private governance from an institutional perspective, focusing on the constitutive and regulative rules, as well as the resulting roles and responsibilities of actors that constitute the governance system as a whole.

To place the analysis of forest certification and corporate environmental reporting in perspective, Chapter 4 engaged in a brief analysis of the phenomenon of global business regulation and its recent transformation to more transnational and private modes. The subsequent case studies have shed light on the process of institutional formation and the functional pathways of influencing actors and structures in global sustainability politics and arguably also beyond.

In sum, this book has attempted to close a research gap in the emerging field of private governance research and the broader global governance debate. At the conceptual level, the book has shed light on the many different uses of the term 'global governance' and argued for an analytical understanding to overcome existing barriers to theory-building. In addition, the discussion has also established 'private governance' as a useful conceptual tool, in particular with regard to emerging rules in the transnational arena. At the empirical level, this book closes a research gap left behind by the scholarly preoccupation with actor-centred approaches and the phenomenon of inter-firm cooperation and business self-regulation. With regard to the theoretical puzzle of institutional formation, I have argued for an integrated model to overcome the shortcomings of functional and other single factor explanations. Another theoretical contribution has been made by proposing three functional mechanisms of influence and carefully applying them to the empirical analysis. Finally, the book has proposed some preliminary explanations for the relative effectiveness of private business co-regulation that can be used as a point of departure for future research.

Science is never a monologue. It reaches its full potential only in constant dialogue, both with its precursors, but also with its future proponents. Therefore, this last paragraph sketches five avenues for future research. A first line of inquiry is about interlinkages between different transnational governance systems and international institutions or among transnational approaches themselves. Research could start from well-established assumptions about regime conflicts and functional interlinkages at the international level, paying attention both to the enhancing and limiting factors. A second possible route is influence/effectiveness. Building on well-established findings from international institutional theory and the preliminary conclusions reached in this book, future research could address the effectiveness of transnational governance in a more systematic manner by including large-n studies and comparison across cases within instruments (for example reporting) and across instruments within issue areas (for example human rights). Thirdly, any serious attempt to understand the emerging area of transnational organisation has to pay attention to the role of the state in this process. Future research therefore needs to assess the role of states in enhancing, preventing, sustaining and shaping governance at the transnational level. In addition, comparative research could also approach the distinct forms of statehood as a scope condition for influence and sustained impact. A fourth line of inquiry could place specific emphasis on the implications of private governance for North–South relations. In particular, future research could address the concrete implications of private governance on developing countries, as well as the potential for the integration of developing countries into private governance arrangements. This research could build on findings that highlight the crucial role of developing countries in global environmental and sustainability politics (Biermann 1998). Finally, the increasing interest in governance at the transnational level could also lead to a greater emphasis on normative questions and critical approaches to transnational governance. Given the widespread talk about partnerships and governance – both in academic and practitioner circles – a more nuanced and critical perspective may engage in further research into the factors that structure, limit or enhance the emerging arena of transnational organisation.

## NOTES

1. Cashore (2002) refers to this specific type of transnational environmental regimes as 'non-state market-driven governance'.
2. In addition to the cost of implementation, one could also study the relation between effectiveness and the cost of devising a private standard in the first place. Here, empirical testing becomes more difficult, because a high level of costs in the formation phase may simply cause some central actors to give up. If so, there may be no formal standard to study rather than a standard with weak influence on stakeholders.
3. However, depending on the individual standpoint, the emergence of alternative schemes could also be interpreted as a positive sign of effective policy diffusion.

# References

Abbott, Kenneth W., Robert O. Keohane, Andrew Moravcsik, Anne-Marie Slaughter and Duncan Snidal (2000), 'The Concept of Legalization', *International Organization*, **54** (3), 401-419.

Abrahams, Désirée (2004), *Regulating Corporations. A Resource Guide*, Geneva: UNRISD.

Albert, Mathias and Tanja Kopp-Malek (2002), 'The Pragmatism of Global and European Governance: Emerging Forms of the Political Beyond Westphalia', *Millennium: Journal of International Studies*, **31** (3), 453-471.

Anonymous (2000), 'CERES', *Green@Work*, **July/August**.

Arts, Bas (2002), 'Green Alliances of Business and NGOs. New Styles of Self-Regulation or Dead-End Roads?', *Corporate Social Responsibility and Environmental Management*, **9** (1), 26-36.

Arts, Bas (2003), *Non-state Actors in Global Governance. Three Faces of Power*, Köln: Max-Planck-Institute for the Study of Societies.

Arts, Bas, Math Noortmann and Bob Reinalda (eds) (2001), *Non-State Actors in International Relations*. Aldershot, UK: Ashgate.

Arts, Bas and Jan van Tatenhove (2000), 'Environmental Policy Arrangements: A New Concept', in H. Goverde (ed.), *Global and European Polity? Organizations, Policies, Contexts*, Aldershot, UK: Ashgate, pp. 223-228.

Association of Chartered Certified Accountants (2005), *CERES-ACCA North American Awards for Sustainability Reporting* 2005 [accessed 17 November 2005], available from: www.accaglobal.com/sustainability/awards/nasra/.

Atteslander, Peter (2000), *Methoden der empirischen Sozialforschung*, 9th edn, Berlin: Walter de Gruyter.

Atyi, Richard E. and Markku Simula (2002), 'Forest Certification. Pending Challenges for Tropical Timber', ITTO Technical Series No 19, Yokohama: ITTO.

Austin, James E. (2000), *The Collaboration Challenge. How Nonprofit and Business Succeed Through Strategic Alliances*, San Francisco: Jossey-Bass.

*221*

Baharuddin, Haji Ghazali and Markku Simula (1996), 'Timber Certification in Transition', ITTO Technical Series No 14, Yokohama: ITTO.

Ball, Jeffrey (2003a), 'Global warming may cloud directors' liability coverage', *The Wall Street Journal*, Wednesday, May 7.

Ball, Jeffrey (2003b), 'State aides mull pension funds and environment', *The Wall Street Journal*, Friday, November 21.

Balling, Richard (1997), *Kooperation. Strategische Allianzen, Netzwerke, Joint-Ventures und andere Organisationsformen zwischenbetrieblicher Zusammenarbeit in Theorie und Praxis*, Frankfurt a.M.: Peter Lang.

Balmaceda, Mary and Todd Larson (2000), 'Changing the Rules of the Game', *Green@Work* (**March-April**), 35-37.

Barnett, Michael and Martha Finnemore (2004), *Rules for the World: International Organizations in Global Politics*, Ithaca and London: Cornell University Press.

Barrett, Scott (1999), 'Montreal versus Kyoto. International Cooperation and the Global Environment', in I. Kaul, I. Grunberg and M.A. Stern (eds), *Global Public Goods. International Cooperation in the 21st Century*, Oxford: Oxford University Press, pp. 192-219.

Bartley, Tim (2003), 'Certifying Forests and Factories: States, Social Movements, and the Rise of Private Regulation in the Apparel and Forest Products Fields', *Politics & Society*, **31** (3), 433-464.

Bass, Stephen (2002), 'Global Forest Governance: Emerging Impacts of the Forest Stewardship Council', Paper presented at SUSTRA Workshop 'Architecture of the Global System of Governance of Trade and Sustainable Development', Berlin, 9-10 December.

Bass, Stephen, Xavier Font and Luke Danielson (2001), 'Standards and Certification. A Leap forward or a Step back for Sustainable Development?', in International Institute for Environment and Development (ed.), *The Future is Now, Volume 2*, London: International Institute for Environment and Development, pp. 21-31.

Bass, Stephen, Kirsti Thornber, Matthew Markopoulos, Sarah Roberts and Maryanne Grieg-Gran (2001), *Certification's Impact on Forests, Stakeholders, and Supply Chains*, London: International Institute for Environment and Development.

Beisheim, Marianne, Sabine Dreher, Gregor Walter, Bernhard Zangl and Michael Zürn (1999), *Im Zeitalter der Globalisierung? Thesen und Daten zur gesellschaftlichen und politischen Denationalisierung*, Baden-Baden: Nomos.

Bélanger, Claude (2003), *Concepts in Social Science and History* [accessed 15 October 2003], available from:
http://www2.marianopolis.edu/quebechistory/events/concepts.htm.

Bendell, Jem (2000), 'Civil Regulation. A New Form of Democratic Governance for the Global Economy?', in J. Bendell (ed.), *Terms for Endearment. Business, NGOs and Sustainable Development*, Sheffield: Greenleaf Publishing, pp. 239-255.

Bendell, Jem (2004), *Barricades and Boardrooms. A Contemporary History of the Corporate Accountability Movement*, Geneva: UNRISD.

Bendell, Jem and David F. Murphy (2000), 'Planting the Seeds of Change. Business-NGO Relations on Tropical Deforestation, in J. Bendell (ed.), *Terms for Endearment. Business, NGOs and Sustainable Development*, Sheffield: Greenleaf Publishing, pp. 65-78.

Bennett, R.J. and G. Krebs (1994), 'Local Economic Development Partnerships: An Analysis of Policy Networks in EC-LEDA Local Employment Development Strategies', *Regional Studies*, **28**, 119-140.

Bernauer, Thomas (1995), 'The Effect of International Environmental Institutions: How We Might Learn More', *International Organization*, **49** (2), 351-377.

Bernauer, Thomas (2000), *Staaten im Weltmarkt. Zur Handlungsfähigkeit von Staaten trotz wirtschaftlicher Globalisierung*, Opladen: Leske+Budrich.

Bernstein, Steven (2001), *The Compromise of Liberal Environmentalism*, New York: Columbia University Press.

Bernstein, Steven and Benjamin Cashore (2004a), 'Non-State Global Governance: Is Forest Certification a Legitimate Alternative to a Global Forest Convention?', in J. Kirton and M. Trebilcock (ed.), *Hard Choices, Soft Law: Combining Trade, Environment and Social Cohesion in Global Governance*, Aldershot, UK: Ashgate, pp. 33-63.

Bernstein, Steven and Benjamin Cashore (2004b), 'The Two-Level Logic of Non-State Global Governance', Paper presented at 45th Annual International Studies Association Convention, Montreal, March 17-20.

Betsill, Michele M. and Harriet Bulkeley (2004), 'Transnational Networks and Global Environmental Governance: The Cities for Climate Protection Program', *International Studies Quarterly*, **48** (2), 471-493.

Biermann, Frank (1998), *Weltumweltpolitik zwischen Nord und Süd. Die neue Verhandlungsmacht der Entwicklungsländer*, Baden-Baden: Nomos.

Biermann, Frank (2002), 'Institutions for Scientific Advice: Global Environmental Assessments and their Influence in Developing Countries', *Global Governance*, **8** (2), 195-219.

Biermann, Frank and Steffen Bauer (2005a), 'Managers of Global Governance: Assessing and Explaining the Effectiveness of Intergovernmental Organisations', Amsterdam, Berlin, Oldenburg: Global Governance Project.

Biermann, Frank and Steffen Bauer (eds) (2005b), *A World Environment Organization: Solution or Threat for Effective International Environmental Governance?*, Aldershot, UK: Ashgate.

Biermann, Frank and Philipp Pattberg (2004), 'Governance zur Bewahrung von Gemeinschaftsgütern. Grundprobleme und Institutionen der Umweltpolitik', in S. Lange and U. Schimank (eds), *Governance und gesellschaftliche Integration*, Opladen: VS Verlag für Sozialwissenschaften, pp. 169-187.

Biersteker, Thomas J. and Rodney Bruce Hall (2002), 'Private Authority as Global Governance', in R.B. Hall and T.J. Biersteker (eds), *The Emergence of Private Authority in Global Governance*, Cambridge: Cambridge University Press, pp. 203-222.

Börzel, Tanja A. (1997), *Policy Networks. A New Paradigm for European Governance?*, Florence: European University Institute.

Börzel, Tanja A. and Thomas Risse (2005), 'Public–Private Partnerships: Effective and Legitimate Tools of International Governance', in E. Grande and L.W. Pauly (eds), *Complex Sovereignty: Reconstituting Political Authority in the Twenty-first Century*, Toronto: Toronto University Press, pp. 195-216.

Bowling, Jill (2000), 'A Workers' View on Sustainable Forestry', in K. v. Gadow, T. Pukkala and M. Tomé (eds), *Sustainable Forest Management*, Dordrecht: Kluwer Academic Publishers, pp. 121-152.

Boyer, Robert and Daniel Drache (eds) (1996), *States Against Markets. The Limits of Globalization*, London, New York: Routledge.

Braithwaite, John and Peter Drahos (2000), *Global Business Regulation*, Cambridge: Cambridge University Press.

Brand, Ulrich (2003), 'Nach dem Fordismus: Global Governance als der neue hegemoniale Diskurs des Internationalen Politikverständnisses', *Zeitschrift für Internationale Beziehungen*, **10** (1), 143-166.

Brink, Patrick ten (ed.) (2002), *Voluntary Environmental Agreements. Process, Practice and Future Use*, Sheffield, UK: Greenleaf Publishing.

Broad, Robin and John Cavanagh (1999), 'The Corporate Accountability Movement: Lessons and Opportunities', *The Fletcher Forum on World Affairs*, **23** (2), 151-169.

Brown, Becky J., Mark E. Hanson, Diana M. Liverman and Robert W. Meredeth (1987), 'Global Sustainability: Toward Definition', *Environmental Management*, **11** (6), 713-719.

Burch, Kurt (2000), 'Changing the Rules: Reconceiving Change in the Westphalian System', *International Studies Review* (Special Issues: Continuity and Change in the Westphalian Order), 181-209.

Burger, D. (2000), 'Making Rio Work. The Vision of Sustainable Development and its Implementation through Forest Certification', in K.

v. Gadow, T. Pukkala and M. Tomé, *Sustainable Forest Management*, Dordrecht: Kluwer Academic Publishers, pp. 153-192.

Burr, Barry B. (2003), 'Climate change: the new off-balance-sheet risk', *Pensions & Investments*, Monday, July 21.

Business for Social Responsibility (2003), *Overview of Corporate Social Responsibility* [accessed 30 November 2004], available from: http://www.bsr.org/CSRResources/IssueBriefDetail.cfm?DocumentID=48 809.

Cable, Vincent (1999), *Globalization and Global Governance*, London, New York: Pinter.

Camilleri, Joseph A. and Jim Falk (1992), *The End of Sovereignty? The Politics of a Shrinking and Fragmenting World*, Aldershot, UK and Brookfield, US: Edward Elgar.

Carson, Rachel (2002 [1962]), *Silent Spring*, Boston: Houghton Mifflin.

Cashore, Benjamin (2002), 'Legitimacy and the Privatization of Environmental Governance: How Non-State Market-Driven (NSMD) Governance Systems gain Rule-Making Authority', *Governance: An International Journal of Policy, Administration, and Institutions*, **15** (4), 503-529.

Cashore, Benjamin, Graeme Auld and Deanna Newsom (2004), *Governing Through Markets. Forest Certification and the Emergence of Non-State Authority*, New Haven and London: Yale University Press.

CERES (1993), *The CERES Principles*, Boston: CERES.

CERES (1995), *CERES Report Standard Form 1994*, Boston: CERES.

CERES (1998), *Annual Report 1997*, Boston: CERES.

CERES (1999a), *Bylaws of CERES, Inc.*, Boston: CERES.

CERES (1999a), *CERES Five-Year Review of Sunoco, Inc. A Collaborative Road to Progress*, Boston: CERES.

CERES (1999c), *CERES Report Standard Form 1998*, Boston: CERES.

CERES (1999d), *Tenth Anniversary Report 1998*, Boston: CERES.

CERES (2001), *Drawing on the Wisdom of Us All. Annual Report 2000*, Boston: CERES.

CERES (2002a), *CERES Performance Review of General Motors Corporation*, Boston: CERES.

CERES (2002b), *CERES Reporting Requirements for Small Enterprises and Non-Profits*, Boston: CERES.

CERES (2002c), *Life in the Edge Environment. Annual Report 2001*, Boston: CERES.

CERES (2003a), *About Us: Frequently Asked Questions* 2003 [accessed 11 December 2003], available from www.ceres.org/about/questions.htm.

CERES (2003b), *About Us: History* 2003 [accessed 11 December 2003], available from www.ceres.org/about/history.htm.

CERES (2003c), *Electric Power, Investors, and Climate Change. A Call to Action*, Boston: CERES.

CERES (2003d) *Our Work: Corporate Accountability Workshop 2003* [accessed 28 December 2003], available from www.ceres.org/our_work/dialogue_orientation.htm.

CERES (2004), *CERES 2003 Annual Report*, Boston: CERES.

CERES (2005a), *About Us* 2005 [accessed 18 November 2005], available from: www.ceres.org/ceres/.

CERES (2005b), *CERES 2005 Conference: Building Equity, Reducing Risk* 2005 [accessed 17 November 2005], available from: www.ceres.org/events/conference/05/.

CERES (2005c), *ExxonMobil Investors Give Record Voting Support to Climate Change Resolution* 2005 [accessed 9 November 2005], available from: www.ceres.org/news/pf.php?nid=115.

CERES (2005d), *Investor Programs* 2005 [accessed 9 November 2005], available from www.ceres.org/investorprograms/shareholder_action.htm.

CERES (2005e), *Sustainability Reporting* 2005 [accessed 9 November 2005], available from www.ceres.org/sustreporting/stakeholder_engagement.htm.

Chayes, Abram and Antonia Handler Chayes (1995), *The New Sovereignty. Compliance with International Regulatory Agreements*, Cambridge: Harvard University Press.

Chisholm, Rupert, F. (1998), *Developing Network Organizations. Learning from Practice and Theory*, Reading: Addison-Wesley.

Clapp, Jennifer (1998), 'The Privatization of Global Environmental Governance: ISO 14000 and the Developing World', *Global Governance. A Review of Multilateralism and International Organizations*, 4 (3), 295-316.

Clapp, Jennifer (2005), 'Transnational Corporations and Global Environmental Governance', in P. Dauvergne (ed.), *Handbook of Global Environmental Politics*, Cheltenham, UK and Northampton, MA, USA: Edward Elgar, pp. 284-297.

Cogan, Douglas G. (2003), *Corporate Governance and Climate Change: Making the Connection*, Boston: CERES and the Investor Responsibility Research Center.

Collier, David and James Mahoney (1996), 'Insights and Pitfalls: Selection Bias in Qualitative Research', *World Politics*, 49 (1), 56-91.

Commission of the European Communities (2001), *Promoting a European Framework for Corporate Social Responsibility*, Brussels: Commission of the European Communities.

Commission on Global Governance (1995), *Our Global Neighbourhood. The Report of the Commission on Global Governance*, Oxford: Oxford University Press.

Confederation of European Paper Industries (2001), *Comparative Matrix of Certification Schemes*, Brussels: CEPI.

Councell, Simon and Kim Terje Loraas (2002), Trading In Credibility. The Myth and Reality of the Forest Stewardship Council, London: Rainforest Foundation.

Cox, Robert W. (1987), *Production, Power, and World Order*, New York: Columbia University Press.

Cutler, A. Claire, Virginia Haufler and Tony Porter (eds) (1999a), *Private Authority and International Affairs*, Albany: State University of New York Press.

Cutler, A. Claire, Virginia Haufler and Tony Porter (1999b), 'Private Authority and International Affairs', in C.A. Cutler, V. Haufler and T. Porter (eds), *Private Authority and International Affairs*, Albany: State University of New York Press, pp. 3-28.

Cutler, A. Claire, Virginia Haufler and Tony Porter (1999c), 'The Contours and Significance of Private Authority in International Affairs', in C.A. Cutler, V. Haufler and T. Porter (eds), *Private Authority and International Affairs*, Albany: State University of New York Press, pp. 333-376.

Dankers, Cora (2003), Environmental and Social Standards, Certification and Labelling for Cash Crops, Rome: FAO.

David Gardiner & Associates, LLC (2005), *Investor Progress on Climate Change. Results Achieved since the 2003 Institutional Investor Summit on Climate Risk*, Boston: CERES.

Davis-Walling, Paige and Stuart A. Batterman (1997), 'Environmental Reporting by the Fortune 50 Firms', *Environmental Management*, **21** (6), 865-875.

de Camino, R. and M. Alfaro (1998), *Certification in Latin America. Experience to Date*, London: ODI.

Department of Environmental Protection Pennsylvania (2005), *Answer to Questions about the Ceres Principles 2005* [accessed 3 November 2005], available from: www.dep.state.pa.us/deputate/pollprev/tech_assistance/toolbox/ceres/answ ers.htm.

Detomasi, David (2002), 'International Institutions and the Case for Corporate Governance: Toward a Distributive Governance Framework?', *Global Governance. A Review of Multilateralism and International Organizations*, **8** (4), 421-442.

Deutscher Bundestag, Study Commission 'Globalization of the World Economy – Challenges and Answers' (2002a), *Schlussbericht der Enquete-Kommission "Globalisierung der Weltwirtschaft"*, Opladen: Leske+Budrich.

Deutscher Bundestag, Study Commission 'Globalization of the World
Economy – Challenges and Answers' (2002b), Short Version of the Final
Report, Berlin: German Bundestag, 14th Legislative Period.

Deutscher Bundestag, Study Commission 'Vorsorge zum Schutz der
Erdatmosphäre' (1994), *Schutz der Grünen Erde. Klimaschutz durch
umweltgerechte Landwirtschaft und den Erhalt der Wälder*, Bonn:
Economica.

Dicken, Peter (1998), *Global Shift – Transforming the World Economy*, 3rd
edn, London: Paul Chapman Publishing.

DiMaggio, Paul J. and Walter W. Powell (1983), 'The Iron Cage Revisited:
Institutional Isomorphism and Collective Rationality in Organizational
Fields', *American Sociological Review*, **48** (2), 147-160.

Dimitrov, Radoslav S. (2004), 'Hostage to Norms: Global Forest Policy and
International Environmental Norms', Paper presented at 45th Annual
International Studies Association Convention, Montreal, March 17-20.

Dingwerth, Klaus (2005a), 'The Democratic Legitimacy of Public-Private
Rule-Making: What Can We Learn from the World Commission on
Dams?', *Global Governance*, **11** (1), 65-83.

Dingwerth, Klaus (2005b), The Democratic Legitimacy of Transnational
Rule-Making. Normative Theory and Empirical Practice, Berlin.

Dingwerth, Klaus (forthcoming), 'Global Governance and the South: The
Affirmative Procedures of the Forest Stewardship Council, *Global
Governance. A Review of Multilateralism and International
Organizations*.

Dingwerth, Klaus and Philipp Pattberg (2006a), 'Global Governance as a
Perspective on World Politics', *Global Governance. A Review of
Multilateralism and International Organizations*, **12** (2), 185-203.

Dingwerth, Klaus and Philipp Pattberg (2006b), 'Was ist Global
Governance?', *Leviathan: Berliner Zeitschrift für Sozialwissenschaft*, **34**
(3), 377-399.

Dingwerth, Klaus and Philipp Pattberg (forthcoming), *The Scale and Scope
of Transnational Rule-making*, Amsterdam, Berlin, Oldenburg: The
Global Governance Project.

Dion, Douglas (1998), 'Evidence and Inference in the Comparative Case
Study', *Comparative Politics*, **30** (2), 127-145.

Dixon, John A. and Louise A. Fallon (1989), 'The Concept of Sustainability:
Origins, Extensions, and Usefulness for Polity', *Society and Natural
Resources*, (2), 73-84.

Djelic, Marie-Laure and Sigried Quack (2003a), 'Governing Globalization –
Bringing Institutions back in', in M.-L. Djelic and S. Quack (eds),
*Globalization and Institutions. Redefining the Rules of the Economic*

*Game*, Cheltenham, UK and Northampton, MA, USA: Edward Elgar, pp. 1-14.

Djelic, Marie-Laure and Sigried Quack (2003b), 'Theoretical Building Blocks for a Research Agenda Linking Globalization and Institutions', in M.-L. Djelic and S. Quack (eds), *Globalization and Institutions. Redefining the Rules of the Economic Game*, Cheltenham, UK and Northampton, MA, USA: Edward Elgar, pp. 15-34.

Doane, Deborah (2005), *The Myth of CSR*, Stanford: Stanford Graduate School of Business.

Dodgson, Mark (1993), 'Organizational Learning: A Review of Some Literatures', *Organization Studies*, **14** (3), 375-394.

Domask, Joseph (2003), 'From Boycotts to Global Partnerships: NGOs, the Private Sector, and the Struggle to Protect the World's Forests', in J.P. Doh and H. Teegen (eds), *Globalization and NGOs. Transforming Business, Government, and Society*, Westport, CT: Praeger, pp. 157-185.

Doremus, Paul N., William W. Keller, Louis W. Pauly and Simon Reich (1998), *The Myth of the Global Corporation*, Princeton, NJ: Princeton University Press.

Dossal, Amir, and Michelle Fanzo (2004), 'Partnerships for a Better World: Working Together to Preserve the Planet', *Natural Resources Forum*, 28, 333-337.

Drezner, Daniel W. (2004), 'The Global Governance of the Internet: Bringing the State Back In', *Political Science Quarterly*, **119** (3), 477-498.

Easton, David (1965), *A Systems Analysis of Political Life*, New York: Wiley.

Ebeling, Johannes (2005), 'Market-based Conservation and Global Governance. Can Forest Certification Compensate for Poor Environmental Law Enforcement? Insights from Ecuador and Bolivia', M.A. Dissertation, Albert-Ludwigs-Universität, Freiburg i. Br.

Eckstein, Harry (1975), 'Case Study and Theory in Political Science', in F.I. Greenstein and N.W. Polsby (eds), *Handbook of Political Science*, Reading: Addison-Wesley, pp. 79-138.

Efinger, Manfred, Peter Mayer and Gudrun Schwarzer (1993), 'Integrating and Contextualizing Hypotheses. Alternative Paths to Better Explanations of Regime Formation?', in V. Rittberger (ed.), *Regime Theory and International Relations*, Oxford: Clarendon Press, pp. 252-281.

Eisler, Riane (1996), 'Creating Partnership Futures', *Future*, **28** (6/7), 563-566.

Eisner, Mark Allen (2004), 'Corporate Environmentalism, Regulatory Reform, and Industry Self-Regulation: Toward Genuine Regulatory Reinvention in the United States', *Governance: An International Journal of Policy, Administration, and Institutions*, **17** (2), 145-167.

Elliott, Chris (1996), 'Certification as a Policy Instrument', in V.M. Viana, J. Ervin, R.Z. Donovan, C. Elliott and H. Gholz (eds), *Certification of Forest Products. Issues and Perspectives*, Washington, DC: Island Press, pp. 83-92.

Elliott, Chris (2004) *Eco-labelling: Short-lived Fad or Growing Trend?* [accessed 20 May 2005], available from: http://www.panda.org/news_facts/newsroom/features/news.cfm?uNewsID =14990.

Elliott, Lorraine (2004), *The Global Politics of the Environment*, 2nd edn, Basingstoke: Macmillan Press.

Enderle, G. and G. Peters (1998), *A Strange Affair? The Emerging Relationship between NGOs and Transnational Companies*, London: PricewaterhouseCoopers.

Environics International Ltd. (1999), *The Millennium Poll on Corporate Social Responsibility*, Toronto: Environics International Ltd.

Eritja, Mar Campins (ed.) (2004), *Sustainability Labelling and Certification*, Madrid: Marcial Pons.

European Chemical Industry Council (2002), *Responsible Care 2002. Status Report: Europe*, Brussels: CEFIC.

Evans, Peter (1997), 'The Eclipse of the State? Reflections on Stateness in an Era of Globalization', *World Politics*, **50** (1), 62-87.

Falk, Richard (1995), *On Humane Governance: Toward a New Global Politics*, Pennsylvania: Pennsylvania University Press.

Falkner, Robert (2003), 'Private Environmental Governance and International Relations: Exploring the Links', *Global Environmental Politics*, **3** (2), 72-87.

Feder, Barnaby J. (2003a), 'Pension funds plan to press global warming as an issue', *The New York Times*, Saturday, November 22.

Feder, Barnaby J. (2003b), 'Report faults big companies on climate', *The New York Times*, Thursday, July 10.

Finkelstein, Lawrence S. (1995), 'What is Global Governance?', *Global Governance. A Review of Multilateralism and International Organizations*, **1** (3), 367-371.

Finnemore, Martha and Kathryn Sikkink (1998), 'International Norm Dynamics and Political Change', *International Organization*, **52** (4), 887-917.

Fiol, Marlene C. and Marjorie A. Lyles (1995), 'Organizational Learning', *Academy of Management Review*, **10** (4), 803-813.

Fligstein, Neil (1996), 'Markets as Politics: A Political–Cultural Approach to Market Institutions', *American Sociological Review*, **61**, 656-673.

Florini, Ann M. (ed.) (2000), *The Third Force. The Rise of Transnational Civil Society*. Washington, DC: Carnegie Endowment for International Peace.

Food and Agriculture Organisation of the United Nations (1993), *Forest Resources Assessment 1990*, Rome: FAO.

Food and Agriculture Organisation of the United Nations (1999), FAO Yearbook. Forest Products 1993–1997, Rome: FAO.

Food and Agriculture Organisation of the United Nations (2001), Global Forest Resource Assessment. Main Report, Rome: FAO.

Frank, Thomas M. (1990), *Power of Legitimacy Among Nations*, New York: Oxford University Press.

Freeman, R. Edward (1984), *Strategic Management: A Stakeholder Approach*, Boston: Pitman.

Friedman, Michael (1970), 'The social responsibility of business is to increase its profits', *New York Times Magazine*, September 13.

Friends of the Earth (2002), *Towards Binding Corporate Accountability: FoEI Position Paper for the WSSD 2002* [accessed 30 November 2004], available from:
http://www.foe.co.uk/pubsinfo/briefings/html/20020730133722.html.

FSC (1999), Roles, Rights, and Responsibilities of the FSC Players, Oaxaca: FSC A.C.

FSC (2000), *FSC Principles and Criteria*, Oaxaca: FSC A.C.

FSC (2001), *2000 Annual Report*, Oaxaca: FSC A.C.

FSC (2002a), Charting Our Future: Annual Report 2001, Oaxaca: FSC A.C.

FSC (2002b), Forest Stewardship Council A.C. By-Laws, Bonn: FSC A.C.

FSC (2002c), *FSC Accreditation Manual*, Oaxaca: FSC A.C.

FSC (2002d), *Statutes*, Oaxaca: FSC A.C.

FSC (2003), *2002 Annual Report*, Bonn: FSC A.C.

FSC (2004a), *FSC Financial Report 2003*, Bonn: FSC A.C.

FSC (2004b), Looking to the Future: 10 Years of FSC, Bonn: FSC A.C.

FSC (2005a), News + Notes. An Information Service of the Forest Stewardship Council. Annual Review 2004, **3** (1).

FSC (2005b) News + Notes. An Information Service of the Forest Stewardship Council, **3** (6).

FSC and WWF-Germany (2002), *Forest Stewardship Council. Political Instrument, Implementation and Concrete Results for Sustainability since 1993*, Frankfurt a. M.: FSC/WWF Germany.

FSC Arbeitsgruppe Deutschland (2005), *Ergebnisse der Fragebogenaktion für Wald21 'FSC-Zertifizierung im Kommunalwald'*, Freiburg i. Br.: FSC Deutschland.

Fuchs, Doris A. (2002), 'Globalization and Global Governance: Discourses on Political Order at the Turn of the Century', in D. Fuchs and F.

Kratochwil (eds), *Transformative Change and Global Order: Reflections on Theory and Practice*, Münster: LIT Verlag, pp. 1-23.

Fuchs, Doris A. (2004), 'Channels and Dimensions of Business Power in Global Governance', Paper presented at 45th Annual International Studies Association Convention, Montreal, March 17-20.

Garcia-Johnson, Ronie (2001), 'Certification Institutions in the Protection of the Environment: Exploring the Implications for Governance', Paper presented at 23rd Annual Research Conference of the Association for Public Policy, Analysis and Management, Washington, DC, November 1.

Garner, B.A. (ed.) (1999), *Black's Law Dictionary*, St. Paul: West Group.

Gereffi, Gary, Ronie Garcia-Johnson and Erika N. Sasser (2001), 'The NGO-Industrial Complex', *Foreign Policy*, **July/August**, 56-65.

Germain, Randall D. and Michael Kenny (1998), 'Engaging Gramsci: International Relations Theory and the New Gramscians', *Review of International Studies*, **24** (1), 3-21.

Gerring, John (2004), 'What is a Case Study and What is it Good for?', *American Political Science Review*, **98** (2), 341-354.

Gerring, John and Paul A. Barresi (2003), 'Putting Ordinary Language to Work. A Min–Max Strategy of Concept Formation in the Social Sciences', *Journal of Theoretical Politics*, **15** (2), 201-232.

Gibson, Robert B. (ed.) (1999), *Voluntary Initiatives: The New Politics of Corporate Greening*, Ontario: Broadview Press.

Giddens, Anthony (1984), *The Constitution of Society. Outline of the Theory of Structuration*, Cambridge: Polity Press.

Gill, Stephen (1997), 'Transformation and Innovation in the Study of World Order', in S. Gill and J.H. Mittelman (eds), *Innovation and Transformation in International Studies*, Cambridge: Cambridge University Press, pp. 5-24.

Gill, Stephen (ed) (1993), *Gramsci, Historical Materialism and International Relations*, Cambridge: Cambridge University Press.

Gilpin, Robert (2001), *Global Political Economy. Understanding the International Economic Order*, Princeton, NJ: Princeton University Press.

Glasbergen, Pieter and R. Groenenberg (2001), 'Environmental Partnership in Sustainable Energy', *European Environment*, **11** (1), 1-13.

Global Reporting Initiative (2002), *Sustainability Reporting Guidelines 2002*, Boston: Global Reporting Initiative.

Goel, Ran (2005), 'Guide to Instruments of Corporate Responsibility. An Overview of 16 Key Tools for Labor Fund Trustees', Toronto: York University.

Goertz, Gary (2003), 'Cause, Correlation, and Necessary Conditions', in G. Goertz and H. Starr (eds), *Necessary Conditions. Theory, Methodology, and Applications*, Lanham: Rowman&Littelfield Publishers, pp. 47-64.

Göhler, Gerhard (1994), 'Politische Institutionen und ihr Kontext. Begriffliche und konzeptionelle Überlegungen zur Theorie politischer Institutionen', in G. Göhler (ed.), *Die Eigenart der Institution. Zum Profil politischer Institutionentheorie*, Baden-Baden: Nomos, pp. 19-46.

Goldsmith, Edward (1972), *A Blueprint for Survival*, Boston: Houghton Mifflin.

Goldstein, Judith L., Miles Kahler, Robert O. Keohane and Anne-Marie Slaughter (eds) (2001), *Legalization and World Politics*, Cambridge: MIT Press.

Gordenker, Leon and Thomas G. Weiss (1996), 'Pluralizing Global Governance: Analytical Approaches and Dimensions', in T.G. Weiss and L. Gordenker (eds), *NGOs, the UN, and Global Governance*, Boulder, CO: Westview, pp. 17-47.

Gordon, Kathryn and Maiko Miyake (1999), 'Deciphering Codes of Conduct: A Review of their Content', Paris: OECD.

Gouldson, Andrew and Joseph Murphy (1997), 'Ecological Modernisation: Economic Restructuring and the Environment', *The Political Quarterly*, **68** (5), 74-86.

Grafstein, R. (1992), *Institutional Realism: Social and Political Constraints on Rational Actors*, New Haven and London: Yale University Press.

Gray, Barbara (1989), *Collaborating. Finding Common Ground for Multiparty Problems*, San Francisco: Jossey-Bass.

Greer, Jed and Kenny Bruno (1996), *Greenwash: The Reality Behind Corporate Environmentalism*, Penang: Third World Network.

Grote, Jürgen and Bernard Gbikpi (eds) (2002), *Participatory Governance. Political and Societal Implications*, Opladen: Leske+Budrich.

Gulbrandsen, Lars H. (2004), 'Overlapping Public and Private Governance: Can Forest Certification fill the Gaps in the Global Forest Regime?', *Global Environmental Politics*, **4** (2), 75-99.

Gullison, R.E. (2003), 'Does Forest Certification Conserve Biodiversity?', *Oryx*, **37** (2), 153-165.

Hall, Peter A. and Rosemary C.R. Taylor (1996), 'Political Science and the Three New Institutionalisms', *Political Studies*, **44**, 936-957.

Hall, Rodney Bruce and Thomas J. Biersteker (eds) (2002), *The Emergence of Private Authority in Global Governance*, Cambridge: Cambridge University Press.

Harding, Alan (1990), 'Public–Private Partnerships in Urban Regeneration', in M. Campbell (ed), *Local Economic Policy*, London: Cassell, pp. 108-127.

Hart, H.L.A. (1961), *The Concept of Law*, Oxford: Clarendon Press.

Hartenstein, Liesel and Ralf Schmidt (1996), *Planet ohne Wälder? Plädoyer für eine neue Waldpolitik*, Bonn: Economica.

Hartman, Cathy L. and Edwin R. Stafford (1997), 'Green Alliances: Building New Business with Environmental Groups', *Long Range Planning*, **30** (2), 184-196.

Harvey, Fiona (2005), 'Severe weather increasing losses, report says', *Financial Times*, 8 November.

Hasenclever, Andreas, Peter Mayer and Volker Rittberger (1997), *Theories of International Regimes*, Cambridge: Cambridge University Press.

Haufler, Virginia (1993), 'Crossing the Boundary between Public and Private: International Regimes and Non-State Actors', in V. Rittberger (ed.), *Regime Theory and International Relations*, Oxford: Clarendon Press, pp. 94-111.

Haufler, Virginia (2000), 'Private Sector International Regimes', in R.A. Higgott, G.R.D. Underhill and A. Bieler (eds), *Non-State Actors and Authority in the Global System*, London, New York: Routledge, pp. 121-137.

Haufler, Virginia (2003), 'New Forms of Governance: Certification Regimes as Social Regulations of the Global Market', in E.E. Meidinger, C. Elliott and G. Oesten (eds), *Social and Political Dimensions of Forest Certification*, Remagen: Verlag Kessel, pp. 237-247.

Heap, Simon (1998), 'NGOs and the Private Sector: Potential for Partnerships?', Oxford: INTRAC.

Heap, Simon (2000), NGOs Engaging with Business: A World of Difference and a Difference to the World, INTRAC NGO Management and Policy Series, Oxford: INTRAC.

Heaton, K. (1994), Perspectives on Certification from the Smart Wood Certification Program, New York: Rainforest Alliance.

Held, David (1995), *Democracy and the Global Order. From the Modern State to Cosmopolitan Governance*, Cambridge: Polity Press.

Held, David, Anthony McGrew, David Goldblatt and Jonathan Perraton (1999), *Global Transformations. Politics, Economics and Culture*, Stanford: Stanford University Press.

Helm, Carsten and Detlef F. Sprinz (2000), 'Measuring the Effectiveness of International Environmental Regimes', *Journal of Conflict Resolution*, **44** (5), 630-652.

Hemmati, Minnu, Felix Dodds, Jasmin Enayati and Jan McHarry (eds) (2002), *Multi-Stakeholder Processes for Governance and Sustainability: Beyond Deadlock and Conflict*, London: Earthscan.

Hewson, Martin and Timothy J. Sinclair (1999), 'The Emergence of Global Governance Theory', in M. Hewson and T.J. Sinclair (eds), *Approaches to Global Governance Theory*, Albany: State University of New York Press, pp. 3-22.

Higgott, Richard A., Geoffrey R.D. Underhill and Andreas Bieler (eds) (2000), *Non-State Actors and Authority in the Global System*, London, New York: Routledge.

Hindess, B. (1997), 'Politics and Governmentality', *Economy and Society*, **26** (May), 257-272.

Hirst, Paul (2000), 'Democracy and Governance', in J. Pierre (ed.), *Debating Governance*, Oxford: Oxford University Press, pp. 13-35.

Hoffman, Andrew J. (1997), *From Heresy to Dogma. An Institutional History of Corporate Environmentalism*, San Francisco: The New Lexington Press.

Hoogervorst, Arend (2005), 'Environmental Reporting', Pretoria: Department of Environmental Affairs and Tourism.

Hooghe, Liesbet and Gary Marks (2003), 'Unravelling the Central State, but how? Types of Multi-level Governance', *American Political Science Review*, **97** (2), 233-243.

Hummel, Hartwig (2001), 'Die Privatisierung der Weltpolitik. Tendenzen, Spielräume und Alternativen', in T. Brühl, T. Debiel, B. Hamm, H. Hummel and J. Martens (eds), *Die Privatisierung der Weltpolitik. Entstaatlichung und Kommerzialisierung im Globalisierungsprozess*, Bonn: Dietz, pp. 22-56.

Humphreys, David (1996), *Forest Politics. The Evolution of International Cooperation*, London: Earthscan.

Innovest Strategic Value Advisors (2002), Value at Risk: Climate Change and the Future of Governance, Boston.

Jagers, Sverker C. and Johannes Stripple (2003), 'Climate Governance Beyond the State', *Global Governance. A Review of Multilateralism and International Organizations*, **9** (3), 385-399.

Jakobeit, Cord (1998), 'Wirksamkeit in der internationalen Umweltpolitik', *Zeitschrift für Internationale Beziehungen*, **5** (2), 345-366.

Jänicke, Martin (2002), 'No Withering Away of the Nation-State. Ten Theses on Environmental Policy', in F. Biermann, R. Brohm and K. Dingwerth (eds), *2001 Berlin Conference on the Human Dimensions of Global Environmental Change: Global Environmental Change and the Nation State*, Berlin: Potsdam Institute for Climate Impact Research, pp. 134-138.

Jenkins, Rhys (2001), Corporate Codes of Conduct. Self-Regulation in a Global Economy, Geneva: UNRISD.

Josselin, Daphné and William Wallace (eds) (2001), *Non-State Actors in World Politics*. London: Palgrave.

Kaiser, Karl (1969) 'Transnationale Politik', in E.O. Czempiel (ed.), *Die anachronistische Souveränität*, Opladen: Westdeutscher Verlag, pp. 80-109.

Kaldor, Mary (2003), 'The Idea of Global Civil Society', *International Affairs*, **79** (3), 583-593.

Karliner, Joshua (1997), *The Corporate Planet. Ecology and Politics in the Age of Globalization*, San Francisco: Sierra Club Books.

Keck, Margaret E. and Kathryn Sikkink (1998), *Activists beyond Borders. Advocacy Networks in International Politics*, Ithaca: Cornell University Press.

Keohane, Robert O., Peter M. Haas and Marc A. Levy (1993), 'The Effectiveness of International Environmental Institutions', in P.M. Haas, R.O. Keohane and M.A. Levy (eds), *Institutions for the Earth. Sources of Effective International Environmental Protection*, Cambridge, MA: MIT Press, pp. 3-25.

Keohane, Robert O. and Joseph S. Nye (1970), 'Transnational Relations and World Politics: An Introduction', in R.O. Keohane and J.S. Nye (eds), *Transnational Relations and World Politics*, Cambridge, MA: Harvard University Press, pp. ix-xxix.

Keohane, Robert O. and Joseph S. Nye (1977), *Power and Interdependence*, Boston: Little, Brown and Company.

Kern, Kristine, Ingrid Kissling-Näf, Ute Landmann and Corine Mauch (2001), 'Ecolabeling and Forest Certification as New Environmental Policy Instruments. Factors which Impede and Support Diffusion', Paper presented at ECPR Workshop on 'The Politics of New Environmental Policy Instruments', Grenoble, April 2001.

Kerwer, Dieter (2002), 'Standardizing as Governance: The Case of Credit Rating Agencies', in A. Heritier (ed.), *Common Goods. Reinventing European and International Governance*, Lanham: Rowman&Littelfield Publishers, pp. 293-316.

King, Gary, Robert O. Keohane and Sidney Verba (1994), *Designing Social Inquiry. Scientific Inference in Qualitative Research*, Princeton, NJ: Princeton University Press.

Kiser, Larry L. and Elinor Ostrom (1982), 'The Three Worlds of Action. A Metatheoretical Synthesis of Institutional Approaches', in E. Ostrom (ed.), *Strategies of Political Inquiry*, Beverly Hills: Sage, pp. 179-222.

Klabbers, Jan (1999), *Forest Certification and WTO*, Joensuu: European Forest Institute.

Koenig-Archibugi, Mathias (2002), 'Mapping Global Governance', in D. Held and A. McGrew (eds), *Governing Globalization. Power, Authority, and Global Governance*, Cambridge: Polity Press, pp. 46-69.

Koenig-Archibugi, Mathias (2004), 'Transnational Corporations and Public Accountability', *Government and Opposition*, **39** (2), 234-259.

Kolk, Ans (2004), 'A Decade of Sustainability Reporting: Developments and Significance', *International Journal for Environment and Sustainable Development*, **3** (1), 51-64.

Kolk, Ans and Mark van der Veen (2002), *KPMG International Survey of Corporate Sustainability Reporting 2002*, Amsterdam: KPMG/University of Amsterdam.

Kolk, Ans, Rob van Tulder and Carlijn Welters (1999), 'International Codes of Conduct and Corporate Social Responsibility: Can Transnational Corporations Regulate Themselves?', *Transnational Corporations*, **8** (1), 143-180.

Kolk, Ans, Mark van der Veen, Danja van der Veldt, Seb Walhain and Susanne van de Wateringen (1999), *KPMG International Survey of Environmental Reporting 1999*, Amsterdam: KPMG.

Kolk, Ans, Mark van der Veen, Jonatan Pinkse and Fabienne Fortanier (2005), *KPMG International Survey on Corporate Responsibility Reporting 2005*, Amsterdam: KPMG/University of Amsterdam.

Kollman, Kelly and Aseem Prakash (2001), 'Green by Choice? Cross-national Variations in Firms' Responses to EMS-based Environmental Regimes', *World Politics*, **53** (2), 399-430.

Kooiman, Jan (ed.) (1993), *Modern Governance: New Government-Society Interactions*, London: Sage.

Kooiman, Jan (2002), 'Governance: A Social–Political Perspective', in J.R. Grote and B. Gbikpi (eds), *Participatory Governance. Political and Societal Implications*, Opladen: Leske+Budrich, pp. 71-96.

Kooiman, Jan (2003), *Governing as Governance*, London: Sage.

Korten, David (1995), *When Corporations Rule the World*, West Hartford: Kumarian Press.

Kouwenhoven, Vincent (1993), 'The Rise of the Public–Private Partnership: A Model for Management of Public–Private Cooperation', in J. Kooiman (ed.), *Modern Governance: New Government–Society Interactions*, London: Sage, pp. 119-130.

Krahmann, Elke (2003), 'National, Regional, and Global Governance: One Phenomenon or Many?', *Global Governance. A Review of Multilateralism and International Organizations*, **9** (3), 323-346.

Krasner, Stephen D. (1983), 'Structural Causes and Regime Consequences: Regimes as Intervening Variables', in S.D. Krasner (ed.), *International Regimes*, Ithaca: Cornell University Press, pp. 1-21.

Krasner, Stephen D. (1999), *Sovereignty. Organized Hypocrisy*, Princeton, NJ: Princeton University Press.

Krasner, Stephen D. (2001), 'Abiding Sovereignty', *International Political Science Review*, **22** (3), 229-251.

Krehbiel, Timothy C. and Homer O. Erekson (2001), 'Characteristics of Self-Regulating Environmental Management Systems: A Survey of Academic Experts', *International Journal for Environmental Technology and Management*, 1 (1/2), 104-126.

Lafferty, William M. (ed) (2004), *Governance for Sustainable Development*, Cheltenham, UK and Northampton, MA, USA: Edward Elgar.

Lawson, Stephanie (2002), 'Introduction: A New Agenda for International Relations?', in S. Lawson (ed.), *The New Agenda for International Relations. From Polarization to Globalization in World Politics?*, Cambridge: Polity Press, pp. 3-18.

Leech, Beth L. (2002a), 'Asking Questions: Techniques for Semistructured Interviews', *Political Science and Politics*, 35 (4), 665-668.

Leech, Beth L. (2002b), 'Interview Methods in Political Science', *Political Studies*, 35 (4), 663.

Lévêque, Francois (1996), Environmental Policy in Europe - Industry, Competition and the Policy Process, Cheltenham, UK and Brookfield USA: Edward Elgar.

Levi, Margaret (1990), 'A Logic of Institutional Change', in K.S. Cook and M. Levi (eds), *Limits of Rationality*, Chicago: University of Chicago Press, pp. 402-419.

Levy, David L. and Peter J. Newell (2002), 'Business Strategy and International Environmental Governance: Toward a Neo-Gramscian Synthesis', *Global Environmental Politics*, 2 (4), 84-100.

Levy, David L. and Peter J. Newell (2005a), 'Introduction: The Business of Global Environmental Governance', in D.L. Levy and P.J. Newell (eds), *The Business of Global Environmental Governance*, Cambridge, MA: MIT Press, pp. 1-20.

Levy, David L. and Peter J. Newell (eds) (2005b), *The Business of Global Environmental Governance*, Cambridge, MA: MIT Press.

Levy, Jack S. (2002), 'Qualitative Methods in International Relations', in F.P. Harvey and M. Brecher (eds), *Evaluating Methodology in International Studies*, Ann Arbor: The University of Michigan Press, pp. 131-160.

Lieberson, Stanley (1994), 'More on the Uneasy Case for Using Mill-Type Methods in Small-N Comparative Studies', *Social Forces*, 72, 1225-1237.

Ligteringen, Ernst and Simon Zadek (2004), *The Future of Corporate Responsibility Codes, Standards, and Frameworks*, Amsterdam and London: Global Reporting Initiative and AccountAbility.

Lijphart, Arend (1975), 'The Comparable Cases Strategy in Comparative Research', *Comparative Political Studies*, 8 (2), 133-177.

Lipschutz, Ronnie D. (1997), 'From Place to Planet: Local Knowledge and Global Environmental Governance', *Global Governance. A Review of Multilateralism and International Organizations*, 3 (1), 83-102.

Lipschutz, Ronnie D. (2002), '"Regulation for the Rest of Us?" Global Civil Society and the Privatization of Transnational Regulation', in R.B. Hall and T.J. Biersteker (eds), *The Emergence of Private Authority in Global Governance*, Cambridge: Cambridge University Press, pp. 115-150.

Lipschutz, Ronnie D. (2005a), 'Environmental Regulation, Certification and Corporate Standards: a Critique', in P. Dauvergne (ed.), *Handbook of Global Environmental Politics*, Cheltenham, UK and Northampton, MA, USA: Edward Elgar, pp. 218-231.

Lipschutz, Ronnie D. with James K. Rowe (2005b), *Globalization, Governmentality, and Global Politics. Regulation for the Rest of Us?*, London and New York: Routledge.

Long, Frederick J. and Mathew B. Arnold (1995), *The Power of Environmental Partnerships*, Fort Worth: Dryden Press.

*Longman Dictionary of the English Language* (1984), London: Longman.

Love, Maryann Cusimano, Mark Hensman and Leslie Rodrigues (2000), 'Private-Sector Transsovereign Actors – MNCs and NGOs', in M.C. Love (ed.), *Beyond Sovereignty: Issues for a Global Agenda*, Boston: Bedford/St. Martin's, pp. 255-282.

Love, Richard A. and Maryann Cusimano Love (2003), 'Multinational Corporations. Power and Responsibility', in M.C. Love (ed.), *Beyond Sovereignty. Issues for a Global Agenda*, 2nd edn, New York: Thomson, pp. 95-118.

Luke, Timothy W. (1995), 'Sustainable Development as a Power/Knowledge System: The Problem of Governmentality', in F. Fischer and M. Black (eds), *Greening Environmental Policy: The Politics of a Sustainable Future*, New York: St. Martin's Press, pp. 21-32.

Mansley, Mark (2003), *Sleeping Tiger, Hidden Liabilities: Amid growing risk and industry movement on climate change, ExxonMobil falls farther behind*, London: Claros Consulting.

Maoz, Zeev (2002), 'Case Study Methodology in International Studies. From Storytelling to Hypothesis Testing', in F.P. Harvey and M. Brecher (eds), *Evaluating Methodology in International Studies*, Ann Arbor: University of Michigan Press, pp. 161-186.

March, James G. and Johan P. Olsen (1998), 'The Institutional Dynamics of International Political Orders', *International Organization*, 52 (4), 943-969.

Maser, Chris and Walter Smith (2001), *Forest Certification in Sustainable Development. Healing the Landscape*, Boca Raton: Lewis.

Mattli, Walter and Tim Büthe (2003), 'Setting International Standards: Technological Rationality or Primacy of Power?', *World Politics*, **56** (October 2003), 1-42.

Mayer, Peter, Volker Rittberger and Michael Zürn (1993), 'Regime Theory. State of the Art and Perspectives', in V. Rittberger (ed.), *Regime Theory and International Relations*, Oxford: Clarendon Press, pp. 391-430.

Mayers, J., J. Evans and T. Foy (2001), *Raising the Stakes: Impacts of Privatization, Certification, and Partnerships in South African Forestry*, London: International Institute for Environment and Development.

Mayntz, Renate (2002), *Mechanisms in the Analysis of Macro-Social Phenomena*, Köln: Max-Planck-Institute for the Study of Societies.

McCracken, Grant (1988), *The Long Interview*, Vol. 13, *Sage University Paper Series on Qualitative Research Methods*, Beverly Hills, CA: Sage.

McQuaid, Ronald W. (2000), 'The Theory of Partnership. Why have Partnerships?', in S. P. Osborne (ed.), *Public–Private Partnerships. Theory and Practice in International Perspective*, London, UK and New York, US: Routledge.

Meadows, Donella H., Denis L. Meadows, Jorgen Randers and William W. Behrens (1972), *The Limits to Growth: A Report for the Club of Rome's Project on the Predicament of Mankind*, New York: Universe Books.

Meidinger, Errol E., Chris Elliott and Gerhard Oesten (eds) (2003), *Social and Political Dimensions of Forest Certification*, Remagen: Verlag Kessel.

Meridian Institute (2001), Comparative Analysis of the Forest Stewardship Council and Sustainable Forestry Initiative Certification Programs. Volume II, Washington, DC: Meridian Institute.

Messner, Dirk and Franz Nuscheler (1996), *Weltkonferenzen und Weltberichte*, Bonn: Dietz.

Meuser, Michael and Ulrike Nagel (1991), 'ExpertInneninterviews – vielfach erprobt, wenig bedacht. Ein Beitrag zur qualitativen Methodendiskussion', in D. Garz and K. Kraimer (eds), *Qualitativ-empirische, Sozialforschung. Konzepte, Methoden, Analysen*, Opladen: Westdeutscher Verlag, pp. 441-471.

Miles, Edward L., Arild Underdal, Steiner Andresen, Jorgen Wettestad, Jon B. Skjaerseth and Elaine M. Carlin (eds) (2002), *Environmental Regime Effectiveness. Confronting Theory with Evidence*, Cambridge, MA: MIT Press.

Mitcham, Carl (1995), 'The Concept of Sustainable Development: Its Origins and Ambivalence', *Technology in Society*, **17** (3), 311-326.

Mitchell, Ronald B. (1994), 'Regime Design Matters: Intentional Oil Pollution and Treaty Compliance', *International Organization*, **48** (3), 425-458.

Mitchell, Ronald B. (2002a), 'International Environment', in W. Carlsnaes, T. Risse and B. Simmons (eds), *Handbook of International Relations*, London: Sage Publications, pp. 500-516.

Mitchell, Ronald B. (2002b), 'Of Course International Institutions Matter: But When and How?', in F. Biermann, R. Brohm and K. Dingwerth (eds), Proceedings of the 2002 Berlin Conference on the Human Dimensions of Global Environmental Change: Global Environmental Change and the Nation State, Potsdam: Potsdam Institute for Climate Impact Research, pp. 16-25.

Mitchell, Ronald B. and Thomas Bernauer (1998), 'Empirical Research on International Environmental Policy: Designing Qualitative Case Studies', *Journal of Environment & Development*, **7** (1), 4-31.

Mittelman, James H. (1997), 'Rethinking Innovation in International Studies: Global Transformation at the Turn of the Millennium', in S. Gill and J.H. Mittelman (eds), *Innovation and Transformation in International Studies*, Cambridge: Cambridge University Press, pp. 248-263.

Mittelman, James H. (2002), 'Globalization: An Ascendent Paradigm?', *International Studies Perspectives*, **3** (1), 1-14.

Morhardt, Emil J., Sarah Baird and Kelly Freeman (2002), 'Scoring Corporate Environmental and Sustainability Reports using GRI 2000, ISO 14031 and other Criteria', *Corporate Social Responsibility and Environmental Management*, **9**, 215-233.

Most, Benjamin A. and Harvey Starr (2003), 'Basic Logic and Research Design: Conceptualization, Case Selection, and the Form of Relationships', in G. Goertz and H. Starr (eds), *Necessary Conditions. Theory, Methodology, and Applications*, Lanham: Rowman&Littelfield Publishers, pp. 25-46.

Murphy, David F. and Jem Bendell (1997), *In the Company of Partners: Business, Environmental Groups and Sustainable Development Post Rio*, Bristol: The Policy Press.

Murphy, David F. and Jem Bendell (1999), 'Partners in Time? Business, NGOs and Sustainable Development', *UNRISD Discussion Paper No. 109*, Geneva: UNRISD.

Murray, Sarah (2003), 'New voices are entering the fray', *Financial Times*, Thursday, October 16.

Murray, Sarah (2004), 'Investors demand action on climate change', *Financial Times*, Friday, January 2004.

Nadvi, Khalid and Frank Wältring (2002), 'Making Sense of Global Standards', Duisburg: INEF.

Nash, Jennifer and John Ehrenfeld (1996), 'Code Green', *Environment*, **38** (1), 16-45.

Nash, Jennifer and John Ehrenfeld (1997), 'Codes of Environmental Management Practice: Assessing their Potential as a Tool for Change', *Annual Review of Energy and the Environment*, **22**, 487-535.

Newell, Peter J. (2001), 'Environmental NGOs, TNCs, and the Question of Governance', in D. Stevis and V.J. Assetto (eds), *The International Political Economy of the Environment: Critical Perspectives*, Boulder, CO: Lynne Rienner, pp. 85-107.

Newell, Peter J. (2005), 'Towards a Political Economy of Global Environmental Governance', in P. Dauvergne (ed.), *Handbook of Global Environmental Politics*, Cheltenham, UK and Northampton, MA, USA: Edward Elgar, pp. 187-201.

Nölke, Andreas (2000), 'Regieren in transnationalen Politiknetzwerken? Kritik postnationaler Governance- Konzepte aus der Perspektive einer transnationalen (Inter-) Organisationssoziologie', *Zeitschrift für Internationale Beziehungen*, **7** (2), 331-358.

Nölke, Andreas (2003), 'Intra- und interdisziplinäre Vernetzung: Die Überwindung der Regierungszentrik?', in G. Hellmann, K.D. Wolf and M. Zürn (eds), *Die neuen Internationalen Beziehungen. Forschungsstand und Perspektiven in Deutschland*, Baden-Baden: Nomos, pp. 519-554.

Norman, Wayne and Chris MacDonald (2004), 'Getting to the Bottom of "Triple Bottom Line"', *Business Ethics Quarterly*, **14** (2), 243-262.

North, Douglass C. (1990), *Institutions, Institutional Change and Economic Performance*, Cambridge: Cambridge University Press.

Northeast Utilities Systems (2005), *CERES and Sustainable Development* [accessed 3 November 2005], available from: http://www.nu.com/environmental/ceres.asp.

Nuscheler, Franz (2000), 'Globalisierung und Global Governance. Zwischen der Skylla der Nationalstaatlichkeit und der Charybdis der Weltstaatlichkeit', in D.S. Lutz (ed.), *Globalisierung und nationale Souveränität*, Baden-Baden: Nomos, pp. 301-317.

O'Brien, Robert, Anne Marie Goetz, Jan Aart Scholte and Marc Williams (2000), *Contesting Global Governance. Multilateral Economic Institutions and Global Social Movements*, Cambridge: Cambridge University Press.

OECD (2001), Codes of Corporate Conduct: Expanded Review of their Contents, Paris: OECD.

Ohmae, Kenichi (1995), *The End of the Nation State. The Rise of Regional Economies*, London: Harper Collins Publishers.

Oliviero, Melanie Beth and Adele Simmons (2002), 'Who's Minding the Store? Global Civil Society and Corporate Responsibility', in H.K. Anheier, M. Glasius and M. Kaldor (eds), *Global Civil Society 2002*, Oxford: Oxford University Press, pp. 77-107.

Onuf, Nicholas (2002), 'Institutions, Intentions and International Relations', *Review of International Studies*, 2 (2), 211-228.

Opello, Walter C. and Stephen J. Rosow (2004), *The Nation-State and Global Order. A Historical Introduction to Contemporary Politics*, 2nd edn, Boulder, CO: Lynne Rienner.

O'Rourke, Dara (2000), *Monitoring the Monitors. A Critique of PricewaterhouseCoopers Labor Monitoring* [accessed 14 December 2004], available from http://nature.berkeley.edu/orourke/PDF/pwc.pdf.

Osborne, D. and T. Gaebler (1992), *Reinventing Government*, Reading: Addison-Wesley.

Ostrom, Elinor (1990), *Governing the Commons. The Evolution of Institutions for Collective Action*, Cambridge: Cambridge University Press.

Ostrom, Elinor (1999), 'Institutional Rational Choice: An Assessment of the Institutional Analysis and Development Framework', in P.A. Sabatier (ed.), *Theories of the Policy Process*, Boulder, CO: Lynne Rienner, pp. 35-72.

Ottaway, Marina (2001), 'Corporatism Goes Global: International Organizations, Nongovernmental Organization Networks, and Transnational Business', *Global Governance*, 7 (3), 265-292.

Overbeek, Henk (2000), 'Transnational Historical Materialism: Theories of Transnational Class Formation and World Order', in R.P. Palan (ed.), *Global Political Economy. Contemporary Theories*, London: Routledge, pp. 168-183.

Overbeek, Henk (2004), 'Global Governance, Class, Hegemony: A Historical Materialist Perspective', Amsterdam: Free University of Amsterdam.

Pattberg, Philipp (2004), 'Private Environmental Governance and the Sustainability Transition: Functions and Impacts of Business–NGO Partnerships', in K. Jacob, M. Binder and A. Wieczorek (eds), *Governance for Industrial Transformation. Proceedings of the 2003 Berlin Conference on the Human Dimension of Global Environmental Change*, Berlin: FFU, pp. 52-66.

Pattberg, Philipp (2005a), 'The Forest Stewardship Council: Risk and Potential of Private Forest Governance', *Journal of Environment & Development*, 14 (3), 356-374.

Pattberg, Philipp (2005b), 'What Role for Private Rule-Making in Global Environmental Governance? Analysing the Forest Stewardship Council (FSC)', *International Environmental Agreements*, 5 (2), 175-189.

Pattberg, Philipp (2005c), 'The Institutionalization of Private Governance: How Business and Non-profit Organizations agree on Transnational Rules', *Governance: An International Journal of Policy, Administration, and Institutions*, 18 (4): 589-610.

Pattberg, Philipp (2006a), 'Private Governance and the South: Lessons from Global Forest Politics', *Third World Quarterly*, **27** (4), 579-593.

Pattberg, Philipp (2006b), 'The Influence of Global Business Regulation: Beyond Good Corporate Conduct', *Business and Society Review*, **111** (3), 241-268.

Peters, Guy B. (1996a) *The Future of Governing: Four Emerging Models*, Lawrence: University Press of Kansas.

Peters, Guy B. (1996b), 'Political Institutions, Old and New', in R.E. Goodin and H.-D. Klingemann (ed.), *Handbook of Political Science*, Oxford: Oxford University Press, pp. 205-220.

Peters, Guy B. (1999), *Institutional Theory in Political Science*, London and New York: Continuum.

Peters, Guy B. (2000), 'Institutional Theory: Problems and Perspectives', Vienna: Institute for Advanced Studies (IHS).

Philpott, Daniel (1997), 'Ideas and the Evolution of Sovereignty', in S.H. Hashmi (ed.), *State Sovereignty. Change and Persistence in International Relations*, University Park: The Pennsylvania State University Press, pp. 15-47.

Pierre, Jon (2000), 'Introduction: Understanding Governance', in J. Pierre (ed.), *Debating Governance*, Oxford: Oxford University Press, pp. 1-10.

Pijl, Kees van der (1997), 'Transnational Class Formation and State Forms', in S. Gill and J.H. Mittelman (eds), *Innovation and Transformation in International Studies*, Cambridge: Cambridge University Press, pp. 118-133.

Poore, Duncan (2003), *Changing Landscapes. The Development of the International Topical Timber Organization and its Influence on Tropical Forest Management*, London: Earthscan.

Prakash, Aseem (2000), *Greening the Firm. The Politics of Corporate Environmentalism*, Cambridge: Cambridge University Press.

PricewaterhouseCoopers (1995), 'Reputation Assurance', document on file with author.

Prittwitz, Volker von (2000), 'Institutionelle Arrangements und Zukunftsfähigkeit', in V. v. Prittwitz. (ed), *Institutionell Arrangements in der Umweltpolitik. Zukunftsfähigkeit durch innovative Verfahrenskombinationen?*, Opladen: Leske+Budrich, pp. 12-40.

Raar, Jean (2001), 'Strategy and the Multiplicity of Variables Associated with Voluntary Reporting of Environmental and Economic Performance: Ullmann Revisited', Paper presented at Governance and Social Responsibility Conference, at School of Accounting & Finance, Deakin University, Burwood, Australia.

Ragin, Charles C. (1994), *Constructing Social Research. The Unity and Diversity of Method*, Thousand Oaks: Pine Forge Press.

Ragin, Charles C. (2003), 'Fuzzy-Set Analysis of Necessary Conditions', in G. Goertz and H. Starr (eds), *Necessary Conditions. Theory, Methodology, and Applications*, Lanham: Rowman&Littelfield Publishers, pp. 178-224.

Ragin, Charles C. and Howard S. Becker (eds) (1992), *What is a Case? Exploring the Foundations of Social Inquiry*, Cambridge: Cambridge University Press.

Rainforest Foundation (2002), Trading in Credibility. The Myth and Reality of the Forest Stewardship Council, London, Oslo: Rainforest Foundation.

Rainforest Information Centre (1998), *RIC Good Wood Guide* [accessed 20 November 2005], available from: www.rainforestinfo.org.au/good_wood/the_fsc.htm.

Rametsteiner, Ewald (1999), 'European Citizens and their Attitude towards Forests, Forestry and Wood', in B. Pajari, T. Peck and E. Rametsteiner (eds), *Potential Markets for Certified Forest Products in Europe*, Joensuu: European Forest Institute, pp. 75-89.

Rametsteiner, Ewald (2002), 'Markets for Certified Forest Products', in UNECE/FAO (ed.), *UNECE/FAO Forest Products Annual Market Review, 2001–2002*, Rome: FAO, pp. 157-164.

Raustiala, Kal (1997), 'States, NGOs, and International Environmental Institutions', *International Studies Quarterly*, **41** (4), 719-740.

Redclift, Michael (1992), 'The Meaning of Sustainable Development', *Geoforum*, **23** (3), 395-403.

Reinalda, Bob, Bas Arts and Math Noortmann (2001), 'Non-State Actors in International Relations: Do They Matter?', in B. Arts, M. Noortmann and B. Reinalda (eds), *Non-State Actors in International Relations*, Aldershot, UK: Ashgate, pp. 1-8.

Reinicke, Wolfgang H. and Francis Deng (eds) (2000), *Critical Choices. The United Nations, Networks, and the Future of Global Governance*, Ottawa: International Development Research Centre.

Reus-Smit, Christian (1998), 'Changing Patterns of Governance: From Absolutism to Global Multilateralism', in A. Paolini (ed.), *Between Sovereignty and Global Governance. The United Nations, the State and Civil Society*, New York: St. Martin' s Press, pp. 3-28.

Rhodes, R.A.W. (1996), 'The New Governance: Governing without Government', *Political Studies*, **44** (4), 652-667.

Rhodes, R.A.W. (1997), *Understanding Governance. Policy Networks, Governance, Reflexity and Accountability*, Maidenhead and Philadelphia: Open University Press.

Richter, Judith (2001), *Holding Corporations Accountable. Corporate Conduct, International Codes, and Citizen Action*, London, UK and New York, US: Zed Books.

Risse, Thomas (2002), 'Transnational Actors and World Politics', in W. Carlsnaes, T. Risse and B.A. Simmons (eds), *Handbook of International Relations*, London: Sage, pp. 255-274.

Risse, Thomas (2004), 'Global Governance and Communicative Action', *Government and Opposition*, **39** (2), 288-313.

Risse-Kappen, Thomas (1995a), 'Bringing Transnational Relations Back In: Introduction', in T. Risse-Kappen (ed.), *Bringing Transnational Relations Back In: Non-State Actors, Domestic Structures and International Institutions*, Cambridge: Cambridge University Press, pp. 3-36.

Risse-Kappen, Thomas (ed.) (1995b), *Bringing Transnational Relations Back In. Non-State Actors, Domestic Structures and International Institutions*, Cambridge: Cambridge University Press.

Ronit, Karsten (2001), 'Institutions of Private Authority in Global Governance: Linking Territorial Forms of Self-regulation', *Administration and Society*, **33** (5), 555-578.

Ronit, Karsten and Volker Schneider (1999), 'Global Governance through Private Organizations', *Governance: An International Journal of Policy, Administration, and Institutions*, **12** (3), 243-266.

Rorty, Richard (1989), *Contingency, Irony and Solidarity*, New York: Cambridge University Press.

Rosenau, James N. (1990), *Turbulence in World Politics: A Theory of Change and Continuity*, Princeton, NJ: Princeton University Press.

Rosenau, James N. (1995), 'Governance in the twenty-first century', *Global Governance. A Review of Multilateralism and International Organizations*, **1** (1), 13-43.

Rosenau, James N. (1997a), *Along the Domestic–Foreign Frontier: Exploring Governance in a Turbulent World*, Cambridge: Cambridge University Press.

Rosenau, James N. (1997b), 'Global Environmental Governance: Delicate Balances, Subtle Nuances, and Multiple Challenges', in M. Rolen, H. Sjöberg and U. Svedin (eds), *International Governance on Environmental Issues*, Dordrecht: Kluwer Academic Publishing, pp. 19-56.

Rosenau, James N. (1999), 'Toward an Ontology for Global Governance', in M. Hewson and T.J. Sinclair (eds), *Approaches to Global Governance Theory*, Albany: State University of New York Press, pp. 287-301.

Rosenau, James N. (2002), 'Governance in a New Global Order', in D. Held and A. McGrew (eds), *Governing Globalization. Power, Authority and Global Governance*, Cambridge: Polity Press, pp. 70-86.

Rosenau, James N. (2003), *Distant Proximities: Dynamics Beyond Globalization*, Princeton, NJ: Princeton University Press.

Rosenau, James N. and Ernst Otto Czempiel (eds) (1992), *Governance without Government: Order and Change in World Politics*, Cambridge: Cambridge University Press.

Rothstein, Bo (1996), 'Political Institutions: An Overview', in R.E. Goodin and H.-D. Klingemann (eds), *A New Handbook of Political Science*, Oxford: Oxford University Press, pp. 133-166.

Rowe, James K. (2005), 'Corporate Social Responsibility as Business Strategy', in R.D. Lipschutz, *Globalization, Governmentality, and Global Politics. Regulation for the Rest of Us?*, London, UK and New York, US: Routledge, pp. 130-170.

Rowlands, Ian H. (2001), 'Transnational Corporations and Global Environmental Politics', in D. Josselin and W. Wallace (eds), *Non-State Actors in World Politics*, London: Palgrave, pp. 133-149.

Ruggie, John G. (1982), 'International Regimes, Transaction Costs, and Change: Embedded Liberalism in the Postwar Economic Order', *International Organization*, **36** (2), 379-416.

Ruggie, John G. (1993), 'Territoriality and Beyond: Problematizing Modernity in International Relations', *International Organization*, **47** (1), 139-174.

Ruggie, John G. (2001), 'Global-Governance Net: The Global Compact as Learning Network', *Global Governance. A Review of Multilateralism and International Organizations*, **7** (4), 371-378.

Ruggie, John G. (2002), 'The Theory and Practice of Learning Networks. Corporate Social Responsibility and the Global Compact', *Journal of Corporate Citizenship*, **(Spring 2002)**, 27-36.

Rundgren, Gunnar (1997), *Building Trust in Organics – A Guide to Setting Up Organic Certification Programmes*, Jamestown: Tholey-Theley.

Rupert, M. and H. Smith (eds) (2002), *Historical Materialism and Globalisation*, London: Routledge.

Sassen, Saskia (1996), *Loosing Control? Sovereignty in an Age of Globalization*, New York: Columbia University Press.

Sasser, Erika N. Benjamin Cashore, Aseem Prakash and Graeme Auld (2004), 'Competition Among Non-Governmental Regimes: Direct Targeting by ENGOs and its Impact on Firm-Level Choice in the U.S. Forest Products Sector', Paper presented at 45th Annual International Studies Association Convention, Montreal, March 17-20.

Saurin, Julian (2001), 'Global Environmental Crisis as the Disaster Triumphant: The Private Capture of Public Goods', *Environmental Politics*, **10** (4), 63-84.

Schlichte, Klaus and Boris Wilke (2000), 'Der Staat und einige seiner Zeitgenossen', *Zeitschrift für Internationale Beziehungen*, **7** (2), 359-384.

Schmidheiny, Stephan (1992), *Changing Course. A Global Business Perspective on Development and the Environment*, Cambridge, MA: MIT Press.
Schneider, Volker (2004), 'Redes de Politicas e a Conducao de Sociedades Complexas', *Civitas*, **5** (1), 29-58.
Schwandt, T.A. (1997), *Qualitative Inquiry: A Dictionary of Terms*, Thousand Oaks: Sage.
Scott, Alan (1997), *The Limits of Globalization. Cases and Arguments*, London, UK and New York, US: Routledge.
Scott, Richard W. (1994), 'Conceptualizing organizational fields: linking organizations and societal systems', in H.-U. Derlien, U. Gerhard and F. W. Scharpf (eds), *Systemrationalität und Partialinteresse*, Baden-Baden: Nomos, pp. 202-222.
Segura, Gerardo (2004), 'Forest Certification and Governments. The Real and Potential Influence on Regulatory Frameworks and Forest Policies', Washington, DC: Forest Trends.
Sellgren, John (1990), 'Local Economic Development Partnerships – an Assessment of Local Authority Economic Development Initiatives', *Local Government Studies*, **16** (4), 57-78.
Senge, Peter (1990), *The Fifth Discipline: The Art and Practice of the Learning Organization*, New York: Currency Doubleday.
Siebenhüner, Bernd (2001), Homo Sustinens: Auf dem Weg zu einem Menschenbild der Nachhaltigkeit, Marburg: Metropolis Verlag.
Siebenhüner, Bernd (2005), 'Sustainable Development Through Social Learning?', *International Journal of Ecological Economics and Statistics*, **3** (5), 42-61.
Simmons, Beth A. and Lisa L. Martin (2002), 'International Organizations and Institutions', in W. Carlsnaes, T. Risse and B.A. Simmons (eds), *Handbook of International Relations*, London: Sage, pp. 192-211.
Simonis, Udo E. (1995), 'Globale Umweltprobleme', in K. Kaiser and H.P. Schwarz (eds), *Die Neue Weltpolitik*, Baden-Baden: Nomos, pp. 123-132.
Simula, Markku (1996), 'Economics of Certification', in V.M. Viana, J. Ervin, R.Z. Donovan, C. Elliott and H. Gholz (eds), *Certification of Forest Products. Issues and Perspectives*, Washington, DC: Island Press, pp. 123-136.
Sinclair, Timothy J. (1999), 'Bond-Rating Agencies and Coordination in the Global Political Economy', in C.A. Cutler, V. Haufler and T. Porter (eds), *Private Authority and International Affairs*, Albany: State University of New York Press, pp. 153-167.
Sinclair, Timothy J. (2002), 'Private Makers of Public Policy: Bond Rating Agencies and the New Global Finance', in A. Héretier (ed.), *Common*

*Goods. Reinventing European and International Governance*, Lanham: Rowman&Littelfield Publishers, pp. 279-292.

Smouts, Marie-Claude (1998), 'The Proper Use of Governance in International Relations', *International Social Science Journal*, **155**, 81-90.

Social Investment Forum (1999), *Leading Socially Responsible Investment Firms Recommit to CERES on 10th Anniversary of Exxon Valdez Oil Spill* [accessed 3 November 2005], available from: http://www.socialinvest.org/Areas/News/CERES.htm.

Socialfunds.com (2005), *CERES Coalition for Corporate Environmental Reporting gains Momentum* 1999 [accessed 3 November 2005], available from www.socialfunds.com/news/aticle.cgi/article27.html.

Soussan, J.G. and A.C. Millington (1992), 'Forests, Woodlands and Deforestation', in A.M. Mannion and S.R. Bolby (eds), *Environmental Issues in the 1990s*, Chichester: Wiley, pp. 79-96.

Sowers, Jeannie, Atul Kholi and Georg Sørensen (2000), 'States and Sovereignty: Introduction', in P.S. Chasek (ed.), *The Global Environment in the Twenty-first Century: Prospects for International Cooperation*, Tokyo: United Nations University, pp. 15-21.

Staden, Alfred van and Hans Vollaard (2002), 'The Erosion of State Sovereignty: Towards a Post-territorial World?', in G. Kreijen (ed.), *State, Sovereignty, and International Governance*, Oxford: Oxford University Press, pp. 165-184.

Stewart, Keith (2001), 'Avoiding the Tragedy of the Commons: Greening Governance through the Market or the Public Domain?', in D. Drache (ed.), *The Market or the Public Domain: Global Governance and the Asymmetry of Power*, London, UK and New York, US: Routledge, pp. 202-228.

Stoker, Gerry (1998), 'Governance as Theory: Five Propositions', *International Social Science Journal*, **155**, 17-28.

Strange, Susan (1996), *The Retreat of the State. The Diffusion of Power in the World Economy*, Cambridge: Cambridge University Press.

Strange, Susan (1998), *Mad Money. When Markets Outgrow Governments*, Ann Arbor: University of Michigan Press.

SustainAbility (2004), 'The 21st Century NGO. In the Market for Change', London: SustainAbility.

Tarasofsky, Richard G. and David R. Downes (1999), 'Global Cooperation on Forests through International Institutions', in R.G. Tarasofski (ed.), *Assessing the International Forest Regime*, Gland: IUCN, pp. 95-110.

Thornber, Kirsti (1999), 'Overview of Global Trends in FSC Certificates', London: International Institute for Environment and Development.

Toman, Michael A. (1992), 'The Difficulty in Defining Sustainability', *Resources*, **106** (Winter), 3-6.

250     *Private Institutions and Global Governance*

Tricker, R.I. (1984), *International Corporate Governance*, Englewood Cliffs, NJ: Prentice-Hall.
Trittin, Jürgen (2003), *Der Schutz der Wälder* [Rede zum Empfang der FSC Arbeitsgruppe Deutschland]. FSC Arbeitsgruppe Deutschland [accessed 15 July 2004], available from: http://www.fsc-deutschland.de/inhalt/news/news/trittin.htm.
Underdal, Arild (2002), 'One Question, Two Answers', in E.L. Miles, A. Underdal, S. Andresen, J. Wettestad, J.B. Skjaerseth and E.M. Carlin (eds), *Environmental Regime Effectiveness. Confronting Theory with Evidence*, Cambridge, MA: MIT Press, pp. 3-45.
UNECE/FAO (2003), State of Europe's Forests 2003. Report on Sustainable Forest Management in Europe, Vienna: UNECE/FAO/MCPFE.
United Nations (1974), Declaration on the Establishment of a New International Economic Order (A/RES/3201 (S-VI)), New York: United Nations.
United Nations (1993), Report of the United Nations Conference on Environment and Development, Rio de Janeiro, 3–14 June 1992, Resolutions Adopted by the Conference, Vol. I, A/CONF.151/26/Rev.1, New York: United Nations.
United Nations (2002), Report of the World Summit on Sustainable Development, Johannesburg, South Africa, 26 August–4 September 2002, A/CONF.199/20, New York: United Nations.
United Nations Conference on Trade and Development (UNCTAD) (2001), *World Investment Report 2001: Promoting Links*, New York: United Nations.
United Nations Environment Programme, Division of Technology, Industry, and Economics (2005), *Corporate Reporting* [accessed 3 November 2005], available from www.uneptie.org/pc/pc/tools/reporting.htm.
Usui, Mikoto (2002), 'The Role of Private Business in International Environmental Governance', Tokyo: United Nations University Institute of Advanced Studies.
Utting, Peter (2002), 'Regulating Business via Multistakeholder Initiatives: A Preliminary Assessment', in R. Jenkins, P. Utting and R.A. Pino (eds), *Voluntary Approaches to Corporate Social Responsibility: Readings and a Resource Guide*, Geneva: NGLS, pp. 61-130.
Utting, Peter (2004), 'Neue Ansätze zur Regulierung Transnationaler Konzerne. Potential und Grenzen von Multistakeholder-Initiativen', in T. Brühl, H. Feldt, B. Hamm, H. Hummel and J. Martens (eds), *Unternehmen in der Weltpolitik. Politiknetzwerke, Unternehmensregeln und die Zukunft des Multilateralismus*, Bonn: Dietz, pp. 96-121.

Viana, Virgilio M., Jamison Ervin, Richard Z. Donovan, Chris Elliott and Henry Gholz (eds) (1996), *Certification of Forest Products. Issues and Perspectives*, Washington, DC: Island Press.

Victor, David G., Kal Raustiala and Eugene B. Skolnikoff (eds) (1998), *The Implementation and Effectiveness of International Environmental Commitments: Theory and Practice*, Cambridge, MA: MIT Press.

Vogel, David (2005), *The Market for Virtue. The Potential and Limits of Corporate Social Responsibility*, Washington, DC: Brookings Institution Press.

Wackernagel, Mathis, Larry Onisto, Alejandro Callejas Linares, Ina Susana López Falfán, Jesus Méndez García, Ana Isabel Suárez Guerrero and Guadalupe Suárez Guerrero (1997), 'Ecological Footprints of Nations. How Much Nature Do They Use? How Much Nature Do They Have?', Mexico: Centro de Estudios para la Sustentabilidad.

Waddell, Steve (1999), 'The Evolving Strategic Benefits for Business in Collaboration with Nonprofits in Civil Society: A Strategic Resources, Capabilities and Competencies Perspective', Washington, DC: The United States Agency for International Development (USAID).

Waddell, Steve (2002), 'The Global Reporting Initiative: Building a Corporate Reporting Strategy Globally', Boston: The Global Action Network Net.

Waltz, Kenneth (1979), *Theory of International Politics*, New York: Wiley.

Wapner, Paul (1997), 'Governance in Global Civil Society', in O. Young (ed.), *Global Governance. Drawing Insights from Environmental Experience*, Cambridge, MA: MIT Press, pp. 65-84.

Webb, Kernaghan (2004), 'Understanding the Voluntary Codes Phenomenon', in K. Webb (ed.), *Voluntary Codes: Private Governance, the Public Interest and Innovation*, Ottawa: Carleton University, pp. 3-31.

*Webster's Third New International Dictionary of the English Language* (1976), Vol. I, Chicago, US and London, UK: Webster.

Weiss, Anne M. (2002), 'Voluntary Codes of Management: New Opportunities for Increased Corporate Accountability', in L. Susskind, W. Moomaw and K. Gallagher (eds), *Transboundary Environmental Negotiations. New Approaches to Global Cooperation*, San Francisco: Jossey-Bass, pp. 85-106.

Weiss, Linda (1998), *The Myth of the Powerless State. Governing the Economy in a Global Era*, Cambridge: Polity Press.

Weiss, Thomas G. and Leon Gordenker (eds) (1996), *NGOs, the UN, and Global Governance*, Boulder, CO: Lynne Rienner.

Weller, Christoph (2003), 'Die Welt, der Diskurs und Global Governance. Zur Konstruktion eines hegemonialen Diskurses – eine Replik auf Ulrich Brandt', *Zeitschrift für Internationale Beziehungen*, 10 (2), 365-382.

White, Allen L. (1999), 'Sustainability and the Accountable Corporation: Society's Rising Expectations of Business', *Environment*, **41** (8), 30-43.

White, Allen L. and Diana Zinkl (1998), 'Green Metrics: A Global Status Report on Standardized Corporate Environmental Reporting', Boston: Tellus Institute.

White, Mark A. (1996), *Corporate Environmental Performance and Shareholder Value*. University of Virginia Online Scholarship Initiative [accessed 30 August 2005], available from http://etext.virginia.edu/etcbin/browse-mixed-osi?id=WHI002&tag=public&images=/lv6/OSI/archive/images&data=/lv6/OSI/archive.

Williamson, Oliver E. (1996), *The Mechanisms of Governance*, Oxford: Oxford University Press.

Winterhalter, D. and D.L. Cassens (1993), 'The United States Hardwood Forests: Consumer Perceptions and Willingness to Pay', Indianapolis: Purdue University.

Witte, Jan Martin, Wolfgang H. Reinicke and Thorsten Benner (2000), 'Beyond Multilateralism: Global Public Policy Networks', *Internationale Politik und Gesellschaft*, (2), 176-188.

Wolfers, Arnold (1962), *Discord and Collaboration. Essays on International Politics*, Baltimore: Johns Hopkins Press.

World Bank/WWF Alliance (2003), 'Progress through Partnership', Washington, DC: The World Bank and WWF International.

World Commission on Environment and Development (1987), *Our Common Future*, Oxford: Oxford University Press.

World Wide Fund for Nature Deutschland (2002), *Faktenservice Wald- und Holzzertifizierung* (October).

World Wide Fund for Nature Deutschland (2004), *Faktenservice Wald- und Holzzertifizierung* (July).

World Wide Fund for Nature Europe (2005), The Effects of FSC Certification in Estonia, Germany, Latvia, Russia, Sweden and the UK. An Analysis of Corrective Action Requests. Summary Report, [accessed 19 February 2005], available from www.panda.org/europe/forests.

World Wildlife Fund United Kingdom (1991), *Truth or Trickery. Timber Labeling Past and Future*, London: WWF UK.

Yin, Robert K. (1994), *Case Study Research. Design and Methods*, Thousand Oaks: Sage.

Young, Oran R. (1994), *International Governance. Protecting the Environment in a Stateless Society*, Ithaca: Cornell University Press.

Young, Oran, Marc A. Levy and Gail Osherenko (eds) (1999), *Effectiveness of International Environmental Regimes: Causal Connections and Behavioral Mechanisms*, Cambridge, MA: MIT Press.

Zacher, Mark W. (1992), 'The Decaying Pillars of the Westphalian Temple: Implications for International Order and Governance', in J.N. Rosenau and E.O. Czempiel (eds), *Governance without Government: Order and Change in World Politics*, Cambridge: Cambridge University Press, pp. 58-101.

Zangl, Bernhard and Michael Zürn (2004), 'Make Law, Not War: Internationale und transnationale Verrechtlichung als Bausteine für Global Governance', in B. Zangl and M. Zürn (eds), *Verrechtlichung – Bausteine für Global Governance?*, Bonn: Dietz, pp. 12-45.

# Index